PRAISE FOR *HUMAN IS THE NEW VINYL*

" *Human Is the New Vinyl* captures the complexity of this new world where AI and human creativity intersect. As someone who works in music, film, television, and publishing, I found Micah's take on all these formats incredibly astute. Like vinyl, human storytelling remains powerful because it's tangible and authentic. The book concludes with big questions about provenance—and who is actually creating what."

—**Craig Martin** | Emmy-nominated producer of *The Good Road* | president of Belltower Pictures and Shockoe Records | co-owner of *The Philanthropy Journal*

" Whether you're just beginning to explore AI or jockeying for a programming position, this book is a gift. The best spaces for discovery are those that foster curiosity over judgment—and Micah does a masterful job of looking back so we can move forward. He helps us imagine a healthy coexistence with AI while holding on to our humanity—a must-read, both individually and in community.

—**Jeremiah Link** | spoken word artist, educator, and community advocate | Philadelphia-area teacher and former Richmond-based creative | champion of justice, faith, and human storytelling

" This thoughtful examination of the implications—and especially the limitations—of AI in the creative arts is a definitive work in its field. An absolute must-read for anyone who wants to understand why AI is not the existential threat its promoters and investors claim."

—**J. Michael Collins** | award-winning voice actor | industry leader in AI and voice rights advocacy

" If you're confused—or just curious—about artificial intelligence and how it seems to be everywhere, especially in areas long considered the realm of human creativity, read this book. Micah explains it with clarity, insight, and just the right touch of humor. A must-read for understanding AI's growing importance."

—**Carolyn Strand Norman** | Professor Emerita of Accounting, Virginia Commonwealth University

" We need human creativity because it feeds our souls. We were made to create—and to be inspired by the creations of others. *Human Is the New Vinyl* celebrates that creative spirit while placing it within the revolutions that have shaped it. Micah engages the current AI shift without fear, making today's changes accessible and less intimidating. Most importantly, the book makes a compelling case for the essential role of human creativity in an increasingly artificial world."

—**Jon Hirst** | co-founder of Generous Mind | Chief Innovation Officer, Innovation in Mission

" Micah Voraritskul's *Human Is the New Vinyl* is just right. It grapples with the ethical and aesthetic complexities AI presents to artists and consumers in a tone that is both accessible and appealing. In fact, Voraritskul's premise—that deep art is engaging because of the humanity inherent in it—is born out in the book itself. His very human, authentic voice with all its concerns and all its hopes makes this a memorable introduction to this rapidly emerging field."

—**Carolyn Dirksen** | Distinguished Professor Emerita of English, Lee University | former Vice President for Academic Affairs | CCCU Senior Fellow

" Human is the New Vinyl is a helpful guide to all things AI. For a non-digital-native like me, it was such a terrific help in understanding the phenomenon and what some of the implications are for the world we enjoy every day. Well written, down-to-earth, this little book is terrific!"

—**Paul Conn** | Chancellor of Lee University (former president, 1986–2020) | bestselling author and Harvard visiting scholar | recipient of the Otis Floyd Award for leadership in higher education

" Voraritskul's exploration of the intersection between human creativity and human values on one hand, and the tools (technologies) we shape—and that in turn shape us—on the other, is timely, insightful, and ultimately hopeful. As we enter the age of AI, we are again called to remember and reimagine what it means to be human—and humane. His case for awe and wonder, for courage and wisdom, for play and accountability—and finally, for a joyful embrace of the creative spirit—is convincing."

—**E. Carson Brisson** | Emeritus Associate Professor of Bible & Biblical Languages, Union Presbyterian Seminary

" A persuasive and beautifully written call to honor human creativity and the slow, deep, edgy, and sometimes agonizing way in which our various art forms are produced. Best read while enjoying a craft beverage in a hi-fi listening bar."

—**Daniel Allen** | founder of CAT3 Leadership Advisors | executive coach for creative leaders and high-impact teams

HUMAN IS THE NEW VINYL

Why Human Creativity Still Wins in the AI Revolution

Micah Voraritskul

WISDOM/WORK

Published by Wisdom Work
Wilmington, North Carolina

This is a VerifiedHuman™ publication.

verifiedhuman.info

© 2025 by Micah Voraritskul

All rights reserved. No part of this book may be reproduced, stored in a retrieval system, or transmitted in any form or by any means—electronic, mechanical, photocopying, recording, or otherwise—without the prior written permission of the publisher, except in the case of brief quotations used in critical articles or reviews.

ISBN: 979-8-9992362-1-0

Subjects: Artificial Intelligence / Creativity / Cultural Commentary

First edition
10 9 8 7 6 5 4 3 2 1

Printed in the United States of America

For Kristy, Ethan, and Molly

"Concern for humans and their future must always be the chief interest of all technical endeavors… so that the creations of our mind are a blessing and not a curse to humankind."

—Albert Einstein

CONTENTS

Author's Note
Foreword
Prologue

PART ONE | REVOLUTIONS
How we built the future—and how it's building us.

Chapter 1 | **Six Hours Early to the Party**
Chapter 2 | **The Rise and Demise of Vinyl**
Chapter 3 | **The Digital World**
Chapter 4 | **The Rise of AI**

PART TWO | THE FIELDS WE CALL OUR OWN
How AI is moving through the work that makes us human.

Chapter 5 | **Those Who Write**
Chapter 6 | **Those Who Visualize**
Chapter 7 | **Those Who Sing and Play**
Chapter 8 | **Those Who Speak**
Chapter 9 | **Those Who Teach and Learn**

PART THREE | THE HUMAN MARK
What we still believe—and why we choose to show it.

Chapter 10 | **People Win**
Hidden Track **—VerifiedHuman**

Acknowledgments
Appendices
Notes
About the Author & VerifiedHuman

Author's Note |

This isn't a typical book about technology. It's a human response to a moment that feels chaotic, creative, and deeply uncertain, and my attempt to take a breath amid the tension. It's the expression of an impulse: We've been here before. Sort of. But this time the shift is faster. The stakes feel higher. I wanted to include this note, written early in the process, to give you a sense of what it felt like as the ground kept shifting beneath us.

Written at the start of this project, February 27, 2024

Working on this book has been exciting, fun, and intense. The pace of AI-related change is dizzying, with new developments unfolding daily. While past innovations are set in the concrete of history, today's reality is swirling, confusing, and uncertain.

At times, writing about it has felt less like assembling a book and more like field reporting from an unstable political region.

Things on the ground shift quickly, and their implications are hard to predict. The rate at which AI is advancing, and the speed at which the media covers it, is staggering. It's a mammoth field to survey, filter, and analyze.

I've been tracking stories from the usual outlets: *The Wall Street Journal*, *NPR*, *The New York Times*, *Wired*, *Fortune*, *Time*, and *Newsweek*. All of them have robust online presences. I also follow a steady stream of tech blogs and industry newsletters.

On an average day, I read around twenty articles about AI, excluding the major players listed above. Today is February 27, 2024. Here's a sample of what landed in my inbox just this morning:

- "Students and AI—The Impending Academic Epidemic"
- "I said, 'Do not train on my content'—Did anyone listen?"
- "The Danger of Deep Fakes and the Importance of Ethics"
- "Amazing Collection of Chat GPT Prompts"
- "Enabling Success in Higher Ed. with Adobe Express + Firefly"
- "AI Automates Google Employees"
- "Why OpenAI's Sora is About More Than AI Videos"

These pieces highlight AI's breathtaking capabilities while raising alarms about its global impact. They cover everything from deepfakes and convincingly fake media to issues of privacy, ethics, job displacement, and the coming academic crisis.

> They affect the lives and livelihoods of billions of people. And it's not even 10 a.m.

When you read this sentence, new developments will already be here. It's a hot, fascinating mess. But you have my commitment: I will keep chasing the most critical insights until the very last possible moment before this manuscript leaves my hands.

—Micah

Foreword |

One of the key differences between humans and other species is our ability to use tools. Even though the human condition is defined by embodied vulnerability, technology has long been the primary means by which we improve our situation.

Indeed, ancient Greek philosophers noted the critical role that technology plays for both individuals and society. These philosophers recognized different kinds of knowledge that emerge as technology is inte--rated into our lives: epistêmê, technê, and phronesis. Whereas epistêmê often indicates a kind of theoretical knowledge, phronesis highlights practical wisdom about how to live well, and technê typically refers to applied expertise in a specific area requiring specialized training.

Although theory and practice are always implicated in each other, it is possible to know "that" something is the case without thereby knowing "how" to deploy one's knowledge in particular ways relative to specific goals. A helpful way to think about this is that humans are not just phone books or encyclopedias.

We don't just store facts. Instead, we decide which facts are significant and then determine how to utilize the tools available to us to create or craft the world as we would like it to be. Technology, then, refers to the tools humans use to shape their existence. Whether those tools be hammers, chairs, computers, or cars, such objects are what they are only relative to the human creativity that produced them.

Although philosophers have long examined the way humans use technology, they have also long warned of its potential dangers. Phenomenological thinkers such as Edmund Husserl, Martin Heidegger, and Michel Henry all worry that as dependence on technology increases, the very meaning of our humanity will likely transform.

Whereas technology once helped facilitate our flourishing (think indoor plumbing, air conditioning, and air travel), it now seems to define what it means to be human in the first place (think cell phones, social media, and teleconferencing). We would do well to take their worries seriously. Contemporary technology doesn't seem to be mainly about the benefit offered by a long lever to move a heavy object, but instead has now, itself, become the object that shapes us and feeds us ideas about who we should want to be.

The advent of Artificial Intelligence has made things much more complicated and much more troubling. AI is likely the most powerful tool that humans have ever designed. It offers enormous potential to revolutionize health care, address environmental challenges, solve traditionally intractable problems, and expand human knowledge to new hori-
-ons. However, it also threatens to dehumanize us in the process. As AI replaces human labor, it also appears poised to replace human thinking and creativity as outmoded relics of a bygone era.

Alarm bells are beginning to ring across society. From tech CEOs to visual artists, and from economists to creative writers, people are highlighting that AI's unlimited potential is precisely what makes it so danger-
-us.

xv

How can we use technology without losing our humanity in the process?

We must not shy away from this question. Instead, we must confront it head-on. *Human is the New Vinyl* does precisely that! Our very existence is at stake in how we answer it.

Micah Voraritskul is a musician, an artist, an entrepreneur, a theologian, a father, a husband, and a member of our shared society. Accordingly, he writes in a way that taps into our very humanity. Combining wit and personal stories with technical expertise and historical precision, Micah's book is not a pessimistic doomsday prophecy. Rather, he offers a vision that is simultaneously hopeful and encouraging.

Tracing how technology has been used in human creative endeavors, Micah never loses sight of the centrality of human creativity itself. In this way, the book is the very best kind of enigma. It is about AI, but more so about the human condition. It is about the future, but as anchored in our experience of the past. It is about the threats to human creativity, but it models why such creativity matters.

As is often the case, books reflect the marks of their makers. Micah is also enigmatically compelling. He is a web designer and founder of the virtual community, VerifiedHuman, and yet he also has a passion for truly great pencils. I can testify that he is happy to spend a long time explaining why a Blackwing pencil might be the most perfect object in existence!

In an era when listening to music on vinyl is retro-cool, it is easy to forget that vinyl recording technology was not so long ago the cutting edge of technological sophistication. Indeed, the very best things in the world manage to be both timely and relevant while also being timeless and stable. This book and its author exemplify that crucial tension.

Reading it will not solve the difficulties presented by AI. Still, I can think of no better way to understand those difficulties. They are challenges that anchor us in our shared circumstances. We are tool users, but we are also dreamers. We are consumers, but we are also creative. We are that strange species that can celebrate the craftsmanship of a pencil and then lean out of windows during a pandemic to join each other in a song of encouragement.

Whatever the recording technology, it is ultimately the song that matters. The song that Micah figuratively sings in this book is one that we all need to hear. And, maybe, just maybe, we will then find our own voices and begin to harmonize with him.

But, yeah, if someone does record the shared music we create, playing it back on vinyl just sounds and feels better.

So whether you take notes on the book with a Blackwing pencil or on an iPad, and whether you read the book in hard copy, audio, or e-book format, what matters is that you think deeply about its ideas and invite others to do the same.

You may find, as Micah suggests, that the coolest way to be retro is to lean hard into the importance of our shared humanity. A conversation, a collaboration, or a coffee with friends might be enhanced by Zoom, Teams, and a fancy espresso maker produced in a global supply chain.

Ultimately, it is not the technology that matters. It is the person with whom you speak, think, and laugh. As Micah so effectively shows, humanity is a vinyl record that will never go out of style!

Sounds good to me!

I guess we should all be thankful that he didn't claim *human is the new 8-track*!

—J. Aaron Simmons

Prologue |

When Fingerprints Leave a Mark

Give me a heartfelt poem written by a ten-year-old kid from Michigan and a perfect sonnet written by an AI model. I'll take Michigan every time. She's real. She's human. She has the experience of living. Her words will mean something.

Likewise, give me a dusty U2 record on vinyl and a digital lossless version. I'll take vinyl every time. It's tangible. I can touch it. It's got my fingerprints all over it.

Those preferences—*Michigan* over AI, and *vinyl* over digital—point to something deeper.

When Human Is the New Vinyl

A metaphor sits at the heart of this book. The "human" part of the metaphor refers to the personal perspective, individuality, and creative intelligence that humans bring to their work, just like a painter, songwriter, or storyteller leaves their mark on the final piece. We're pitting the heart of human creativity against AI's boundless computational power.

The "vinyl" part of the metaphor draws from the global resurgence of vinyl records over the past two decades, an era that has been almost entirely dominated by digital music.

> Why has vinyl made such an incredible comeback despite all logic?

It's delicate. Inconvenient. Expensive. It skips. It wears out. It's a hassle. *So why go back?*

Digital audio is superior in nearly every way. It's cleaner, more portable, and more durable. You can stream anything, anytime, anywhere, including every song you've ever loved, and millions more you haven't even discovered yet.

In theory, that should've been the end of the story. Yet vinyl thrives even though it's the opposite of easy. Vinyl offers something digital can't: texture, tangibility. A record has weight. Grooves. Two sides. You drop the needle. Hear the crackle. Study the cover art. Read the lyrics. You don't skip around. You sit with it. You stay.

> Vinyl asks something of you—*your presence.*

And in return, it gives you something rare: a sense of connection. A warm sound. A tactile experience. Its comeback was a little bit *nostalgia* and a little bit *rebellion* against the perfection and convenience of the digital age. It marked a shift. A longing for warmth over polish, friction over frictionless, presence over automation. It didn't surprise me that *authenticity* was Merriam-Webster's word of the year in 2023. The hunger for what's real and what's human goes way beyond music.

Take the enduring legacy of Hatch Show Print, a traditional letterpress shop in Nashville that's been cranking out hand-inked posters since 1879. Their prints are bold and unmistakably human. That's the point.

Or artists like Jessica Hische and Stefan Sagmeister, celebrated for the distinctive quirks in their hand-drawn typography. Their work is inconvenient. Inefficient. Imperfect. That's precisely what makes them matter.

> And that's what this metaphor captures.

AI thrives in a world of hyperproduction, über-efficiency, and relentless optimization. A world racing to satisfy the appetites of faceless market segments, where everything becomes easier, faster, and cheaper. *Ad infinitum*.

AI is reshaping the creative game, changing how we make, share, and experience all kinds of content. So our metaphor has to carry that kind of weight. And I think it does. Vinyl didn't disappear when digital took over, and I don't believe human work will disappear either. It'll stand out. It'll still count. Maybe more than ever.

Human creativity may be initially overshadowed by AI, much like vinyl was by digital. But it doesn't have to stay that way. Just as vinyl made room for digital, human-made work must now make room for AI.

This shift goes beyond tools and mediums. It calls for a cultural and existential metamorphosis. We're only beginning to glimpse AI's emerging societal and philosophical identity. And its influence will only continue to grow.

But we don't have to be swept away, mindlessly or unquestioningly. Enduring revolutions help us remember where we've been, recover what we've lost, and redefine what's worth holding on to.

> Digital nearly wiped out analog.
> But something scrappy and real in vinyl
> helped it survive and rise again.

With its dust, scratches, and wonky grooves, vinyl is more than just a medium for sound. It's a symbol of memory, story, and moments in life. Now, AI's generative superpowers loom larger than life, threatening to obscure human contribution.

Like vinyl, something scrappy and real in the human spirit will help it survive and rise again. Human-created work bears the imprint of its creator: her perspective, his lived experience, and their unique story. And as artificial intelligence continues advancing at breakneck speed, vinyl's reawakening reminds us: We're far from done.

> Vinyl found its way in a digital world. So will we.

That hope is what set me on this path—tracing AI's impact on human creativity—because the pattern felt familiar, like a movie I'd seen before, only never at this speed and never with such global gravitas.

By the end of our journey here, I hope we'll be able to:

1. Recognize the long arc of innovation – how invention reshapes the ways we live and create.
2. Understand the "Differentiation Problem" – why blurred lines between human and AI work threaten trust.
3. See the "Vinyl Paradox" – how we trade texture for convenience, only to long for the real again.
4. Trace AI's impact on creative culture – in writing, art, music, voice, and education, noticing both what humans still bring and where the seams are already fraying.
5. Walk away equipped – with sharper language, better questions, and a clearer sense of why human creativity endures in an AI-driven world.

When We Choose the Right Lens

Before we proceed, I would like to offer a word about *perspective*. We all have unique experiences, countries of origin, upbringings, and other factors that shape our perception of the world. Writing this book has made me acutely aware of the *limitations* of my own lens, particularly when researching and writing about the intersections of history, art, and technology.

For example, I recently learned that the Chinese invented modern paper and movable type centuries before Gutenberg's press appeared in Germany. This fact is often overlooked in Western narratives because Chinese printing largely flew under the radar of most European merchants, who were primarily chasing spices and silks, rather than scrolls. Plus, most of the world couldn't read, much less read Chinese.

Some innovations happen in a flash. Others are the slow result of many people in many places, all pushing in the same direction for years, even centuries, like mapping the human genome. It wasn't the work of a lone genius, but the layered result of many decades of global collaboration across genetics, biology, and computational science.

Parallel invention is one of my favorite phenomena: it occurs when discoveries emerge independently in different parts of the world, often around the same time, like the development of Chinese printing and Gutenberg's press, flight, calculus, and the invention of the telephone. Alexander Graham Bell and Elisha Gray even filed their patent for the telephone on the same day. The world is just *ready* for an idea, and it emerges in more than one place.

> All of it makes attribution messy and kind of beautiful.

I usually rely on prevailing opinions in my research, knowing that *prevailing* doesn't mean *correct*. It just means prevailing. For example, I've bantered with my Brazilian best friend about whether the American Wright Brothers or Brazil's Alberto Santos-Dumont were actually *the first to fly*.

In this book, I may give credit to one inventor or artist where it seems due, and inadvertently overlook another one from a different time, place, or background who may be more deserving. If that happens, I hope you'll know it wasn't intentional.

I was born in Bangkok, raised in the US, Thailand, and the Philippines, educated in a liberal arts environment, and steeped in global philosophy. My mixed heritage, being half Chinese Thai and half American, shapes how I see the world. I can't help but write through this lens.

> It's the only lens I've got.

Over the years, I've held firm beliefs, only to *change* them, sometimes even *reverse* them.

But I've always learned the most in spirited, mutually respectful conversations with friends who see things differently than I do. We may disagree fiercely, but we honor the relationship and choose understanding over consensus.

When People Win

I don't see the human–AI tension as a *contest*. I see it as a *confluence*. And in that confluence, humans must always define the win. Machines are here to assist their architects, and hopefully toward benevolent ends. But the direction, values, and vision for the work must always remain human.

I hope you'll stand with me in preserving human creativity as technology advances. We don't want to stiff-arm progress or spark a new wave of Luddites.

We want to raise essential questions while there's still time to shape the answers:

> *How can artificial intelligence improve our lives without compromising what makes us human?*
> *Can we pursue progress without losing the parts of ourselves that make life worth living?*

> Let's work together to find the answers.
> Not so machines lose,
> but so people win.

Now you know where I'm coming from. Let's take a trip through creative revolutions, past and present, and follow the human thread running through them all.

PART ONE |

REVOLUTIONS

How we built the future—
And how it's building us.

Chapter 1

Six Hours Early to the Party |

When a Spin Is a Revolution

Our heads spin, our clocks spin, our wheels spin, our planet spins. And the moon, its faithful dance partner, spins in graceful synchrony. Our Earth revolves around the sun, our solar system around the galaxy, and it just keeps going.

Physically, a revolution is simply a rotation, a complete turn. Revolutions surround us. Civil revolutions have their own distinctive sound: masses assembling and boiling over, law enforcement pleading for calm through megaphones, crowds shuffling their feet, chanting in unison, voicing collective outrage and hope. In this way, revolution sounds like a coup d'état, the forcible overthrow of a government.

Vinyl records also have a revolutionary sound. They spin in revolutions per minute, or RPM.

But in the broader creative world, revolutions are more than whimsical shifts in style. They introduce entirely new modalities of expression, reshaping how creators work and how audiences connect with what they see, hear, and feel.

Throughout history, the creative fields have witnessed revolutionary changes: the printing press, the camera, the phonograph, and television. Each of these has altered *how* humans create and *what it means* to create.

Of all these shifts in history, two recent ones stand out:

> (1) The rise of digital music from analog roots.
> (2) The rise of generative AI across creative fields.

Both have radically reshaped how we create, and both echo each other in remarkable ways. This book is about those echoes, and what they tell us about where we're headed.

The digital revolution has reinvented the music industry, redefining how music is produced, distributed, and consumed. And now, the AI revolution is doing the same across nearly every field of human creativity, challenging long-held assumptions about what it means to write, design, compose, and perform. What I was about to discover was just how personal this second revolution would become.

When the Signal Got Weird

In late March 2023, my friend Brian and I hunkered down in a café at the public library next to Lee University over a couple of wedge salads. We had just heard that Elon Musk, Steve Wozniak, and other tech giants had signed an open letter calling for a six-month pause on the development of powerful AI systems, long enough for safety protocols to catch up.

I had to stop chewing when I heard the news, just to let it sink in.

Wait. The "Hey, let's colonize Mars" guru and Apple's co-founder want the world to tap the brakes on AI?

> *What the hell is going on?*

One thing was obvious: Icons like Wozniak and Musk saying such things were signs of genuine fear and chaos behind the tech curtain. What rattled them was AI's unbelievable *general* ability, general in the sense that it could do *everything*.

AI's knack for writing catchy headlines or organizing inboxes wasn't exactly apocalyptic. But it could write code, answer complex questions, crush standardized tests, generate photorealistic art, make music, and mimic human conversation. And do it convincingly, at scale. No brakes.

Their open letter didn't call for a shutdown. Just a pause. A minute to think. To figure out what the reins might even look like. That call told me everything: The people who built the system suddenly feared they might lose control.

When We Couldn't Do Nothing

There was a palpable tension building in the upper echelons of AI leadership, an unsettling notion that machines might get so advanced, they figure out how to take over, wipe out humans, and end the world.

> You know, *Terminator*.

But I wasn't worried about that. The Apocalypse is well above my pay grade. I was worried about the end of something much more immediate and personal: *creative expression*.

A new kind of urgency hit me as I sat with the scope and speed of AI's rise. AI isn't *evil*. AI is *easy*.

> And *easy* has a funny way of winning.
> Even when it shouldn't.

Late at night, questions began tumbling around in my mind:

> How will AI impact my friends, who are authors, photographers, painters, sculptors, architects, songwriters, and musicians?
> What millions of jobs might automation supplant?
> Will teachers know if a student or AI wrote a paper, poem, or essay?
> Can we tell what a machine has created from what a person has?
> *Will anyone care either way?*

As the questions circled, I realized I couldn't just sit on my hands, knees bouncing. So I started reaching out, calling, and texting a handful of friends: writers, visual artists, musicians, voice actors, filmmakers, philosophers, engineers, and HR professionals. I kept wondering: was there a way to verify human authorship—not through legislation, detection tools, or encryption and watermarks (because those will always fall short)—but through *values*? Through *trust*?

With their insight and encouragement, I launched VerifiedHuman, a small, grassroots platform designed to explore and address the growing challenge of AI's impact on creative work. At the center of our work was what I began calling the differentiation problem: the increasingly blurry line between human-made work and AI-generated content.

And right away, I discovered how messy that line had already become.

In writing, AI detection tools like Grammarly or Originality.ai can, with some accuracy, root out machine-written text. But detectors often get overzealous in their pursuit. They're notorious for false positives. And detectors are met head-on by evasion tools like Undetectable.ai, which can "humanize" machine-written content with stealthy precision. It's become an endless game of cat-and-mouse like the 1983 movie *WarGames*, where a supercomputer plays against itself in millions of unwinnable rounds of tic-tac-toe.

In the visual arts, AI can now generate lifelike images that are often indistinguishable from those created by humans.

In music, arguably the most complex of the fields, differentiation becomes even more challenging. Many songs are made of dozens of layered tracks and elements: some recorded by humans, some played on real instruments, others produced by synthesizers, pulled from samples, or generated by AI.

As I continued to explore these questions and track the media's frenzied coverage, something else came into focus: lawmakers don't have a prayer of keeping up. But that shouldn't surprise us. Legislation almost always trails technology. It's reactive, not proactive, and painfully slow. By the time laws are passed, they're often out of step with reality or ignored altogether.

Anyway, after years of reading and reflecting on human behavior, I've come to believe something deeper: *values* drive human behavior, *not laws*. People usually do what they believe is right. Sometimes what they know is wrong. And always justify their actions if they're not sure.

As I leaned in more, I found myself on a twisting path, taking early positions and then reevaluating them as the human–AI story kept unfolding. My views on what human–AI collaboration means, how AI is shaping the fields I care about, and even how to talk about it with nuance, let alone offer solutions, have remained in flux.

What hasn't changed is the heart of the project I'd set in motion: VerifiedHuman.

At its core, VerifiedHuman is a growing circle of stubborn, humanistic optimists. We have great faith in human adaptability, a trait that has shown up throughout history, even in the face of extinction-level threats. Humans are scrappy. And if history tells us anything, it's this: we don't give up easily, especially when the real stuff is on the line.

We didn't hire a PR firm, spend money on ads, or seek out venture capital. But we've got an unshakable mission:

> **To preserve the authenticity of human-created work in an AI world, by offering a transparent, values-based model rooted in human trust.**

We may not be sitting on the *financial opportunities* side of the AI market. But we're standing firmly, and joyfully, on the *human* side.

When the Mic Dropped

By spring 2023, AI had become a global phenomenon, sparked by the release of ChatGPT in November 2022. It cast a dazzling light of possibility, and at the same time, long, ominous shadows over the future.

The "Chat" in ChatGPT refers to how intuitive and simple it is to use. Type a prompt in the window. Blink twice. Out comes a remarkably coherent response.

"GPT" stands for Generative Pre-trained Transformer, a robust algorithm trained to respond to natural language by predicting the next best word or thought. ChatGPT shocked the world with what it already seemed to grasp: math, medicine, law, and even philosophy.

But what *really* stunned the world was its unbelievable ability *to write*. ChatGPT churned out human-level text, fluently and convincingly, across a broad swath of subjects in nearly any style or tone. It instantly set off tsunamis across education, technology, and the creative industries. Early 2023 marked the seismic shift, and the whole world stopped and stared.

> The mic had dropped.
> AI was here, and it wasn't going away.

Within two months, ChatGPT had surpassed 100 million users, making it one of the fastest-growing consumer applications in history. And it was just the start.

Even before ChatGPT, early adopters had been tinkering with text-to-image models, like DALL·E, Midjourney, and Stable Diffusion, to generate photorealistic or stylized images from simple text prompts.

These models were erasing the line between digital and physical reality. If AI could create stunning images from words, I realized that soon it would gatecrash music production, making it possible for machines to generate entire soundscapes from a few lines of text.

2025 UPDATE | AI Floods the Playlist

Over the past year, AI-generated music has flooded platforms like Spotify. Thousands of tracks were covertly added to playlists, often without listeners realizing that algorithms, not humans, generated them. It's raising troubling questions about authenticity, ownership, and the future of music.

The biggest mess has been AI tracks mimicking famous artists. Songs like "Heart on My Sleeve" imitated Drake and The Weeknd so convincingly that they garnered millions of streams before being pulled for copyright infringement. Now, record labels, streaming platforms, and artists are all asking the same thing: Who owns the sound? What counts as real? How do you protect creativity when the boundaries keep dissolving?

What struck me about AI's arrival was how quickly it made creativity feel *effortless*. And a quiet question rose in me:

> When it's that easy to generate,
> does it still carry the same creative weight?

When Everything Hit Home

Some still insisted AI would always feel just a little off. I didn't buy it. I needed to know if the differentiation problem—the risk of not knowing what's human—was already here. The proof came from an unexpected place.

The problem wasn't just theoretical. Back at the café, I told Brian how I was a big fan of Jeremy Cowart, a celebrated Nashville portrait photographer. His portfolio includes notable figures like the Kardashians, Tim Tebow, Taylor Swift, and President Obama. Cowart has also done global humanitarian work for the UN.

In a March 2023 email to his news list titled "Houston We Have a Problem," Jeremy Cowart described something that stopped me cold: even with his "very trained, professional eye," he had inadvertently mistaken AI-generated images for real photographs. It was deeply unsettling.

Cowart is a seasoned professional who has carefully shot, developed, and scrutinized tens of thousands of portraits, spending years studying the shape, expression, and unique presence of the human face.

> If Jeremy Cowart can't distinguish
> a human photo from an AI-generated image —
> Who *can*?

Houston, we *definitely* have a problem.

By the end of lunch, Brian and I had reached some conclusions. They felt disheartening.

He said, "Micah, I think we're getting close to a point where it will be nearly impossible to tell what's human and what's AI: writing, visual arts, music, film, whatever."

I frowned, imagining a world so saturated with generative content that AI quietly becomes the *assumed* creator behind it all.

"I think you're right," I said. "Pretty soon, the default reaction will be: AI probably made this, unless proven otherwise."

It felt plausible. Even inevitable. My conversation with Brian shook me. But it crystallized a hunch that had been nagging me for weeks.

When Levi's Lost the Thread

What I didn't know yet was how quickly that hunch would be put to the test.

> The timing alone told a story.

On March 22, 2023, Jeremy Cowart sent his email. That very same day, Levi Strauss & Co. announced a partnership with the digital fashion studio Lalaland.ai to use AI-generated models in their online product photos, framing it as a push for diversity and inclusion. A week later came the AI pause storm: Musk, Wozniak, and hundreds of tech leaders urging the world to hit the pause button on AI.

Photography. Fashion. Technology. All blinking red. The Levi's announcement was caught in the heart of this perfect storm.

> It backfired immediately. People weren't having it.

It's ironic. The company that owes its legacy to a Bavarian immigrant solving a gritty, real-world problem with canvas, rivets, and grit now stumbled trying to fix a PR problem with an algorithm.

Some said, *I don't care what an* AI model *looks like in these jeans. I want to see a* real person *who looks like* me *in these jeans.* Others bristled at the idea that AI might be replacing real, paid human models.

It got me wondering: Why are people okay with AI *souping up* their phones, but not their jeans? There was something about it that just felt off. Like AI had wandered into a space it didn't belong in. Jeans are personal. Worn in, lived-in, full of stories. And suddenly an algorithm is wearing them? *What is that?*

Beyond the real fear of job loss, the deeper issue was something harder to name:

> What we give up when expression becomes code, and presence gets replaced by simulation.

Caught off guard, Levi's tried to walk it back. But their clumsy response showed just how hard it is for brands to adopt AI without stumbling over human trust. AI offers efficiency and low-cost experimentation. But companies must weigh that against something harder to measure: the value of human connection, especially in industries already struggling to represent inclusivity and authenticity.

I want to give Levi's some grace. They're a spirited, iconic American brand that stumbled while trying to innovate. But this misstep is worth our attention. It's an early warning for other companies adopting AI: Balance matters. Human connection matters. Fashion is about celebrating people. And customers haven't forgotten.

When the Fields Come Into View

Every generation in human history has faced its technological nemesis, a shift from one way of living or working to a supposedly better one. From hunting alone to hunting in packs. From writing with sticks to writing with ink. From home-cooked meals to TV dinners. From analog everything to digital everything. We're repeat offenders.

> We trade what's meaningful for what works, and what's real for what's easy.

And every time, we're left asking:

> What have we gained?
> What have we lost?
> Do we still recognize ourselves on the other side?

I'm not a scholar. I'm not a specialist. I'm a hopeless generalist, curious about almost everything. My friends call it *intellectual promiscuity*. I call it *pathological curiosity*.

In my research travels, five domains kept surfacing, each showing the same underlying pattern:

- **Writing:** of all kinds, for all purposes, from ChatGPT's explosive debut to content flooding markets.
- **Visual arts:** photography, film, and design, where even seasoned experts can't tell real from synthetic.
- **Music:** composition, performance, and production as AI-generated tracks flood the platforms.
- **Voice acting:** a more pervasive field than most realize, now facing synthetic competition.
- **Education:** where students learn to create and learn to be human, a world I've spent much of my life in.

Surveying innovation across five disciplines may sound ambitious. It is. But I've done so deliberately. I want to show how inventive, resourceful, and resilient humans have been when creative tools disrupt the status quo.

The historical glimpses remind us that people have survived and flourished, even when innovation brought unintended consequences. Like any powerful tool, AI holds both promise and peril. It can improve our lives in countless ways. But beyond the apocalyptic headlines lies a more immediate risk: losing sight of human value.

That's what finally pushed me from observation into action, launching VerifiedHuman on the belief that people would need it *immediately*. It felt urgent.

> Turns out, I was early—*really* early.

Over the next few months, more than a hundred people joined the VerifiedHuman consortium, each one a reminder I wasn't alone. The early adopters (for whom I'm deeply grateful) gave me hope. But they also raised a couple of questions: *Was my effort too small?* Or *was the conversation still too undefined?* I wasn't sure, so I started reaching out.

I wanted a clearer read on how people in the industry were feeling, especially in music, where it's always mattered who made what. So I called my friend Andy, who's well-connected in the Nashville scene.

> "Hey, man. What are professional musicians saying about the idea of AI making music?"

Andy asked around and called me back a few days later. He'd talked to successful, seasoned musicians across the Nashville scene: bands, duos, solo artists. I won't name names.

> "Micah," he said. "They're just not sure. Most people under forty, they said, don't really care how music gets made. If AI writes a song that sounds good, younger listeners just say, 'Cool. Works for me.'"

Audiences over forty, he said, were more troubled. They were more likely to say, "I'm not sure how I feel about a song written by a machine. What even *is* that?" But they didn't know what to do with that concern. And honestly, neither did the artists themselves.

For many of Andy's musician friends, that was the deeper tension: What do people actually want? Some fans said, "I don't care if it's an AI song." Others said, "I kind of care… It's just weird." And a few were clear: "*Hell no.* I don't want to listen to a song written by a *robot*. I want a song written by a *person*." Not panic, just a low, persistent malaise.

When Andy brought up the idea of verifying whether a human made something, one of them put it perfectly:

> "Andy, your friend Micah's like
> a guy who shows up *six hours early* to a huge party.
> There's no one there yet—just a big, empty, lonely house.
> But hang out for a few hours, and the food,
> the music, and everyone else will get there."

It stuck with me because it felt true.

I had seen something coming that felt urgent. But the world wasn't ready yet. Everyone seemed to be in wait-and-see mode. They weren't okay with it but weren't sure how to name what felt off. Even the media, even everyday people, carried this subtle hesitation. Not fear. Not excitement. Just a kind of ambient caution.

And I was sitting there, alone in the quiet, convinced the party was supposed to start. In those early hours, here's what I began to understand:

in a world where anyone can generate a song, write a story, or create an image with a prompt, the work shaped by lived experience, emotional truth, and intentional craft becomes more valuable, not less—like vinyl records in the age of streaming: scarce, tactile, irreplaceably human.

> As AI proliferates, people are going to want more of that. They'll seek out what's real.

The party is starting. The house is filling up. People are beginning to feel what I felt in that café with Brian: a quiet recognition that something fundamental is shifting under our feet.

This book is about that shift. It's an expression of what I sensed in those early hours and what we need to be talking about as others begin to show up.

Chapter 2

The Rise and Demise of Vinyl |

When My Walkman Was My World

My first Sony Walkman was one of the most meaningful presents I ever unwrapped with giddy fingers. Christmas 1985 was my rite of passage, my pre-teen entrée into the enchanting universe of portable, high-fidelity music.

I found two AA batteries, jammed them into the back, and snapped the hatch. I positioned the orange-padded headphones over my bated ears. I didn't realize this small ritual would shape so many decades of my life.

My brain exploded when I slid the cassette into that black plastic magic-maker, locked the lid, and pressed play. Instantly, I was no longer in our small Texas farmhouse. I had teleported to Prince's recording studio, hearing his raw lyrical genius come to life, performing for an audience of one: *me*.

My brain kept exploding through my teenage years as my bond with music deepened and my gear got more sophisticated.

I remember a definitive moment in 1987. I had elevated my listening game to a waterproof Sony Sportsman with bass-enhancing earbuds.

When I first heard the opening acoustic riff of U2's "Running to Stand Still," I couldn't believe my ears. It was completely immersive.

Paranoid, I glanced around, half-convinced there was someone playing guitar in our tan and brown conversion van. There wasn't. It was just a utopian recording of The Edge bending steel strings in Danesmoate House, Ireland, 1986. That signal had traveled thousands of miles and passed through countless invisible iterations before it reached a teenager's ears in central Texas.

When the CD Skipped In

Our 1970s rancher on West Upshaw Avenue was home to three record players.

The first was a Fisher-Price model, circa 1978, featuring a red base, a white turntable, and a robotic yellow arm. It spun its own proprietary tech: indestructible, multi-colored plastic disks with thick grooves. It filled the air with favorites like "Jack and Jill," "Humpty Dumpty," "Camp-town Races," and "Farmer in the Dell."

> There was no end to our listening pleasure.

The second was a silver-finished Sony component turntable with a signal amplifier and 10-band equalizer. It sat in Mom's fancy rack with a clear glass front.

> We weren't allowed to touch it.

The third was a Pioneer turntable connected to low-voltage speakers in my brother's room.

> That's where the real magic happened.

For hours, I binged on healthy servings of Journey, Stevie Nicks, Meatloaf, Foreigner, and the *Rocky Horror Picture Show* album, lost in the universe of the cover art as the licks drifted into the Texas night.

In 1987, my older brothers Mitch and Jim, flush from their server jobs at The Pelican's Wharf, unboxed a new digital delight in their bedroom: a compact disc player. This simple act marked the dethroning of the empress, the record player, and the dismissal of her court: the once-revered vinyl.

When Vinyl Got Forgotten

> Such a strange and simple tragedy.

Just the day before, our Pioneer turntable was the darling of our musical universe.

Now, she lay, unplugged and abandoned, a pariah on the carpet. A dense stack of vinyl was laid to rest in a lowly milk crate, exiled to a closet, stacked beside dusty sweatpants and broken dreams.

Beaming with infatuation, Jim handed me a CD to examine. I turned the flat plastic disc over in my hands. My eyes widened at the colorful artwork, the thin margin at the edge, and the half-dollar-sized clear plastic center.

"Hey, watch out. Don't touch the bottom. You'll get fingerprints on it," Jim said.

The smooth underside mirrored my enchanted face: no grooves, no lines, just a faint pattern beneath a silvery crystal veneer.

Mitch attempted to explain the newfangled medium. "Yeah. So the needle's a laser," he said as if to inspire reverence.

"A laser?" I wondered. "But how does the laser know what sound the record is making?"

"It's all digital, bro. There's no physical contact. It happens in its brain. It just knows." He leaned in. "And get this, you can skip to any song you want. Just press this button."

Amazing. Unlike cassettes, where you had to search for the beginnings of songs through trial and error, CDs could jump to the track of your choice. All that old-world alchemy now happened in its brain.

> *Wow.* It just knows.

We christened the first CD, *A Momentary Lapse of Reason*, by Pink Floyd. We all sat back, grinning and high-fiving each other with our eyes as the music ascended.

I almost cried when the thundering guitars and David Gilmour's ghostly vocals on "Learning to Fly" came through in a clarity I couldn't believe. The words mirrored exactly how I felt: Like I was being drawn away across some vast, empty landscape, past the point of no return. A dangerous kind of beauty had taken hold of me, and I couldn't pull away.

I was hooked. The digital sound of these bright, mysterious beauties was exquisite compared to my grubby, road-weary tapes, crisper than the vinyl we had so rudely forsaken. They didn't distort, crackle, or slump when the batteries got tired. CDs were the new cool kids. Sleek, flawless, compared to their nerdy musical cousins.

> I've noticed something about cool kids. Cool never lasts. The spotlight moves on, and pretty soon, they're just out there mowing the lawn like everyone else.

When You Could Still Feel the Music

Author and humorist Dave Barry once joked that the four building blocks of the universe were: "Fire, water, gravel, and vinyl." A playful nod to vinyl's reign, sudden fall, and improbable return.

> Why did vinyl make such a surprising comeback?
> Wasn't digital supposed to be superior?

Legendary BBC Radio DJ John Peel once said,

> "Somebody was trying to tell me that CDs are better than vinyl because they don't have any surface noise. I said, 'Listen, mate, *life* has surface noise.'"

Vinyl doesn't hide surface noise. It embraces it.
That's part of the draw.

People love vinyl for its warm, round sound, often described as more "authentic" than the sterile precision of digital formats. John Lydon, Johnny Rotten of the Sex Pistols, put it more bluntly:

> "I hate the technological rip-offs that pass for music formats these days and go back to vinyl to hear a good record because the sound is always so much fuller."

Vinyl's charm lives in its weight, its nostalgia, its perfectly imperfect sound. Vinyl lovers often point to science: a needle glides over intricate grooves, producing silky, unbroken sound waves. Zoom in on an analog waveform, and you'll find a perfect curve, flowing seamlessly from one point to the next.

Digital audio, on the other hand, is made of tiny discrete steps, like a staircase. Each step is a specific sound value at a specific moment, encoded as data. More steps, or "bits," bring it closer to the analog curve, but can't match its fluency. No matter how refined, a staircase can never become a perfect waveform.

Electronic artist Beck reflects on the physical difference:

> "When I pull out vinyl, there's a different physiology happening between the sound waves and the body that doesn't happen with music off the computer."

Vinyl's allure lives in the liturgy. The devotion you shared with fading cover art and liner notes. The sacred act of dropping the needle, closing your eyes, and just listening. Jack White says, "There's an inherent romance to it. When you see the disc moving around, and you get up to put the needle down, you feel connected."

When the Needle First Dropped

Vinyl's story is a fascinating blend of innovation, culture, and a deep love of music. In the early days of sound recording, inventors in the US and Europe were zeroing in on similar ideas.

In 1877, American inventor Thomas Edison introduced the phonograph, a device that used a foil-wrapped cylinder to record and play back sound. A decade later, German engineer Emile Berliner unveiled the gramophone, which played flat shellac discs, a closer cousin to modern records.

In 1901, the Victor Talking Machine Company (famous for the iconic Victrola phonograph, the wooden box with the horn on top) released the first commercially successful record. Featuring world-famous Italian tenor Enrico Caruso, The Red Seal record became an instant hit.

Suddenly, the unimaginable became real: people who might never attend an opera could now hear world-class tenors in their living rooms. The triumph of Red Seal Records sparked serious interest and investment in recording technology.

Then, in 1925, recording and playback got an electrical upgrade. Even with Berliner's shellac discs, which offered better fidelity, durability, and ease of use, the Edison-style stylus and drum still lingered in many systems.

Recording orchestras and vocalists proved tricky. Orchestras overwhelmed the setup, and mechanical methods couldn't capture the full range of sound.

HEAR THE DIFFERENCE FOR YOURSELF |

You can hear the contrast between low and high-fidelity sound in Pink Floyd's "Wish You Were Here," where a grungy, radio-filtered guitar gives way to a clean acoustic lead around the 56-second mark.

Sheryl Crow's "All I Wanna Do" does something similar, starting with a narrow, vintage sound before opening into a bright, polished mix around fifteen seconds in. Both tracks show how production shapes what we hear.

Electricity added a new dimensionality, powering amplifiers, multiplying microphones, and capturing a broader sonic spectrum. Electromagnetic recording heads carved detailed inscriptions onto each record. Electric instruments sparked sonic experiments: the haunting Theremin, early electric organs, and a growing arsenal of amplified tools.

When Radio Sang

Vinyl didn't emerge in a vacuum. It came of age in a world humming with stories, signals, and the static of change.

For much of the twentieth century, radio was king. It delivered music, news, dramas, and sports straight into the living room. My stepdad, David, used to tell us how, in the 1940s, his family in Peekskill, New York, would huddle around the radio each evening, eager for whatever came through the speakers.

By the end of the 1920s, the US had more than six hundred licensed stations, and the "Golden Age of Radio" was in full swing.

> **FIRESIDE CHATS** | During World War II, radio became a lifeline, bringing news from overseas and lifting morale at home. FDR's "Fireside Chats" offered comfort, his steady voice making the war feel a little less far away.

Radio fueled demand for recorded music, and vinyl was how DJs brought those songs to the airwaves. Jazz and blues gained popularity, led by Black artists like Bessie Smith, Louis Armstrong, and Duke Ellington. They played alongside white and Latino musicians, proving music could cross racial lines. Big Bands lit up dance halls, and the bouncing knees of youth confirmed Swing's rise.

As its reach grew, radio became a magnet. Advertisers, politicians, and reformers all wanted in. It stirred the public, amplified voices. And helped create the media machine we love to hate.

When "Vinyl" Sounds Cooler Than "PVC"

Vinyl made its debut in the 1930s as polyvinyl chloride (PVC), also called Vinylite, a name only a chemist could love. It was less brittle and delivered a clearer sound than shellac, its stuffy predecessor. The world took a few years to catch on, but once it did,

> The nickname *vinyl*, clipped straight from polyvinyl, stuck for good.

Through the 1930s and early 1940s, engineers experimented with "microgrooves" and slower rotation speeds to fit more music on each record. In 1948, Columbia Records dropped a bombshell: the first long-playing (LP) record, a wide, thin, twelve-inch disc spinning at a steady 33 1/3 RPM. LPs were a breakthrough. Each side could hold over twenty minutes of music. They spread like wildfire, allowing labels to release full-length works, artists to take bigger creative swings, and listeners to get hopelessly lost in the music.

When DJs Packed .45s

Starting in the 1930s and developing over the next several decades, radio DJs took to the national airwaves—chatting with listeners, spinning stories, and setting the tone for every record they played. Like pre-social media influencers with turntables, DJs such as Martin Block, Alan Freed, and later Wolfman Jack made listening fun and interactive. They added a third-party voice to the conversation between artist and listener, shaping tastes, breaking artists, and giving genres like R&B and rock and roll a shot at the mainstream.

Radio and record companies began tracking listener preferences, which led to the pop charts, ranking songs and albums by popularity.

It was a golden era for American music. Latin sounds—mambo, rumba, cha-cha-chá—were building momentum, especially in border cities, Caribbean communities, and major markets like Miami, LA, and New York. Jazz, born in New Orleans, was spreading nationwide, filling dance halls with big band swing.

I always remember my dad proudly declaring:

> "Son, jazz and country music were born right here in the United States."

Crooners like Bing Crosby, Frank Sinatra, and Rosemary Clooney leaned into the mic, introducing a smoother, sentimental sound. At the same time, folk, country, and Western music were finding their foothold across the country. The Grand Ole Opry, founded in 1925 and featured on NBC radio by 1939, relocated to the Ryman Theater in 1943, solidifying Nashville's status as the "Country Music Capital."

In 1949, RCA Victor dropped another vinyl bombshell: the 45 RPM single. Smaller than its twelve-inch big brother, the 45 measured just seven inches in diameter and became the standard for single-track releases. With the 45, labels could release songs as one-offs without releasing a full album. More portable and less expensive, 45s made "hot" songs instantly available to the public, who could play their favorite tracks over and over to the face-palming bewilderment of everyone else nearby.

When Love Cost a Quarter

Jukeboxes deserve a tip of the hat. Their bond with 45s was a match made in heaven. Big, glowing machines with buttons and vinyl behind glass stood ready to play whatever song your change could buy.

I remember the instant gravitational pull jukeboxes had on me, every time, everywhere. As soon as we sauntered into a restaurant and I saw one glowing weirdly, like a spaceship in the corner, my parents would sigh. They knew exactly what was coming.

> "Hey, Mom, can I have a quarter?
> Just three songs? Please?"

They rarely caved and smacking it like Fonzie never worked. So, I lurked in the shadows, a tiny jukebox stalker, waiting for some patron to walk up and select a song. All manners aside, I'd tiptoe in for a look, beaming as the mechanical arm pulled the record, dropped it on the turntable, and the music sprang to life.

By the 1930s, jukeboxes were popping up in bars, diners, and clubs.

> While the etymology is fuzzy, "juke" is thought to be slang for *rowdy behavior*.

By the 1950s and 1960s, jukeboxes had developed a culture all their own. Trimmed in chrome and lined with rows of vinyl under glass, they perfectly reflected Americana's spirited ethos and tidy pragmatism. They reflected the diversity of the cultures they came from, an eclectic mix of singers, dancers, and revelers sharing songs and space, who could be known to get a little rowdy.

When Vinyl Ruled the World

At the end of World War II, everything boomed. The US was booming with cash and babies. Electric guitars were booming on car and home radios. Jukeboxes were booming in diners and dive bars. The recording industry boomed, too, feeding America's insatiable appetite for music.

The technological and cultural shifts of the 1950s set the stage for rock and roll's world-shaping arrival. Elvis Presley, Chuck Berry, Little Richard, and Buddy Holly became early rock icons, driving record sales to record heights.

The Beatles hit like a meteor. The Rolling Stones swaggered in close behind. Together, they christened the British Invasion and jolted global rock and roll with new energy.

The 1950s and 1960s kicked off the era of high-fidelity sound and the advancement of stereo recording techniques. In 1957, Audio Fidelity released the first commercial stereo LP, featuring distinct tracks sent to the left and right speakers, which created a sense of dimension and offered a more realistic sound experience.

The 1950s through the early 80s were the "Camelot" decades for the vinyl industry. While Les Paul pioneered multitrack recording in 1955, it was Ampex engineer Ross Snyder who developed the first system to record eight discrete tracks on a single tape. The new tech gave editors and mixers the freedom to create beautiful, balanced masters from clean, isolated vocal and instrumental tracks.

The 1960s, 1970s, and 1980s saw further advancements, with synthesizers and electronic keyboards revolutionizing music production, enabling greater complexity and experimentation. These innovations ush- -red in new genres, including progressive rock, electronica, and hip-hop, underscoring the growing influence of technology on contemporary music.

The results were invigorating. Studio-recorded music sounded as good as, or better than, live performances, capturing nuances with impossible clarity, to the delight of a new kind of music obsessive: *the audiophile.*

> Records sounded incredible.
> And vinyl was the queen bee.

Its impact on global culture is impossible to overstate.
Consider the legacy of the era's most iconic titles:

- **Bob Dylan** – *Highway 61 Revisited* (1965). Redefined folk rock with biting lyrics and raw sound. "Like a Rolling Stone" was more like a seismic shift.

The Beach Boys – *Pet Sounds* (1966). Blended tight harmonies, emotional resonance, and studio precision. A masterclass in how to craft a pop album that still sings.

Aretha Franklin – *I Never Loved a Man the Way I Love You* (1967). Put soul on the global radar. Demanded *respect* with hits like "Respect." Crowned Aretha as the Queen of Soul.

The Beatles – *Sgt. Pepper's Lonely Hearts Club Band* (1967). With new studio techniques. Sold over thirty-two million copies and became the high watermark of sonic ambition.

Marvin Gaye – *What's Going On* (1971). Expanded soul's voice, merging social commentary, spiritual depth, and sonic beauty. Motown never sounded more urgent.

Led Zeppelin – *Led Zeppelin IV* (1971). Showcased LZ's range. Balanced mystic acoustics alongside booming electric riffs. With over thirty-seven million copies sold, it remains hard rock's gold standard.

David Bowie – *The Rise & Fall of Ziggy Stardust & the Spiders from Mars* (1972). Made glam rock legit and theatrical storytelling essential, a cultural shockwave in platform boots.

The Rolling Stones – *Exile on Main St.* (1972). Melted rock, blues, and country into a rambling, glorious mix. It sold over ten million copies, becoming one of the most respected rock albums of the era.

Pink Floyd – *The Dark Side of the Moon* (1973). Spent 937 weeks on the Billboard charts and sold over forty million copies. Few albums have ever been more revered from conception to production.

- **Fleetwood Mac** – *Rumours* (1977). Turned personal chaos into pop perfection. A timeless example of how heartache can fuel genius. It sold over forty million copies.

- **Michael Jackson** – *Thriller* (1982). Revolutionized pop music, music videos, and superstardom. With over 70 million copies sold, it remains the best-selling album of all time.

- **U2** – *The Joshua Tree* (1987). Dialed in their signature sound and cemented their legacy. "With or Without You" and "Where the Streets Have No Name" pushed rock lyrics to new depths.

We could have listed fifty more. But even these twelve prove just how monumental vinyl has been for generations.

Vinyl's influence reached far beyond the US. The UK's punk movement, Jamaica's reggae and dub scenes, and Japan's audiophile culture have all thrived on vinyl. Vinyl created a deep, transcendent bond between music lovers and their albums. It earned tangible and emotional equity, transcending genres and reaching ears worldwide.

However, that magic, fragile, physical, and grounded in ritual, had a bumpy road ahead.

When the Music Left Home

The shift didn't feel dramatic at first. It was a regular night in 1987 when my brothers brought home that CD player. It looked sleek, futuristic, with a digital counter and glowing buttons. You could skip tracks, play the whole album straight through, no flipping, no needle, no hiss, no wobble.

The discs were slim and gleaming. Clean and Fast. They auto-glided into place with a whisper, and just like that, the music began. It's funny, they were silver. They'd end up being the silver bullets that ended vinyl's reign. And the trigger was nothing more than a tiny button.

> It was easy. That was the draw.
> The old way of listening faded fast.

In truth, vinyl had been taking a slow beating for years, from something smaller, tougher, and even more portable than a CD: the cassette tape.

Tapes were indestructible. Didn't care where you played them. They rattled around in glove boxes, got tossed into backpacks and gym bags, and flung across bedrooms, yet still worked most of the time. Tapes weren't precious. But they *were* personal. Scratched, dubbed, Sharpied, and re-recorded.

Cassettes were versatile for the savvy and affordable for kids like me. If you didn't like the tape you bought, simply cover the top edge with a little adhesive and record right over it. If it snapped, you didn't toss it. You found a screwdriver, cracked open the shell, found the broken ends, and surgically spliced them with a piece of Scotch tape. They were resilient. They were hackable.

> They were totally *yours*.

Cassette players were rough. They hissed, chewed, and warbled. I'm pretty sure they made sparks. They warped in the heat. The batteries sputtered. The front covers broke off and dangled by wires. But somehow, they just kept trucking along.

The cassette tape had arrived in 1963, developed by Philips as a compact, durable alternative to reel-to-reel audio. Inside that plastic shell were two tiny reels, spooling a thin ribbon of 0.15-inch magnetic tape. Initially, they were primarily used for dictation and interviews. But by the late '60s, the Mercury Company began distributing music albums on cassette.

And from there, they spread fast. Throughout the 1970s, cassettes and vinyl shared space on record store shelves. People with turntables bought vinyl. Those who wanted portable music chose tapes. They followed us around. In boomboxes to barbecues and beaches. In dashboards for decades. For music on the road, your choices were simple: whatever was on the radio or whatever tape was on the front seat.

Cassettes were gritty enough to survive alongside CDs for more than a decade. And for a quarter-century, they coexisted with vinyl, delivering warm, analog sound to us all. They were the scrappy middle children of the analog age, but their role was never in question.

MIXTAPES AND MEMORIES |

It would be a crime to discuss tapes without mentioning mixtapes. Most people over forty have either made or received one:
A handmade playlist, lovingly compiled by a friend or a crush.

> | If you haven't, it's never too late.

Mixtapes were special because they took time, intention, and effort. Never mind the copyright issues. You had to cue up the exact moment, hit *record* with precision, and wait for the song to finish in real time. If you were *good*, you added the standard four seconds of silence between tracks. If you were *outstanding*, you slipped in your own DJ commentary, maybe even a few cryptic words of affection.

Mixtapes were time-consuming. Wildly inefficient.

> | But they *meant something*
> | because they *required something* from the maker.
> | And that effort gave them weight.

I have a drawer full of old cassettes and occasionally worry about their condition. I know they won't last forever. Lying dormant are priceless recordings from the eighties and nineties, memories hanging on by thin magnetic threads. Sometimes we'd throw a dinner party and just hit *record* on the tape deck, capturing the whole night, just for the hell of it. The sounds of my friends and family—cooking, laughing, and talking—are priceless now.

Among the treasures in my drawer is a mixtape I made in Cambridge, England, for a sweetheart back home in the States. I packed it with songs that said what I couldn't and dropped it in the mail. We've been happily married for a long time now. It paid off.

Other tapes in the drawer, stacked neatly, were ripped from the radio, complete with a DJ's lead-in or a long-gone station's unique ID. To younger generations, they're strange, ancient alchemy. But to many of us, those rugged, friendly little tapes still hold a sacred place.

When the Record Scratched

It isn't accurate to say that vinyl died in the 1990s, but it came very close to extinction. Sales collapsed from 1.1 billion units in 1981 to under a million by 2001. That's a billion-unit freefall in just two decades, the heartbreaking end of an era.

> Vinyl disappeared for one simple reason: People got *mobile*.

Vinyl record players are homebodies, sedentary creatures happiest on flat, solid ground. The hair-thin needle, nestled in a spinning vinyl microgroove, was delicate. One heavy footstep and the record skipped.

Cassettes and CDs let us take our music anywhere. And lugging a turntable on vacation is hard. It doesn't work in cars, won't play on trails, and hates the beach.

> Portability had won the day.

To make matters worse, digital audio formats and MP3 players completely rewrote the rules of music consumption. I can still see Steve Jobs on stage, holding up an iPod, proclaiming, "1,000 songs in your pocket." I remember thinking: *Wow. I could carry almost all my music with me wherever I went.* MP3 players made listening easy and practically infinite: tight, lightweight, and able to hold thousands of tracks. And they only sped up vinyl's decline.

Another tantalizing draw was the price. Online music stores sold songs for 99¢ each, making it a snap to buy a handful from your favorite artist or album. Why pay ten bucks for the whole thing when you only liked three songs? For broke kids like me or anyone with just a casual interest in music, it felt steep. I remember a conversation with a friend who insisted on buying full albums out of respect for the artist.

"Bro, you have to hear the song in the context of the album," he'd say. "If you cherry-pick a few songs, you're missing the artist's full creative vision."

"I get it," I'd reply, "But why pay for the whole thing when I only like a few songs? Drudging through the rest is exhausting. It's like pulling teeth. Besides, singles were nothing new. Think about it. Radio. MTV. 45s. That's how we have always gotten music. No one plays the whole album."

My friend wasn't wrong. But I had a short attention span and a tight music budget. Some artists set "Album Only" restrictions, hoping to protect their project's integrity or encourage fans to experience the whole thing. But a ten-dollar album was often beyond a listener's spending-to-desire threshold. They'd shrug. "Meh," and move on.

By the early 2000s, the market data was clear: vinyl was all but dead. Consumers had shifted from full albums to singles, ironically, a return to the 45's heyday half a century earlier. Vinyl still stood for something real. But *real* wasn't enough to win. Newer, sleeker formats sent the industry into a death spiral.

> The messy, meaningful experiences got edged out by the frictionless convenience.

It felt like the beginning of the end. But vinyl wasn't dead yet. Its roots ran deep, and its diehards wouldn't let go. Through the digital storm, they held the line, standing by Richie Finestra from HBO's *Vinyl*: "When I find something real, I hang on to it."

It was just another chapter. Even bigger shifts were coming: new tools, new questions, new chances to trade away texture for speed. And as usual, the quiet work began: deciding in the middle of all that noise, what we would keep, what we would let go, and what was still worth calling *real*.

Chapter 3

The Digital World |

When the Computer Came Home

If you were born in the US in the mid-1970s, your school years kept pace with the rise of personal computers.

My first encounters with those early machines were burned into my memory. In elementary school, I approached the Tandy Radio Shack TRS-80 (1977), one of the first mass-produced personal computers, with equal parts awe and curiosity.

The Apple IIe started appearing in classrooms from then on, deepening my fascination. However, it was the Macintosh (1984) that redefined reality. Its innovative, all-in-one design along with the legendary Super Bowl ad directed by Ridley Scott, ignited a sales frenzy and captured the public's imagination.

When Computers Got a Face

As humans, we *really* get it when we see it. Our brains are biologically wired to make sense of what we see: shapes, textures, patterns, and contrast. The natural human tendency for *visual* processing is why graphical user interfaces, GUIs, became the way we use computers. We needed an intuitive way to interact: clicking on icons, placing items in containers, and dragging elements around on the screen.

We just didn't know it until we did.

Innovative engineers at Xerox developed the first GUI in the 1970s, laying the foundation for the visual computing we take for granted today. We can hardly imagine our computer or phone screens without the visual elements we expect: icons, applications, and pictures.

The first personal computers weren't visually friendly. They relied on text interfaces consisting of letters, numbers, and symbols displayed on a one-color screen. You had to decipher code just to do anything, which made them a non-starter for most people.

The back-and-forth was cryptic and complicated. What was happening between the user and the machine wasn't always clear. Prompts had to be phrased perfectly, or they failed. Some will even remember the dreaded *?_SYNTAX ERROR*. For most of us, getting the computer to cooperate was exasperating.

There was no desktop with folders, just a curious blinking cursor, waiting for orders. For younger generations, it's hard to imagine a world without interactive visuals, like apps, games, calculators, notepads, documents, clocks, and trash cans.

When We Learned to Click

As the perfect complement to the GUI, the Apple Macintosh platform introduced another innovation to mainstream use: *the mouse*. Before that, a mouse was just a tiny mammalian classroom pet. Suddenly, it became the extension of our hand, gliding, selecting, and dropping a cursor right where we wanted it.

I remember my first encounter with a mouse. On a break from basketball in the Texas heat, my friend Kevin and I retreated to his chilly, dark living room. His family had just gotten the new Mac. I was dying to see it.

"Oh, yeah. You've got to check this out," Kevin said, motioning to the tan object with a single button on top. "It's called a mouse. Try it! You can select stuff by gliding over it and clicking the button."

Amazed, I followed the pointer on the screen as it responded to my hand movements.

"What the—?! How does it know what my hand is doing?" I marveled as it translated the tiniest motion of a ball into movement on the screen. Magic. Navigating a computer finally made sense: easy, intuitive, fun. The mouse had outgrown its cage, and computing had entered a new age.

When Work Got Wings

Laptop computers entered the mainstream in the late 1980s, offering a portable alternative to desktop PCs at prices that were affordable to the general public. This mobility changed how people worked, studied, and communicated. No longer chained to a desk, they began working in coffee shops, libraries, and even on *planes, trains, and automobiles.* Students could bring computers to class. Note-taking got easier. So did collaboration and homework.

Despite their early quirks, minimal battery life, and lackluster screens, laptops became essential for anyone who needed on-the-go flexibility. The boundaries at the office, in the classroom, and even at my desk started to dissolve.

Laptops were the parents of portability, giving rise to a whole line of digital offspring: tablets, PDAs, and smartphones, which are tucked neatly into handbags and pockets. Ever draining. Ever recharging. Always on. Always connected.

When Our Pockets Got Smart

After college, I stepped into adult life and joined the wave of eager consumers hooked on ultra-portable PDAs, like Palm and BlackBerry, during their brief historic run from the mid-1990s to the mid-2000s. They combined computing, networking, internet capabilities, contacts, calendars, email, and browsers, all in a handheld size. These devices also paved the way for music players like the iPod, revolutionizing how people consumed music on the go.

For a few years, my pockets snugged a Palm Pilot to my thigh and some iteration of a Nokia phone to my hip.

> We were all *packin' heat*—
> the lithium-ion-powered, microprocessor kind,
> not the gun kind.

PDAs quickly faded into historical obsolescence after the launch of the iPhone and other sexy new smartphones. But they still deserve credit for pushing mobile computing downfield a few more yards, paving the way for more tightly integrated technologies.

When Everyone's Pockets Started Buzzing

My family has lived and traveled extensively in Southeast Asia. In the early 2010s, we lived in the Philippines and traveled through Thailand, Hong Kong, China, Macau, Vietnam, and South Korea.

After landing at whatever city, we'd grab our bags and head straight into town. Every time, we'd ask the taxi driver:

"Before we get to the hotel, can you take us to a good cell phone store?"

Connecting our phones to fast local networks was mission-critical. As we sauntered along each sidewalk, we needed navigation apps, translation tools, and a way to Google everything. Staying connected was the only way to avoid missing the things that really mattered: gnarly markets and crunchy spring rolls.

The rise of mobile phones has been nothing short of revolutionary. Almost everyone relies on one now. *More than 85% of the world's adults own a cell phone.* On the eve of the iPhone's 2007 launch, Steve Jobs's famous line reverberated:

> "Every once in a while, a revolutionary product comes along that changes everything."

And did it ever. The new device whipped the mobile world into a frenzy over ever sexier, touch-sensitive works of art. With its sleek design, friendly interface, and a promising app ecosystem, the iPhone became *the* benchmark for everything a smartphone could be.

Not long after, Google's Android joined the scene as Apple's fiercest rival. Its open-source platform enabled companies worldwide to enter the smartphone race, driving innovation and creating phones for everyone, especially those who couldn't afford an iPhone.

In 2007, there were 122 million smartphone users worldwide. By 2016, that number had hit 2.5 billion. By 2023, 6.8 billion. In the US, smartphone ownership jumped from 2% in 2005 to 81% in 2019. They didn't stay rudimentary for long. Today, they're mini supercomputers, connecting us to everyone, everything, and all our music, too. Their impact on our daily lives is difficult to overstate. We use them constantly: making calls, sending texts, playing games, getting directions, and making mobile payments.

The real challenge used to be trying to fit them in our pockets. Now it's trying to survive without them for five seconds.

The smartphone revolution is underhyped. Smartphones have transformed entire industries, including healthcare, education, transportation, trade, and media. Journalist Andrew Keen captured the scale when he noted a 2013 UN report that more people on the planet had cell phones than access to running water, a mind-boggling measure of how technology has outpaced basic infrastructure.

Globally, smartphone subscriptions exceeded non-smartphone subscriptions for the first time in 2016. By 2027, they'll account for over 90% of mobile subscriptions.

When a Phone Became a Jukebox

In the mid-2010s, smartphones pushed music consumption further into the era of portability. They became the near-perfect digital nexus. They combined a browser, a phone, a suite of apps, and a music player, cramming everything necessary, helpful, and fun into the palm of your hand.

It wasn't long before we wirelessly connected our phones to car audio systems and Bluetooth speakers everywhere. With streaming platforms and fast mobile bandwidth, we can download entire albums and play them instantly, anywhere.

This *always-on-our-person* access means more opportunities to interact with music throughout the day, even in the bathroom. In the kitchen. On the way to school or work. On vacation. At the gym. At lunch and dinner. Anytime, anywhere.

| It's great. Sort of.

A few days ago, while writing in the den of our Tennessee home, I stopped everything and put on a Johnny Cash record. The vinyl crackled to life. It had been a while. And it was beautiful.

I have all Cash's songs on my computer and phone. Engineers have remixed them. The lows are lower, and the highs are crisper. Cash's vocals cut through the mix with absolute purity. His guitar sounds incredible.

The files are *lossless*, meaning they're perfect digital reflections of the original. And I *own* them. But the experience isn't any *better*. It isn't even close. That gap left me wondering how digital music has changed my listening habits, and what it may have *quietly taken* from me.

For collectors like me and many of my friends, it's cool to have music files that can float around the ether. Instant, contactless. But they've also *distanced* us, as listeners, from the music, from the tactile engagement of handling a physical record, CD, or tape. We're connected at the ear level, but not much else. We don't get to de-sleeve the vinyl. Handle it. Blow the dust off. Set it in place. Flip it over twenty minutes later to hear what comes next.

With digital music, many of us felt it, even if we couldn't quite explain it: Convenience, clarity, even pristine sound, *don't* mean better. Even when digital files sound indistinguishable from analog,

> "Digital lossless audio" is an oxymoron. We have clearly lost *something*.

When We First Logged On

Change never stops on just one front. Even as music went digital, a different kind of revolution was taking shape: one forming under, in, and around all the hardware: *the internet*. Not long ago, "Internet" was capitalized. Over time, it has become familiar, a part of daily life, so we see the capital *I* dropping off. Today, no one needs to explain the internet.

I'll never forget the day I met email, my first glimpse of the internet. You probably have a story like this if you're over forty. In the fall of 1992, I was studying in the library at Lee College in Tennessee. During a break, I wandered over to a pay phone (I know. *Pay phone*—attached to the wall and everything) and called my close friend Nate at Biola University in La Jolla, California.

Early in the call, Nate asked me something strange.

"Hey, do you guys have *email* yet?"

> "Huh? Did you say 'e-mail?'
> What's email?" I asked.
> I didn't even understand the question.

That's when Nate started explaining this odd and wonderful new thing called *the internet.*

"Yeah, so all these university computers are connected together," he said. "You can jump on and see what's going on in other places. The coolest part is that I can send you a letter, from LA to Tennessee, and you'll get it in like five seconds."

I was stunned. "What? That is insane!" I rubbed my temple in awe.

"Yeah. I could even send you a three-hundred-page document," Nate added, "and it'd take about the same time."

I spent my teenage years as a dutiful letter writer, pen to paper, with an envelope and a stamp. Mailing took days, sometimes weeks. Suddenly, my whole approach felt antiquated. That moment marked the beginning of much larger changes.

Soon, it would be *pedal to the floor.* From the late 1960s to the 1990s, the internet quietly rewired how we live, work, and communicate. Its impact has reached every corner of the planet. Calling it a quantum leap for humankind still doesn't capture it. The internet redefined human life on a global scale.

Before it connected the world, the internet began as a humble, decentralized network known as ARPANET. In 1969, ARPANET made its first successful link between UCLA and the Stanford Research Institute. The network continued to grow through the 1970s and 1980s as governments, universities, and researchers came online.

Other early projects, such as CYCLADES, NPL, and NSFNET, eventually converged into what we now know as the Internet. These systems were built on breakthroughs from the 1970s, including the work of researchers like Vint Cerf and Bob Kahn, who developed TCP/IP —the rules that *still* govern how information moves online.

1989 was a big year. Computer scientist Tim Berners-Lee, working at a research lab in Europe, invented the World Wide Web.

> He created the first-ever website.
> You can still see it today: *https://info.cern.ch*.

In 1990, Berners-Lee also built the first web browser. By 1993, *Mosaic* hit the scene. It was the first browser that could display text and images *together*. That's when the web started spreading beyond research labs. The internet quickly morphed from an academic tool to a global platform, reshaping how we share information, connect, and create.

Acronyms swirled around us: .com, .net, .gov, .org, .edu, suddenly part of everyday vocabulary. We stumbled through *"www-dot-whatever,"* but we said it anyway, as if it made perfect sense. HTTP, HTML, and URL became standard terms, rules for sending, styling, and locating content online, turning us all into creators and consumers of a different kind.

Years later, in 1996, I bought my first home computer. My wife and I cleared the kitchen table, unboxed it, and hooked up the four-pin phone cord. We dialed in through a noisy modem, accompanied by clicks, buzzes, and robotic wheezes.

> Then we heard it: "Welcome. *You've got mail.*"
> Suddenly, we were in a completely new universe.

The early web felt raw, imperfect, and full of possibility, like the hiss before the first track starts on a record. But the internet superhighway's on-ramp was remarkably short. Netscape Navigator. Internet Explorer. Search engines. Soon, we were *Googling* like it had always been a verb.

Little did I know that from then on, digital music, email, images, documents, and even the early stirrings of today's AI would be inextricably woven into my everyday life.

When the Feed Buried the Lede

Most people have heard the term *Web 2.0*. However, few can tell you what it means. It subtly altered how the web functioned and who it served.

Web 1.0 was static. You read. You clicked. That was it. Web 2.0 turned up the volume. Now you post, comment, remix, and connect. It turned users into creators. And websites into platforms. The internet morphed into a living space. You *participated*. Your contribution shaped it. You had a kind of ownership in it.

The shift arrived quietly. It felt as familiar as logging on. But in hindsight, the level of change was dramatic. And fast. Between 2002 and 2005, the web reinvented itself.

> Friendster (2002) introduced the concept of the social graph.
> LinkedIn (2003) made resumes interactive.
> MySpace (2003) gave users customizable profile pages.
> Facebook (2004) went from college chums to global news feed.
> YouTube (2005) gave everyone a stage.

AJAX code made web pages feel like personal software. *Google Maps* made the world feel familiar. *Wikipedia* and blogs handed the mic to the crowd. Just like that, the *read-only* internet became *read-write*. It got social. Personal. Alive. The transformation was so continuous, we almost missed it. It's like watching your kids grow.

You don't notice the difference in them until your aunt Janet comes over and says, "Oh my gosh. Your babies are adults now! When did this *happen?*"

By 2006, it had. Twitter launched. Facebook exploded. YouTube logged *billions* of viewers. The web wasn't *on* your screen. It *was* the screen. And expanding access to widespread broadband made everything even faster, richer, and more interactive.

> Today, Facebook, Twitter (now X), and Instagram have grown into sprawling digital societies with their own currencies, customs, and codes.

They have also given a voice to everyone: from old friends to oversharing presidents. Social media extends beyond selfies, group chats, and status updates. It has become an indispensable tool for businesses, political campaigns, and massive social movements.

Millions of people. Moving as one. The #MeToo movement used social platforms to expose the global epidemic of sexual abuse and harassment. The Green Movement in Iran, after the disputed 2009 presidential election, was also fueled by social media. Its protests were organized, broadcast, and amplified almost entirely online. Black Lives Matter. Arab Spring. Hong Kong. Parkland. The web became the front line.

On a personal level, social media's reach is undeniable. It reunites long-lost classmates and sometimes stirs up relationships that are better left in the past. "Facebook" shows up in a surprising number of divorce filings.

A few months ago, a friend said something that stuck with me: "Micah, Facebook is archiving our adult lives. Our great-grandkids will be able to trace our digital trail." That idea floored me. I recall how difficult it was to find any substantive information about my grandparents from Thailand and China. I found a couple of old photos. Their names were listed in some registry. And that was it.

For kids born after the mid-2000s, life online starts before they can walk. Their baby photos are geotagged. Their first words and first steps get likes.

> Their entire lives, from birth to death, will leave digital footprints.

Those over forty witnessed the birth of the internet. Millennials watched it blow up. Gen Z has never known a world without it. And the generations coming up now will inherit the world of Web 2.0, built with all its speed, ferocity, and permanence.

Even faster, more invasive platforms would follow: With its algorithmic death grip on Gen Z, TikTok made Web 2.0 look quaint by comparison. It marked a turning point. The feed became the front page.

> And we *became* what we posted.

When the Cloud Got Deep

But all that posting, streaming, and sharing had to live somewhere. Underneath it all, TikTok, Instagram, Netflix, and even your notes app all run on the same invisible backbone: *the Cloud*.

When you think of a cloud, you may picture a soft puff drifting across a blue sky. You probably don't picture endless concrete buildings, cold, expansive spaces lined with blinking servers and whirring fans. But *that's* the cloud. It's a vast, invisible network that stores our files, photos, and videos, accessible from anywhere. Our data resides on these always-on computer servers, backing up our lives and freeing up our de--ices.

Cloud computing, online services, and big data didn't arrive with fanfare. They slipped quietly into our lives. No announcements. No unveilings. Just part of the deal now. Yet we depend on the cloud more than we might realize.

Imagine if every server in the US failed at once. Power grid gone. Data centers blacked out. Cloud storage offline. Airports grounded. Banks frozen. No email, no tap-to-pay, no Google Maps. Streaming services, gone. The apps we rely on for food, work, rides, and communication, dead. No DoorDash. No Slack. No Venmo.

And that's just the first few hours. Without servers, the grid can't be balanced, fuel can't be routed, supply chains can't be tracked. Deliveries stall. Stores stop restocking. Communications vanish. Emergency response grinds to a halt. Hospitals lose access to patient records, lab results, and critical systems. It wouldn't just be inconvenient—it would be *The Walking Dead* without the zombies.

Tools like Google Drive, Dropbox, and iCloud, along with infrastructure giants such as Amazon Web Services, have transformed cloud computing from a convenience to a necessity. It's embedded in the bedrock of daily life. We can't see it or touch it, but we need it—for storage, communication, collaboration—for everything.

When Numbers Know Who You Are

Big data may be the cloud's most profound consequence: the massive collection, storage, and analysis of human behavior.

One story says it all. In 2012, *The New York Times* reported that Target figured out a teenage girl was pregnant before her family did. Her parents began receiving maternity ads in the mail and were baffled: "Why in the world is Target sending us diaper coupons?"

And Target essentially responding, "We've been tracking your daughter's data, running models to predict her needs. Yes—diapers. Oh, you didn't know she was pr—? Well, we did."

As disturbing as this story is,

> Big data isn't to blame. Data is just numbers. It doesn't care, it doesn't choose, it just sits there.

The trouble comes from how it's collected, bought, sold, and analyzed by governments, tech giants, and advertisers, anyone trying to figure out what people want and how to show up just in time to win, or at least cash in.

Targeted marketing usually annoys me. But I have to admit, more often than not, the algorithm nails it. Big data isn't all bad: it finds the fastest, safest driving routes, helps doctors tailor treatments, builds playlists you didn't know you needed, and serves up eerily relevant articles.

Like it or not, big data is woven into daily life, shaping what we see, choose, and even think about, often without our knowledge. And that influence, alongside the cloud and all our connected tools, is only growing. As Google CEO Sundar Pichai put it: "Cloud is the engine that drives the modern world." And that engine shows no sign of slowing.

When Fires Rage and Thieves Steal

Most people don't think about the condition of the original recordings when they listen to music. But the artists and archivists who have safeguarded those analog treasures understand the value of digitization.

Digitizing provides a powerful way to protect history and keep the music alive.

For decades, the music industry has used reel-to-reel decks to record onto dense magnetic tape, establishing it as *the* gold standard. We're talking Studer A-800s here, not cassette tapes or 8-tracks. Audiophiles will tell you: reel-to-reel is analog at its finest.

Unfortunately, the magnetic tape on which these recordings reside is fragile, comprising layers of plastic, glue, and chemicals that degrade over time and can fail instantly. Digitization lets us capture pristine versions before they're lost to moisture, fire, or theft.

In 2008, a fire tore through Universal Studios Building 6197, the vault housing tape libraries and film reels owned by Universal Music Group (UMG). In minutes, priceless master recordings were reduced to ashes, including tapes from Chuck Berry, Aretha Franklin, and Nirvana.

These weren't copies. They were the original masters, the highest-quality sources from which all future versions were made. Roughly 500,000 songs vanished in the flames, a tragic loss to music history.

Then there's a different kind of disaster—less fire, more facepalm. From the 1950s to the 1970s, broadcasters like the BBC recorded over old tapes to save money and shelf space.

> That short-sighted "efficiency" erased vast chunks of cultural memory,

including early episodes of *Doctor Who* and live TV performances by The Beatles, David Bowie, and Jimi Hendrix, lost forever.

Other losses highlight the vulnerability of analog recordings. In the 1970s, unreleased Rolling Stones session tapes were stolen, bootlegged, and never fully recovered. And in 1979, Tom Petty's master tapes for

Damn the Torpedoes were stolen during production, delaying the album and nearly ending in disaster.

These stories remind us of how fragile the soundtrack of a generation truly is. Digitization provides a new way to protect and preserve the music that has shaped our memories.

While researching recording technologies for this book, I wondered: *Why not just transfer audio from one analog master to a newer tape?*

Here's what I found: For purists, creating new analog copies still holds aesthetic value. It preserves an unbroken lineage of analog recordings. But the sound-on-sound problem remains. Every analog copy is second-generation, and with it comes inevitable degradation: added noise, distortion, and the loss of high-frequency detail.

The best digitization techniques are complex and hotly debated. But if we can preserve the priceless originals—Andrés Segovia, Django Reinhardt, Miles Davis, Whitney Houston, and Prince—painstakingly archived on redundant servers,

> People will still be able to *party like it's 1999* with nearly the same fidelity in 2999.

Digitizing them now is the smartest way to future-proof the classics for generations to come.

When the Edge Is Now

We have covered a lot of ground already: computers, phones, and the tools that tether us to the digital world. Some shifts have been loud. Others have come quietly, the ones running in the background, reconfiguring how we build, share, and verify things.

Open-source platforms like Android and Linux are built by global contributors and shared freely. They've shaped a generation of collaborative tools.

Blockchain arrived with big promises: a secure way to verify ownership. A digital ledger that couldn't be faked. It aimed to solve the problem of provenance: who made what and when.

The Internet of Things (IoT) encompasses a wide range of devices, including smartphones, smartwatches, refrigerators, thermostats, and security systems. My garage door opener is smarter than I am.

Increasingly, AI is what runs it all. It listens, learns, nudges, and responds, sometimes when we ask, sometimes on its own. The tools evolved. Now they act.

When Everything Is Everywhere, All at Once

The digital world changed how we live, fast. It reshaped how we communicate, connect, and even how we raise our children. As a dad, I'm acutely aware of how much digital technology affects my own children.

> My daughter could swipe an iPad before she could talk.

We may not control the systems, but we shape the culture, set expectations, and raise our voices for accountability and justice. When we care about privacy, fairness, and access, we're just saying: hey, *people* matter.

The digital revolution is merely the latest chapter in a long human story of invention, adaptation, and innovation. We dream, explore, and tinker until the impossible becomes possible, and the possible becomes real. But now, that drive has brought us something different. More than a tool we hold or a technique we use, this one responds, reasons, and creates.

> The digital world has revolutionized how we live.
> Now, AI is poised to change *how we express*
> what makes life worth living.

And that's when the revolution gets personal.

Chapter 4

The Rise of AI |

When the Shift Shifted Everything

The digital revolution changed the world. And it also changed us: how we live, learn, connect, and create. Nowhere was that more visible than in music. The shift from analog to digital technology changed how music was created, shared, and experienced. But music wasn't the only field that felt the impact. The same transformation also extended to writing, visual art, voice, and education.

Now AI is pushing that change even further. AI may well become history's most powerful technological force, surpassing even the impact of the digital revolution. Some say it's too early to tell. But I'd be willing to bet on it. Here's why:

> Digitization changed the *format*.
> AI changes the *role*.

Digitization redefined how we *store* and *move* information. AI redefines how machines act, *decide*, and *create*, and how we respond in kind. It's altering *how* technology interacts with everything we do. Every job, every tool. No sector of the expression industry is untouched. No field is unaffected.

We'll explore all of that soon. But first, we need to understand its origins and how it fits into the broader narrative of human invention and ambition.

When Two Centuries Outran Two Millennia

Between the late eighteenth and early nineteenth centuries, the Industrial Revolution transformed the world.

The spinning jenny and the power loom modernized textile production. Manufacturing advanced significantly with the introduction of interchangeable parts and the assembly line. Steam engines and locomotives revolutionized transportation. The telegraph revolutionized long-distance communication, paving the way for modern telecommunication.

The twentieth century brought too many innovations to list, but a few comparisons stand out:

> The Ford Model T, the first mass-produced automobile, cost $825. The 2025 Tesla Model S, at $90,000, can almost drive itself.

Orville and Wilbur Wright's first flights from the sandy dunes of Kitty Hawk in 1903 are a far cry from Atlanta International, the world's busiest airport, with 2,700 flights arriving and departing each day.

Consider how radios, televisions, microwave ovens, vacuum cleaners, antibiotics, computers, and the internet have become ever-present in nearly every corner of the planet.

Applied science has advanced significantly, particularly in computing. Bulky switchboards shrank over two generations into sleek cell phones. Room-sized computers, weighing thirty thousand pounds, reincarnated a few years later in slender bodies and were many times more powerful. Some may recall the first pocket-sized calculators by Texas Instru--ents in the early 1970s, which made math teachers everywhere be--oan the future of math education.

A few innovations have quietly crept into our lives, like cloud computing. Others, like the iPhone, burst onto the scene with dramatic flair: sexy visuals and rousing music. Each one lapped its predecessors and permanently redefined the human game.

When a Prompt Painted My Life

The world's fascination with artificial intelligence surged after its thunderous arrival in the visual arts scene, driven by two breakout platforms: Midjourney and Stable Diffusion. ChatGPT was right on their heels.

In the summer of 2022, I was immersed in the home-improvement vortex, remodeling one of our bathrooms, when my son, Ethan, a double major in math and computer science, introduced me to text-to-image generation using Midjourney and Stable Diffusion.

He poked his head around the corner and said,

"Dad, you're going to freak. This program can create entirely new pictures from the words you provide. Try it!"

I said, "Wait, *what*? You can just tell it to draw a picture, and it'll draw anything?"

He grinned. "Yep. You can tell it to draw a dog riding a bicycle while eating a banana, in the style of Degas. It'll do it in seconds."

I replied, "Really? Wow. Tell it to draw a half-Asian guy, frustrated, installing a vent fan in a small bathroom."

Within a few seconds, it generated stylized graphics, impressionistic renderings, and even photorealistic versions of me doing exactly what I was doing in that instant. Images that hadn't existed in the universe thirty seconds earlier. Some weren't remarkable, but others blew me away.

I shuddered. "Holy moly. This is unbelievable. I feel bad for visual artists. This is going to crush them."

I was a little worried about AI ending civilization, a little. But what bugged me more was how it might affect people I know. Especially those who create work for a living.

A few months later, in December, I was chopping veggies in the kitchen, the local news babbling in the background. Ethan came back with his laptop.

"Hey, Dad. There's this new language-driven thing called ChatGPT. You can give it a prompt, and it'll write *anything*: poems, reports, outlines, whatever you want."

We experimented with it for an hour, asking it to generate a few simple pieces, like essays, poems, and short papers, as well as other random content. It blew me away. I imagined how easy it would be for students to write papers with just a basic prompt.

> Wow. This is insane, I thought.
> Students are going to love this.
> Teachers, not so much.

When Smarter Gets Weirder and Closer

I can't say this more clearly:

> AI doesn't just *seem* different.
> AI *is* different.

Artificial intelligence now operates on a global scale, with remarkable depth and reach, drawing on tools like language processing, machine learning, and massive data models.

It's transforming medicine through deep data science: predictive forecasting, personalized care, radiological imaging, accurate diagnoses, outbreak modeling, and genetic research.

Over the past few years, AI has quietly become an integral part of nearly every facet of our lives. It powers tools like Google Search, Grammarly, and Photoshop. It runs Alexa and Siri, filters email, flags fraud, and powers smart homes and self-driving cars.

We carry AI in our pockets, backpacks, and purses. It sits on our countertops and nightstands, waiting for our queries, simplifying our routines, tilting daily life toward ease and automation.

It's terraforming the software industry. Between 2022 and 2024, global AI investment surged to nearly $170 billion. And this is just the beginning.

We will likely remember artificial intelligence as *the defining* technological leap of our lifetime. Max Roser put it bluntly:

> "A development as powerful as this should be at the center of our attention."

AI's meteoric rise and the speed and depth of its inroads into our lives are both exciting and unsettling.

It's like discovering a powerful, unpredictable superhero living in your basement. Still, you're not sure if they're for you, against you, or too busy growing up to realize they're even living with you. Welcome home.

What we now call AI got its start long before computers. It began with ancient philosophical stirrings and became a formal field in the mid-twentieth century. Visionary thinkers laid the foundation for what we're beginning to see today.

When Logic Met Legends

The origins of artificial intelligence stretch back farther than most people realize, to ancient myths and stories where humans first imagined machines that could think and move independently.

Ancient myths are filled with legendary *automata*, robot-like figures built by gods or human inventors, long before real machines existed. Those imagined creations captured a centuries-old dream.

In ancient Greece, Aristotle taught his students *syllogistic reasoning*:

> All dairy products are made from milk.
> Cheese is a dairy product.
> Therefore, cheese is made from milk.

This simple, step-by-step form of logic became the foundation that AI still relies on today.

In the 1800s, British mathematician George Boole took it further. Boole built a system of algebra based on pure logic. Yes or no. True or false. Zero or one. The same binary logic is at the heart of modern circuits.

Other legends followed. Charles Babbage envisioned machines capable of running programs. Ada Lovelace saw their potential to process symbols, patterns, even language and music, a glimpse of human reasoning inside the machine. By the twentieth century, AI had graduated from myth to math, and the race to build thinking machines was underway.

When Imitation Became the Game

The concept of artificial "beings" has been a part of human imagination for centuries. However, it wasn't until the mid-twentieth century that AI became a serious scientific pursuit, thanks to the brilliant minds of individuals like John von Neumann and Alan Turing.

Years before most people even knew what a computer was, Turing published a groundbreaking 1936 paper, On Computable Numbers, proposing a universal machine capable of solving any computable problem. A few years later, he helped crack the Enigma code and turn the tide of World War II. Somehow, between war work and deep theory, Turing still found time to wonder about the future of intelligent machines.

> "It seems probable," he wrote, "that once the machine thinking method had started, it would not take long to outstrip our feeble powers."

Then, in 1950, he proposed another mind-bender: a simple test with a profound premise. We now refer to it as the Turing Test. First, he asked, Can machines think? Then he asked something more challenging: How would we even know if they *could*?

Since the 1950s, the Turing Test has been a widely referenced benchmark for evaluating machine intelligence and a fixture in ongoing debates about whether machines can exhibit human-like awareness. At its core, the Turing Test is a simple game:

> Can someone tell if they're talking to a machine or a human?

A computer would deserve to be called intelligent, Turing wrote, "if it could deceive a human into believing it was human."

Here's how it works: A human judge sits in *one* room, unaware whether the subject in the *other* room is a person or a computer. Their task is simple: Can they identify which agent is which based solely on their responses? To evaluate a machine's intelligence, the tester might ask questions like:

"How is a dog like a rock?"
  Tests creativity and humor.

"How do you know if someone is happy?"
  Challenging emotional reasoning.

"What does it mean to 'spill the beans'?"
  Checks for idiomatic fluency.

"How would you help a friend find their phone?"
  Measures problem-solving and handling incomplete information.

"Outstanding! Traffic! How great is that?"
  Determines whether the subject can recognize sarcasm or irony.

2025 UPDATE | AI Just Out-Humaned Humans

In 2025, researchers at UC San Diego ran a tougher, three-party version of the classic Turing test. GPT-4.5, posing as an introverted, slang-savvy young adult, fooled human judges 73% of the time. Even more unsettling, it was rated as more human than the actual person.

AI could out-human humans.

That shouldn't feel surprising. The machine wasn't showing up as a single person. It was an amalgam of all discoverable humans, blended together.

For almost a decade, I led a massive youth choir with 150 teenagers. We had 70 altos. One thing I learned fast: to sound great, I only needed a handful of strong singers, maybe 5 to 10 percent. The rest filled in the gaps, added volume, and followed the confident voices. Even the off-key moments got buried in the mix. The collective always came out smoother, more polished, even supra-human, bigger than any one person alone.

That's how GPT-4.5 pulled it off. It wasn't competing as a person. It was performing as a collective, a stitched-together reflection of millions of voices, patterns, and emotional cues. There's real nuance in that. Real power. And it's unsettling.

A single human didn't stand a chance.

And that takes us right back to the heart of the differentiation problem. If a machine can beat us at sounding like us by remixing the best and hiding the flaws, what exactly are we measuring? Intelligence? Authenticity? Originality? Or just the illu--ion of being a person—by being a super-person?

When Four Guys Gave AI Its Name

In AI's early days, researchers focused on building systems to perform narrow, well-defined tasks, an approach now known as *narrow AI*, like playing chess or solving math problems. One early example was the Logic Theorist, a program developed in 1956 by Allen Newell, Herbert Simon, and Cliff Shaw.

It simulated human problem-solving and proved mathematical theorems using symbolic logic. The Logic Theorist was a breakthrough. It demonstrated that machines could perform complex cognitive tasks and inspired researchers to develop a systematic approach to the field.

The *Dartmouth Conference*, held at Dartmouth College in the summer of 1956, is widely considered the birthplace of AI as a formal field. Organized by John McCarthy, Marvin Minsky, Nathaniel Rochester, and Claude Shannon, the workshop brought artificial intelligence into formal academic study.

McCarthy developed LISP, one of the first programming languages for AI. Minsky, co-founder of the MIT AI Lab, advanced early machine learning and neural networks. Rochester led IBM's first AI efforts, and Shannon, the father of information theory, laid the foundations for logical systems.

The conference became a turning point in computer science, bringing together top minds to explore how machines might one day mimic human intelligence.

> It was also the moment they introduced a new term to the world: *Artificial Intelligence.*

Their ambition was remarkable. They imagined a future where machines could eventually replicate every aspect of human learning and intelligence. The conference created the framework for decades of innovation in teaching machines to think and learn like humans, focusing on four key areas: reasoning, language use, learning, and perception.

It didn't lead to immediate breakthroughs, but it set the field's long-term goals and challenges:

–Natural language processing: *getting computers to understand and respond in everyday language.*

- Neural networks: *systems able to learn like a brain by making connections.*
- Computer vision: *teaching machines to recognize what they see, like faces or objects in a photo.*

When Winters Waxed and Summers Waned

Dartmouth's optimism captured the era's zeitgeist. The conference foreshadowed the breakthroughs and setbacks that would shape AI research for the next 50 years.

But its legacy didn't stop there. Ideas like symbolic reasoning, general intelligence, and machine learning remain central today.

What followed, though, was a long and often sluggish quest to build machines able to think like humans. AI's early decades moved in fits and starts: *AI summers*, marked by seasons of progress and funding, often gave way to *AI winters*, characterized by stalled momentum and vanishing cash. Developers endured the cycle: hope, hype, disappointment, repeat. History may help frame the current AI boom, and whatever comes next.

In the 1980s and 1990s, new hope returned. Machine learning and neural networks re-emerged. Expert systems, rule-based programs used in medicine and finance, began to achieve real-world success.

The next breakthrough came in 1986, when David Rumelhart, Geoffrey Hinton, and Ronald Williams popularized the backpropagation algorithm, enabling computers to learn from their mistakes and train deep, layered neural networks. Hinton, later nicknamed the "Godfather of AI," played a central role in advancing deep learning, influencing everything from speech recognition to image analysis in the decades that followed.

When Machines Started Learning (and Swearing)

If you've been reading about AI lately, you've probably come across curious terms like *machine learning* and *deep learning*. They're key to understanding what makes AI so powerful.

Here's a quick breakdown. In *machine learning*, developers train systems using a massive amount of example data. They use it to identify patterns, similarities, and differences.

To teach a machine human language, programmers feed it unbelievable amounts of written text, billions of examples from which it starts learning grammar, tone, and context rules. Eventually, when you give it a prompt, it can generate a coherent, context-aware response.

However, learning can be messy, even for computers. After training on Urban Dictionary—an online slang dictionary known for its colorful and often explicit language—

> IBM's Watson started swearing like a sailor.

Every response was laced with profanity. The team had to wash its mouth out with digital soap.

Watson wasn't the only system to go sideways. In 2016, Microsoft launched a chatbot on Twitter. Their model, "Tay," was designed to learn from public interactions in real-time. It was a very quick faceplant. Within 24 hours, Tay was parroting conspiracy theories, slurs, and toxic nonsense. AI learns from our best ideas *and* our worst instincts.

Let's go back to fruit. Say you want a computer to recognize apples, oranges, and bananas. You'd write a program that spells out their shape, color, and texture, step by step. That's called *explicit programming*: giving the machine a fixed set of rules to follow.

But if you wanted the computer to learn on its own, you'd take a different approach. In *machine learning*, you'd feed the computer thousands of fruit photos. Then it identifies patterns, colors, shapes, and sizes independently. The more it sees, the better it gets.

When Learning Got Deep

> *Deep learning* is a type of machine learning modeled after the human brain.

Our brains contain billions of interconnected neurons working together to process information. The "deep" comes from this stacking concept: multiple layers, each building on the last, allow the system to tackle more complex tasks.

The first layer may detect simple shapes or edges in a model trained to recognize fruit. The next layer picks color and texture. Later layers detect even more subtle variations, and the process continues, leading to even more accurate classification.

Connections between units work like roads. They widen or shrink in response to their performance. If a particular pathway consistently helps solve the problem, it grows broader, like a highway adding lanes as traffic builds. These dynamic adjustments help the system prioritize the most successful connections. The more layers it has, the deeper the patterns it can decode.

This is the power behind tools like ChatGPT and Claude. Their language sounds human: layered, structured, and intentional. The same technology drives platforms like DALL·E, turning simple text prompts into images with stunning realism and complexity. These systems stack decisions, building language, visuals, and ideas that feel surprisingly purposeful.

When the Layers Get Stacked

In the 1980s, my mom worked full-time, raised five kids, and typed her master's papers on a manual typewriter. One evening, I wandered into her room, drawn by the clack-clack of the keys. She had just changed the ink ribbon and was testing it with the sentence:

> The quick brown fox jumps over the lazy dog.

She told me it was to make sure every letter left a nice, inky mark. It's a well-known little sentence, a pangram using all twenty-six letters of the alphabet at least once. It's often used to test typewriters, keyboards, or font styles.

For fun, I prompted two well-known LLMs to write ten alternate versions for me, keeping them light. Here are the three I liked best:

- The nimble russet vulpine vaults above an indolent canine.
- The speedy cinnamon reynard bounces beyond a slothful hound.
- With zest, a swift sienna fox skips over a napping tail-wagger.

They're a little over the top, but the range of vocabulary is wild. Think about it. To transform "The quick brown fox jumps over the lazy dog" into "The speedy cinnamon reynard bounces beyond a slothful hound," the models had to make a series of layered decisions: finding synonyms, preserving meaning, reworking the structure, and matching the tone. They had to consider meaning, find equivalent words that worked in the context, avoid redundancy, and stay, as I asked them to, "fun."

They're surprisingly creative, even a little imaginative. If I had read those unquestioningly, I would have made assumptions about the writer. This person comes across as playful and inventive, someone with a strong vocabulary, pulling in words like vulpine for fox, somnolent for sleepy, and russet, cinnamon, and sienna for brown. Most readers would likely envision a native-speaking, college-educated writer with a solid grasp of the English language.

| But the writer isn't a person. It's an LLM.

With the same layered approach, these tools can produce writing that feels grounded, experienced, and even expert.

A few months ago, our lifelong friends Carl and Debbie visited us at our new place in Tennessee. Carl had just retired after a long career adjusting insurance claims for high-end agribusiness: ranches, farms, equipment, and the occasional million-dollar thoroughbred racehorse.

Between meals, I wanted to show them what I'd been working on, so we started talking about ChatGPT. They'd heard of it but had never seen it in action.

"Everybody's talking about it. What's the big deal?" they asked.

I came up with a prompt on the spot: *Write me a brief on insuring farms, ranches, and estates in the Eastern US.*

In less than fifteen seconds, ChatGPT generated nearly ten pages of detailed, specific, industry-level content.

It read like a brief written by a person with years of experience: clear structure, technical language, nuanced examples, and even references to emerging risks and market trends. It broke down the real-world complexity of the sector, connecting dots most outsiders wouldn't even know existed.

Carl stared at the screen, nodded, and grinned. "Whoa. That's my entire career. You could print that out and hand it to any recruit. They'd instantly get a feel for the sector. Wow." Chat wrote it in under fifteen seconds.

When the Machines Started Winning

Strategic board games offer a vivid lens into AI's growing capabilities. Chess and *Go*, two of the world's most respected games, have long served as ultimate tests. They require logical precision. They demand foresight, pattern recognition, depth, and intuition—the kind of quiet brilliance we tend to associate with humans, not machines.

I've always enjoyed chess, even if my game could use some profound love. So, in 1997,

> When IBM's Deep Blue beat Garry Kasparov, the world champion, something in me died a little.

A machine had outplayed a grandmaster on the world stage for the first time. It was a pivotal moment, proof of how *far* machines had come, and how *fast*.

Nearly two decades later, it happened again, this time in the popular game of *Go*. In 2016, Google DeepMind's AI, AlphaGo, faced off against Lee Sedol, one of the greatest *Go* players in history. Go is exponentially more complex than chess, with more board combinations than atoms in the universe. For years, it stood as the final stronghold of human strategic dominance.

> Sedol *lost*.

What's remarkable about the victories of Deep Blue and AlphaGo is that almost everyone watching got it wrong. We naively believed intuition, creativity, and deep human strategy would still prevail over raw computing power.

In the final game, AlphaGo made a few moves so bizarre and out-of-left-field that even serious amateurs and world-class Go players thought they were *mistakes*.

> But they weren't. They were brilliant.

The AI wasn't imitating human logic. It was making independent decisions far outside the range of human comprehension. It was playing its *own creative game*. Sedol fought hard. But in the end, he bowed.

I remember seeing videos of people, all over the world, literally weeping after the match. Maybe they were mourning the fall of their mortal champion.

> Maybe their tears represented something deeper: a quiet grief over humanity's loss to a machine of its own making.

When Language Became a Superpower

These breakthroughs are just a glimpse of what's coming. Over the past five years, AI progress has accelerated significantly, driven by massive datasets, powerful hardware, and the emergence of large language models (LLMs). Models like GPT (OpenAI), Claude (Anthropic), and Gemini (Google) have been trained on vast portions of online data. They've parsed nearly the entire body of human writing: books, articles, websites, and social media posts.

Their goal is to learn how humans communicate: What words do they use, and in what combinations do they use them? What ideas go together?

From there, they predict the most likely, or most useful, response. Now, we can ask an LLM to do almost anything: write a story, answer questions, and organize vast amounts of information in seconds.

It's like having a supercharged research assistant, always ready to work on your problem, always just a click away.

Last week, I received a set of *Office Actions* from the US Patent and Copyright Office: dense documents packed with precise legal language. I immediately felt overwhelmed. I then uploaded the files to ChatGPT and asked, "What does this say? Break it down for me. What's the best way to respond?"

Within ten seconds, it summarized the documents and handed me a clean, comprehensive list of action steps to choose from.

LLMs are also multilingual, fluent in all of the world's major languages: English, Chinese, Spanish, French, German, Russian, Portuguese, Italian, Arabic, and Japanese. In all these languages, LLMs can now write and respond with fluency that rivals, or even surpasses, most human writers and speakers.

They've also achieved proficiency in dozens of other languages: Korean, Dutch, Swedish, Turkish, Polish, Hindi, Indonesian, Thai, Czech, and Greek. Many of us, including writers, translators, and language professionals, have closely followed this evolution, watching as LLMs improve their linguistic performance.

At this point, it's safe to say: LLMs can now write well in more than 100 human languages, depending on how you define "writing well." And they're still advancing. Over the past two years alone, LLMs have made significant strides in generating human-like language. And with more time and training, they'll only get sharper. As I like to say:

> While we sleep, the AIs are doing ten trillion push-ups, getting faster, stronger, and smarter.

But here's the part we can't forget: LLMs don't understand content the way humans do. They generate responses by predicting patterns, rather than grasping meaning or forming original thoughts. Critical thinking, deep comprehension, and genuine insight remain distinctly human.

When Machines Began to Dream

We have spent a lot of time with LLMs. Now, let's turn to generative AI, a technology that extends beyond writing copy and into the creative realm: images, music, and video. Specialized models like Midjourney and Stable Diffusion are known for generating elaborate, often breathtaking visuals. Others, like OpenAI's Jukebox and AIVA, focus on music composition. In late 2024, OpenAI released Sora, a model capable of transforming simple prompts into cinematic short films.

> **2025 UPDATE | AI Got Faster Than the Debate**
>
> Generative AI hasn't slowed down. It's sped up. OpenAI's Sora continues to raise the bar, creating cinematic scenes with unsettling depth and realism, all from text prompts.
>
> Midjourney's Version 7 advanced image quality with smarter prompts, faster drafts, and near-photorealistic results. ChatGPT-4o can now create images on the fly, with DALL·E built right into the chat.
>
> Many artists, musicians, filmmakers, and creative pros are experimenting with folding these tools into their workflows. However, critics are asking tough questions about ownership, sourcing, and the essence of the work.

Like LLMs, these generative models are trained on massive datasets, learning the fine-grained patterns that define their domains. These are images rivaling fine art, music fit for a concert hall, and cinematic scenes that feel strikingly real.

There's a fascinating intersection where LLMs and generative models meet. Text-to-image tools sit right at this edge, where linguistic precision meets visual imagination. You describe what you want in words. The model interprets, then switches gears, tapping its generative power to deliver striking visuals. The canvas of visual creation has stretched in ways no one could have predicted.

> The revolution is here. It landed while everyone was arguing about whether it had wings.

When *Babel* Went Backwards

There's a fascinating story in Genesis, a sacred text shared by Christianity, Judaism, and Islam, which together represent more than half the world's population.

(A classic illustration of the Tower of Babel appears in the appendices.)

According to the story, in the earliest days of human history, everyone spoke *the same language.* They came together and began building a massive city using their newly developed *brick* technology. Stackable shapes made everything square up. Smart. Odd-sized rocks don't stack well.

As they built tall towers, ziggurats, the deity grew curious and went down to check things out in person. (God's concern probably *wasn't* that humans were in danger of storming the gates of heaven with a skyscraper. More, that humans were getting ahead of themselves and attempting to become the gods of their own ambition.)

After all, God *had* instructed them to spread out, multiply, and fill the earth. But instead, they clustered into dense cities and built massive buildings.

To thwart their progress, the story recounts how God "confused" their single language into many languages, rendering it so that large groups could no longer understand one another. Work stopped immediately due to a lack of linguistic coordination.

So, people locked arms with those they could still understand, maybe five to ten thousand per group, and headed off to find their own land and do their own thing.

> Here's the moment I almost fell out of my chair.

In April 2023, I watched a captivating TED Talk by Tristan Harris and Aza Raskin from the Center for Humane Technology. The two presented their thoughts about the sudden, steep spike in AI development.

Harris and Raskin explained that, before 2022, AI progress was primarily confined to research silos, including robotics, genetics, medicine, linguistics, and computer science. Each field advanced slowly and steadily, moving up and to the right. But when LLMs arrived, everything shifted.

Because LLMs process and generate human-like language, they could translate and connect information across disciplines. The models became a bridge between specialists. Suddenly, the diaspora of fields could "talk to each other."

> They were speaking *the same language.*

Through language-driven LLMs, researchers, developers, and companies could share insights, collaborate, and innovate faster than ever before. As a result, AI development skyrocketed. The curve went vertical in a matter of months.

> I thought: *Whoa.* This is like *anti*-Babel: Languages are coming back *together* again.

AI is breaking down interdisciplinary barriers and enabling unprecedented collaboration. It's a reversal of Babel's confusion, uniting humans for collective progress and casting AI as a powerful catalyst.

Some friends have asked whether this anti-Babel shift gives me theological pause. Honestly? I'm not sure. I'm not sure what to make of it.

> I just notice it.

The flywheel is spinning fast. With breakthroughs shared freely, the pace of innovation continues to climb. In 2022, Max Roser noted that AI development was accelerating, and it has only continued to gain steam.

> "Since about 2010, this exponential growth has now sped up to a doubling time of just about six months. That's astonishingly fast."

These technologies are now more accessible to a wider range of people in more places, enabling a broader range of applications. Over the past two years, the LLM community has grown, focusing on improving models, addressing bias and privacy concerns, and exploring new, meaningful uses for AI.

When Everybody Ate Their Cake

Given all this, it's no surprise that AI has become a media obsession. Throughout 2023 and 2024, AI stories ran daily on every platform, every channel, nonstop. Reports buzzed with speculation, from cataclysmic predictions to promises for humankind.

Major outlets ran AI-related stories after AI-related stories. *The New York Times* ran a series on AI's promises and risks, from job loss to privacy to inequality. *The Wall Street Journal* focused on the business side, with headlines like "AI Poised to Disrupt Major Industries" and "CEOs Grapple with AI Integration Challenges." Local syndicates also piled on, covering ethics and implications.

But one moment floored me. I was watching 60 Minutes, late 2023, when reporter Scott Pelley closed his AI segment with this:

> We'll conclude with a note that has never appeared on 60 Minutes, but one that you may hear often in the AI revolution: *The preceding was created with 100% human content.*

What? I did a double-take. Didn't he just say *VerifiedHuman*? As in, "*Hey, world, this story came from people*"?

2025 UPDATE | Still Waiting for a Clear Voice

Since 2023, the conversation around attribution has continued, but it hasn't settled around any one field or consistent leader. Some outlets now include AI disclosures, noting when generative tools were used for research, drafting, or editing. Others label "human-written" content as premium.

Even in early 2023, before VerifiedHuman was ever scribbled in a notebook, I sensed the conversation would unfold slowly. I kept hoping someone would step up and lead.

I still believe someone can.

When Meta Got Personal

In 2023, concerns over AI's risks and unintended consequences got louder. Stories of machine "hallucinations" surfaced: AI spitting out nonsense and bad information, even causing real harm.

Governments started taking notice. In February 2023, the US issued an Executive Order outlining a national AI strategy that balances innovation with ethics, safety, and security. The European Union followed in

April with the proposed AI Act targeting high-risk applications and setting new rules for transparency and oversight.

Fears about AI's potential for chaos abound.

- What happens when AI-generated deepfakes of world leaders spread misinformation?
- How will hackers utilize AI for more sophisticated cyberattacks?
- Biased data leads to biased outputs. Can developers make AI fair?
- Who gets credit, or paid, when generative AI remixes real people's work?
- What protects human-made art when AI mimics it at scale?

When We Couldn't Peer Into the Black Box

AI grows more capable every day. It's easy to see *what* it can do. But one persistent problem is that no one understands *how* it's doing it. Not even the people who built it.

LLM systems are often referred to as "black boxes." You feed them data, they spit out answers, but what happens in the middle, no one can say. They're opaque because of their design.

Each query triggers hundreds of billions of micro-operations, firing across layers of neural networks. It's impossible to untangle what's influencing what.

> Even the engineers behind the models can't explain precisely why they respond the way they do.

The black box problem is technical *and* societal. It complicates accountability. When no one fully understands the system, determining who should be held accountable for any resulting harm becomes an ethical and legal nightmare. Consequences fall through the cracks. These concerns loom large in the minds of policymakers, technologists, and the public.

AI ethics researcher Timnit Gebru, co-author of the influential "Stochastic Parrots" paper, puts it this way: "We must develop and deploy it responsibly." Then her warning pushes harder: "We can talk about ethics and fairness all we want, but if our institutions don't allow this work to happen, then it won't." Harvard computer scientist Finale Doshi-Velez echoes the urgency: "There's a much greater recognition that we should not be waiting for AI tools to become mainstream before making sure they are ethical."

However, the moment has passed. The tools are built. The future is surprisingly uncertain, even for the futurists. No one knows what's coming. The experts don't know. Geoffrey Hinton doesn't know. Sam Alt--an doesn't know. Wozniak and Musk don't know.

When the Cash Got Crazy

As soon as the breakthroughs made headlines, the opportunists moved fast, eager to slap "AI-powered" on anything they could brand, sell, or spin. Developers scrambled, flooding the market with tools that looked slick but often didn't deliver. Some barely worked. Others rebranded old tech with new AI labels.

Investors poured in billions, hoping to cash in before the novelty faded. In 2023, the startup scene exploded: Inflection AI raised $1.3 billion. Anthropic secured over $2 billion. Hugging Face landed $235 million. OpenAI soared to an $86 billion valuation. Cohere pulled in $445 million. The message was clear: AI wasn't just hot. It was a roaring inferno.

2025 UPDATE | Everyone Wants In

As promised, I've kept an eye on the numbers, and they've only gotten bigger. OpenAI has now secured $13 billion in funding and hit a $157 billion valuation. Anthropic raised $7.3 billion with its valuation climbing to $60 billion.

Mira Murati launched a startup with no product, chasing a $2 billion valuation. Andreessen Horowitz is raising a $20 billion AI fund. The EU is mobilizing €200 billion for AI innovation. Everyone wants in.

Some analysts predict a cooldown as the hype cycle runs its course, echoes of the AI summers and winters that have always defined this field. I guess we'll see.

When the Human Touch Still Counts

Vinyl. Digital. AI. Each was an inflection point, a moment when the rules changed and the world got weird. We embraced speed, clarity, and convenience, but started missing what felt real. This is the paradox. We trade touch for the contactless and then find ourselves longing for the very thing we left behind.

> What do solid people do when things get weird?

When the biopsy results tilt their world sideways, they feel disoriented, unsure about what's happening, how to read it, or what to do.

> They stay calm. Try not to panic.
> Try to figure out what the hell is going on.

Humans have always needed time to process new tools. But AI moves so fast, so deep, so invisibly. And it's reshaping how we make *and* how we trust.

Over the past two years, I've waxed and waned, been swayed by hype, unsettled by headlines, disappointed by developments, and sometimes lost in the complexity of it all.

> It's going to be okay. Take a breath. Give it a minute. Then try to do what solid people do: Stay calm.
> Seek clarity.
> Clarity about what's crucial. Clarity about what's ours to hold onto and protect.

So far, we have traced the arc from analog to digital to AI: revolutions that changed our tools, reset our expectations, and redefined how we express ourselves in the world.

Next, we'll discuss the creative fields: writing, visual art, music, and voice. Fields that have always been deeply, and recognizably, human. Fields where the line between machine and maker is suddenly unclear. Where is AI showing up in the creative process as a helpful tool? As a collaborator? As a competitor? Or as an impostor?

> We want to understand which aspects of AI can help humans do their best work and which might be more costly than we're willing to pay.

The stakes are high for the real people behind the work, those who make a living by, or better yet, who live to write the lines that stay with us, make images that move us, compose music that rings true, and give voice to what we recognize as part of who we are, and who we're becoming.

> It doesn't have to be *perfect*.
> It just has to be *real*.

Beyond the creative fields, we'll also examine education, where teachers shape the next generation. Today's educators face a double challenge: stopping students from misusing AI while preparing them to lead in a world increasingly immersed in it. Their work goes far beyond policies and tools. They're forming minds to think critically, hearts to feel with empathy, and character to act with integrity.

Across every field we'll touch—the arts, writing, music, and voice—the same tension emerges: between what new tools can do and what they can't, or shouldn't, replace.

My hunch is that it's not a tension we'll resolve, but one we have to learn to live with. There are so many promises out there for tidy answers and quick fixes. However, life rarely works that way. Most of the time, we carry the tension with us, asking better questions, knowing good questions rarely come with easy answers:

> How do we harness AI to elevate human creativity? Can we do it without losing what makes our work and our voices uniquely human?

There's no straightforward way through. But these are the right questions. And now's the time to ask them.

PART TWO |

THE FIELDS WE CALL OUR OWN

How AI is moving through
the work that makes us human.

Chapter 5

Those Who Write |

When Words Define What's Real

Learning language is an essential part of human development and sits at the heart of our conversation. Human beings are wired to communicate. Throughout history and across cultures, writing has captured our thoughts and helped us define what's essential. It's how we have passed down memory, declared belief, carried grief, carved law, and preserved wonder.

> The instinct to do so, *to put words to the world* around us, is part of what sets humans apart from all other creatures.

While studying human development during my undergraduate years as an English education major, I stumbled upon a fascinating discussion that captivated me. Almost thirty years later, I'm still intrigued.

Two linguists, Edward Sapir and Benjamin Whorf, posed a theory with implications for anthropology, linguistics, psychology, and cognitive science. The teacher and protégé suggested that the structure of a language does more than simply define how people speak—it may dictate how they see the world. The more widely accepted version of their hypothesis goes like this: *The structure and vocabulary of a language determine how its speakers perceive and think.*

Their most famous examples asked whether the Inuit and Yupik languages, with many words for snow, might lead to a more nuanced understanding of whiteness. The Navajo verb system, which associates motion with physical properties, may influence how speakers attend to movement, what they register, and how they interpret it. Sapir and Whorf wanted to know:

> Does the *structure* of our language,
> and the breadth of its vocabulary,
> *shape how* we experience reality?

Others haven't been convinced they were asking the right question. In *The Language Instinct*, Steven Pinker argues that children possess an *innate capacity* to learn language, an idea long promoted by MIT linguist Noam Chomsky. Unlike Sapir and Whorf, Pinker believes human *language* is *independent* of *thought*. Ideas come *first* and can exist even *without* being spoken or written. In this view, language is simply a means by which we express our thoughts.

I'm not astute enough to dissuade Sapir-Whorfians or Chomsky-Pinkerians. But as a writer, I can't help but feel the connection. Something about *shaping* words *reshapes* how we think and how we live. Choosing language forces us to slow down, look closer, and sort what's worth saying. It brings us to a deeper question:

> What does it mean to use artificial intelligence,
> a "brain" that's not human, to write so widely
> about the human experience?

When Illegible Was Good Enough

In the spring of 1994, I sat at a high-top table in a dim pub called *The Cow* on Corn Exchange Street in Cambridge, England. It's where I handwrote most of my long papers.

I worked best under pressure, so I cranked them out just a few hours before they were due. Then I raced them by bicycle to my professor's office at Homerton College. The papers were probably not good. I'm sure I only got A's because they were long and largely illegible.

A few friends and I spent a semester in Cambridge through a university-sponsored program. We had the opportunity to take classes taught by professors from the University of Cambridge. It was inspiring and intimidating. We had no laptops or word processors, just a library card, a stack of loose-leaf paper, and a pen.

Later that year, back home in the States, and tasked with a thirty-page final paper, I got access to WordPerfect and a dot-matrix printer. It took some time to get used to composing on a screen instead of in my head or with a pencil on paper. But it was faster. My legibility jumped to 100%. And I could spellcheck.

I still miss those early days of word processing, yellow Courier text glowing unnaturally on a deep blue screen.

> It's wild how far writing tools have come in thirty years.

Human writing has constantly progressed. New waves of tools have redefined how we create, share, and preserve language, from symbols on stone to Underwood typewriters, word processors, and digital platforms. Each breakthrough has built upon the last, expanding how we express ourselves, pass on knowledge, and invite more voices into the conversation.

Writing transcends mere information transmission. It's part of how we remember, wrestle with meaning, and make sense of the world. With the rise of artificial intelligence, we're standing at the edge of another writing revolution.

> And this time, our tools are doing something odd: *they're writing back.*

AI is already redefining how humans write. But every leap like this is built on the past, just another reflection of our broader history. To fully understand this moment, we need to rewind the story.

When Marks Became Memory

The invention of writing systems was the first significant breakthrough in how humans captured memory and meaning.

Thousands of years ago, prehistoric people began leaving marks on cave walls, pottery, and objects meant to outlast them and carry their stories forward. They drew to decorate but also to communicate, remember, and make ideas stick.

One troglodyte bent on aesthetics might have said, "*It would look charming if you painted your hunting trip with Gad on the living room wall.*"

Another, more practical, might have urged, "*Yes, Gad. Draw that. That's a good one. We don't want to forget it.*" We'll never know. But they clearly understood that anything worth keeping needed to be marked.

As humans discovered fire and forged tools, they also developed language and gradually found more efficient ways to feed themselves. Then they did what humans like to do: cluster into communities, build systems, and complicate life.

As civilizations matured, writing systems emerged: Egyptian hieroglyphs, Mesopotamian cuneiform, and Elamite script. These early scripts began as simple drawings —visual symbols representing ideas rather than sounds —and evolved generation by generation. Eventually, people realized clay tablets were easier to carry than buildings. Papyrus, thin, organic, portable, was easier still.

When Letters Unlocked Language

Roughly two millennia later, the next breakthrough arrived, and it was seismic. The Phoenicians introduced something the world had never seen: writing that captured *sounds* instead of *symbols* or *ideas*.

> This shift, from *visual scripts*
> to *phonetic characters*,
> was the most profound linguistic leap
> in human history.

They created the first *alphabet* —a small, elegant system of marks to represent the *sounds* of any word —simply by rearranging the characters. Writing got portable. It crossed dialects. It allowed for precision. People could accurately record what they saw, what they did, and what was said about it. Speech sounds represented as symbols could be copied and scaled.

Their idea stuck. And the writing world as we know it blossomed from there.

> I would argue that the word *'phonetic'*
> should be *'Phoenetic'*
> as a proper nod to its originators.

Meanwhile, China, "The Middle Kingdom," thrived in its own cultural and artistic ecosystem. Largely insulated from outside influence, it experienced a stunning wave of innovation *from within*. Chinese script traditions developed from early pictographs into the intricate systems still used today.

In the East, writing has always been more than functional. It's considered a beautiful and complex representation of life.

Visit any park in China, and you might see someone, often an elder, painting Hanzi on the pavement with a giant calligraphy brush dipped in water. No ink. No permanence. The characters appear, shimmer briefly, then vanish. Ironically, the alphabet promises permanence and pragmatism.

But Hanzi offers something more delicate, more organic, a beauty meant to be seen, not just stored.

When Plants Became Pages

Before pens or keyboards, ink or pixels, you have to start with something simpler: *the surface.*

> You can't write without one.

Writing surfaces reveal human ingenuity, how each era responded to the needs of its moment. Papyrus, made from its namesake plant, became the primary material for documents and scrolls for thousands of years. It was lightweight, portable, and durable, built to travel. We still have papyrus records from the Pyramids at Giza that date back nearly 5,000 years. It boggles the mind.

Another early writing surface was parchment, a medium made from animal skin. It was more rigid than papyrus and painstaking to produce. (I try not to think of parchment as leather paper.) Despite the cost, parchment became the medium of choice for legal documents, sacred texts, and scholarly works across the Greco-Roman world and medieval Europe. Some parchment manuscripts still survive, giving us rare glimpses into ancient literature, law, and society. These early documents helped lay the foundations of written civilization.

The Chinese invented paper as we know it, a flat surface made from pulp or plant fibers. Paper dramatically lowered the cost of writing and expanded the global reach of the written word. Papermaking gradually migrated westward, reaching the Islamic world by the eighth century, where it helped ignite a golden age of scholarship and science.

In the following centuries, universities and academies sprang up across the East and Europe, and scholastic life got going. Paper finally reached Europe by way of Spain in the eleventh century, just in time to fuel another revolution: mass book production and distribution, driven by the printing press.

> **ANALOG BY DESIGN** | TAKING NOTES ON PAPER
>
> Paper still wins. In a University of Tokyo study, students who took notes by hand finished 25% faster—and remembered more—than those using tablets or phones. Why? Paper creates stronger memory cues. Texture. Sequence. Spatial anchors. You place it, feel it, recall it. The physical tracing helps the mind hold on.

When Words Went Viral

Although the Chinese had developed woodblock printing nearly six hundred years earlier, it had little effect on the West, a striking case of parallel invention, where distance, language, and need shaped separate sparks of genius.

In Europe during the Middle Ages, books were still meticulously copied by hand. Illuminated manuscripts, crafted by monks and artists, were among the most treasured. Intricately detailed, they blended calligraphy, illustration, and devotion, becoming sacred objects and cultural heirlooms.

Gutenberg's press arrived quietly as a whisper, world-shaking as thunder. And *everything* changed, quietly at first, then all at once. It's hard to overstate the ingenuity behind Gutenberg's vision. I imagine him thinking: *What if we made reusable letter blocks?*

> *Instead of copying every book by hand,*
> *we could ink the blocks and print page after page,*
> *faster, cheaper, better.*

It worked. And it triggered one of the most pivotal inflection points in human history. Books became reproducible, ideas became portable, and knowledge could scale. Literacy rose. Questions multiplied. What was once owned by a privileged few spread like wildfire.

For the first time, ordinary people had access to books and the chance to read them. They could interpret the Bible *for themselves*. This power shift helped spark the Protestant Reformation and fuel the Renaissance. The press redefined who could *write*, and also who got *read*.

It took time for the technology to reach the rest of the world. Its adoption in the Middle East, India, and China lagged by centuries, slowed by cultural, linguistic, and geopolitical barriers. But Gutenberg's spark lit the fuse, and the world was altered forever.

When Keys Replaced Cursive

I have a few 1930s Underwood typewriters on bookshelves in my home and office. I love them because they're solid, thick, and nostalgic. The sound of manual typewriters is music to my ears, though I haven't heard it in years. The soft tapping of laptop keys has replaced it.

The invention of the typewriter in the nineteenth century revolutionized how people wrote, read, and understood the written word. Mark Twain submitted the first-ever typed manuscript to a publisher, then cursed "its perplexities" to friends.

> Think about it. Before its adoption, people only saw words in two forms: *handwritten* or printed by a printing *press*.

Credit for developing the typewriter belongs to more than one person. But in 1868, Christopher Latham Sholes introduced the first commercially successful model: the Remington No. 1. It featured the QWERTY keyboard layout, which remains the standard for keyboards to this day. The typewriter was a windfall for businesses and authors alike, making writing faster, more efficient, and legible.

And it was perfect for writers like Hemingway. Written dialogue became punchier, more clipped, and closer to how people spoke. But Hemingway wasn't alone. All writers found a new kind of flow.

The typewriter also had a *social* impact. It opened a door for women to join men in the professional world, first as typists or secretaries, at a time when most people still believed their place was at home, raising children. It wasn't a wide door. But it marked the beginning of our ongoing struggle for gender equality in the workplace.

When Old Ways Held Their Ground

The typewriter's active lifespan stretched well through the end of the twentieth century, teeing up the rise of word processors and computers. But it also revealed something stubborn and deeply human: *our tendency to cling to what's familiar.* The status quo has weight. Inertia. To break it, something more substantial has to come along, something that nudges us out of what we know and edges us into something new.

We have seen this before. Berliner's discs were a clear upgrade from Edison's cylinders. They were flatter, more portable, and better sounding. However, the US recording industry adhered to the old way for nearly thirty years, not because it was *better*, but because it was *familiar*. It just worked, and that was enough.

The same is true for keyboards. The QWERTY layout was carefully designed to prevent typebar jams on early mechanical typewriters by spacing out commonly used letters. Today's keyboards might get sticky, but they don't jam. And yet QWERTY *remains* standard.

> (My son has experimented with faster keyboard layouts, but I have to wonder: *Isn't 120 words per minute fast enough?*)

Even when personal computers took off in the 1980s, electric typewriters doggedly held their ground through the 1990s in homes, schools, and offices. They were cheaper, simpler, and crucially, more familiar. For many adults, computers felt intimidating. Plus, filling out forms on a dot matrix printer was a real pain.

I remember learning to type in ninth grade (1989). At my high school, Typing 101 was required for first-year students. But I didn't exactly rise to the challenge. Instead of honing my accuracy or boosting my GWAM (gross words a minute), I spent the semester clacking out love notes to a girl I liked.

My final grade reflected my utter inattention to the craft. But my bleeding heart could not have cared less.

When Writing Got Rolling

Inkwells and quills served writers for centuries. Fountain pens followed. But in 1938, a humble new invention won the race for pragmatism: the *ballpoint pen*, patented by Hungarian Argentinian inventor László Bíró. The ballpoint smoked its grandiloquent predecessors thanks to a tiny ball-bearing tip rolling out quick-drying ink from a simple, slender tube.

It had serious advantages: smooth writing, long-lasting, ink-efficient, leak-free, and surprisingly reliable. These self-contained ink tubes could write for miles, literally. They upended writing, much like the typewriter had. Writers could move *faster*: no more dipping into inkwells, no more refilling fountains, no more blowing on the page to dry the ink.

The timing was perfect. Public education was expanding across much of the world in the mid-twentieth century. Teachers and students needed writing tools to be affordable, reliable, and easy to use. Ballpoint pens became everyday essentials, perfect for taking notes, writing letters, or jotting down ideas before they slipped away. They were a worldwide hit.

And now, everyone's got a junk drawer full of them.

When Mistakes Come With Erasers

> Pencils don't get nearly enough credit.

They date to the 1500s, when shepherds discovered graphite in the hills of Borrowdale, England. Early users wrapped the strange black clumps in string or sheepskin to keep their fingers clean while writing or sketching. In 1565, Swiss naturalist Conrad Gesner devised a method for encasing graphite in wood.

During the Napoleonic Wars, the British Navy blockaded graphite exports to France, including that bloody-good stuff from England. The French artists and engineers desperately needed their pencils. Napoleon saw the problem and acted. He commissioned inventor Nicholas-Jacques Conté to devise a method for producing pencils that did not rely on imported graphite. Conté delivered. He created pencil leads by mixing powdered graphite with clay and firing the blend in a kiln. By adjusting the ratios, he could make leads with different hardness levels, from soft to hard.

I've got a thing for pencils. Here's why.

In 2019, I made two New Year's resolutions.

The first one was to cook dinner from scratch for my family 300 times in 365 days.

I hit my goal by November 18, just before the holidays. I chose cooking because I wanted to learn new dishes and spend more time with my loved ones, rather than working late on projects that seem critical now but will likely be forgotten in a decade. It was a good choice.

The second resolution was to write only in pencil for the entire year unless I had to sign something in ink.

Why pencils? They take me back to my childhood, a time in my life when drawing, writing, and creating were simply expressions of who I was. Plus, they smell good when you sharpen them. They're simple. Familiar. And they come with an eraser, so you can fix your mistakes if you want to.

So, if I were going to write in pencil for an entire year, I was determined to find the *best damn pencil* in the world. And I did. Introduced in the 1930s, the Blackwing pencil found its way into the hands of legends:

Walt Disney, John Steinbeck, Leonard Bernstein, and Quincy Jones. Artists. Composers. Writers. Grammy, Emmy, Pulitzer, and Oscar winners.

I got giddy and ordered a few boxes of the classic 602 model and a swanky one-step, long-point sharpener. It was love at first sight. I was instantly, permanently hooked. Since 2019, I haven't stopped. Pencils help me slow down. Stay focused. Think with my hands. Be creative. They're forgiving, flexible, and analog enough to keep me present. You should give pencils a try. Again.

ANALOG BY DESIGN | WRITING BY HAND

Like vinyl, fountain pens, and even high-quality pencils like the Blackwing are making a quiet comeback, especially among millennials drawn to slower, more tactile tools.

Writers describe the same pull vinyl lovers know: the scratch of the nib, the weight of a well-made pencil, the ritual of ink or graphite on the page. It's deliberate. Textured. Unmistakably human.

When Words Finally Got Their Chance to Dance

Word processing turned writing into choreography. You could suddenly dance between sentences, cut without consequence, and play your way to clarity. Writing by hand or on a typewriter felt heavier. The words hit the page with *weight*. Crossing them out felt like undoing something permanent.

With word processing, writers could move fluidly: composing, backspacing, revising, rearranging, and even trying out different phrases before moving on. They could effortlessly reorder paragraphs or restructure a section without retyping entire pages, something brutally slow on a typewriter.

Personal computers of the 1980s went hand in hand with word processing, with programs such as WordPerfect and, later, Microsoft Word. For the first time, writers had absolute control over the look and feel of their text. They could choose their fonts, adjust their margins, and set custom layouts. Spellcheck and grammar tools became standard. And when "track changes" arrived, the craft shifted again. Writers, editors, and teams could now build drafts together in real time.

> But maybe the most significant shift wasn't mechanical.

With the development of word processors, writing became more accessible. Anyone with a computer could create professional-quality documents from their kitchen table.

Some people argue that this explosion of digital content has cheapened the craft. Maybe. But it has also opened the door for more people to find their voice. And one of the beautiful parts of the human experience is this:

> Everyone has the right to write.

When Writers Got the Whole World

Long before the internet took over, my writing life smelled like old paper and busted backpacks full of Xeroxed sources.

Then the ground shifted. Digitized archives appeared. Search engines sped up. Wikipedia, love it or not, became a reasonable place to start wrapping your head around a topic. A global, virtual library opened its doors and never closed. We stopped leaving home to find knowledge and started pulling it toward us: messy, living knowledge, reconfigured as we touched it.

But that shift brought new problems. Previously, reliable information was available, but it required effort to locate. Now, access is instant, but volume is overwhelming. Thousands of results. Contradictory claims. Confusing headlines. We have moved from scarcity to saturation. And it changed the writer's job.

Today, the work goes beyond finding information. The search part is easy. The hard part is making sense of it, sorting what's credible from what's careless, or worse, manipulative. We skim. We cross-check. We read with skepticism, listen for ulterior motives, and verify sources.

> More facts do not equal more clarity.

The internet gave us everything except understanding. Good writing has always depended on judgment. Now, it begins in quieter places: what we notice, what we question, and what we trust.

When the Gates Came Down

> The tide of digital publishing has blown a hole in the old system's hull.

Today's writers don't need permission to matter. Writers can reach readers directly, without agent queries, editor pitches, or waiting for someone in a New York office to decide their work deserves attention.

Blogs and personal websites turned out to be powerful tools: simple to launch, easy to share, built for honest conversation between writer and reader. The entry barrier fell to zero. Writers began sharing what moved them: niche obsessions, personal histories, bold experiments, even complete novels.

E-books bent the model early, then broke it completely. A writer could finish a manuscript on Tuesday and publish it by Friday.

They could avoid incurring printing costs, warehouse fees, or gatekeeper expenses. Then the platforms made the break deeper.

Wattpad provided teens and young adults with a platform to post stories and poems directly from their phones, allowing them to vote, comment, and encourage one another as they wrote.

Medium offered something quieter and more polished, a space between blog posts and op-eds, open to anyone but built for long-form, thoughtful writing. It became a pleasant intersection of essayists, journalists, experts, and regular people with something to say.

Substack re-centered the writer's voice, part blog, part newsletter, and for many, part paycheck. It enables writers to build followings, set their terms, and get paid without chasing clicks.

Readers also got something extraordinary: access to voices, genres, and stories they might never have found in a bookstore or seen in print at all. All of it added up to something new: a literary scene, livelier, weirder, and more open than ever.

> With more voices, more genres, and fewer walls, the stories got wilder, sharper, and more human.

However, every story has a conflict. Lowering the barrier to entry was a breakthrough, but it came with a roar. The volume is relentless. Everyone can publish. Almost no one gets heard. Platforms that opened the floodgates also flooded the stage. One voice barely breaks the surface. Readers scroll, skim, and move on.

And then there's the issue of flat-out theft. A world built for sharing makes it easy to rip off ideas, paragraphs, and entire voices. Credit gets lost. Work gets scraped into training sets. And algorithms don't care who said it first.

When Research Got a Robot

Research used to be a grind. Writers had to dig through stacks of books, scroll through microfiche, wait weeks for interlibrary loans, or photocopy hundreds of pages. It was excavation: digging in the right places, lifting shovelfuls of dirt, sifting signals from noise, and piecing scraps together until something emerged.

Now, AI can do the heavy lifting. Large language models can scan and sort hundreds of links in minutes, synthesizing, summarizing, reframing, and turning hours of legwork into a few quick prompts. Models like ChatGPT and Claude can answer almost any question.

They can also help you follow trails, spot gaps, and catch logical inconsistencies. Some models even pull clean summaries from peer-reviewed sources. A solo writer can work at the speed and scale of a research team. The tools free you to focus on higher-order thinking: interpreting, shaping arguments, and deciding which ideas to elevate. But they're not perfect. Not even close.

> *Hallucinations* still dog most language models, even the very best models like ChatGPT 5: false claims, fabricated citations, and straight-up bull.

Users have to be aware enough to spot it, push back, and call the machine's bluff. It takes a responsible person to drive the process. So human discernment still leads. Ideas still need testing. Facts still need checking.

When Fast Got Good Enough

LLMs crush content creation. A coherent article, report, story, or even a poem is now just a few prompts away. The results sometimes have the "meh" quality of an MP3. But for most readers, it's good enough.

And it's everywhere: tech, healthcare, finance, retail, media, even the news. AI is shaping search, shopping, cars, healthcare, and quietly writing more headlines than most people realize. For quick, low-friction content, LLMs are hard to beat. For stuck writers, they help surface ideas. For those who are overwhelmed, they offer structure.

Professionals everywhere are reverse-integrating AI into their creative process. Screenwriters, marketers, freelancers, and content creators, especially those churning out work for fast-paced platforms, are paying attention. Things are moving fast. And serious writers have had to stop and ask:

> What's my approach to this?
> Where do I draw the line?

These aren't hypothetical questions anymore. The tools are here. The work is shifting. And for every writer reckoning with it, something deeper is on the line.

When Homework Died

You can understand why authors are worried. There's a volume problem. Generative AI is flooding the market with lower-quality work, some of which is built directly from their models. Imagine a day when half the books in a store, physical or online, are generated by AI. We may already be close. I've read several that I'm convinced were mostly machine-made. Not because the content was flimsy, but because the prose felt wooden. It didn't ring true.

Some readers can still spot AI writing, or at least its shades. Plenty of articles will tell you how: watch for giveaway words like "fosters" or "tapestry," phrases like "as a poignant example," and AI-ey patterns, like corrective contrasts: *It's not X, it's actually Y.*

However, it's becoming increasingly difficult to distinguish, even for the experts. I kept thinking of Malcolm Gladwell's story about the Getty Kouros statue in *Blink*: an ancient-looking sculpture, supposedly priceless, presented with flawless credentials. Experts should've been wowed. But the real ones bristled. They couldn't even explain why, just something felt off.

> They said it looked "too fresh."

And they were right. It turned out to be an elaborate counterfeit: right stone from the right historical quarry, flawless technique, even chemical aging to match carbon dating. But no amount of forgery could manufacture feeling. Their gut instinct told them: It looks right. But it's not real.

Atlantic writer Kaitlyn Tiffany put it this way: "ChatGPT can write you anything, but can't write you anything good." For a while, I thought the same might be true of AI writing. That we'd sharpen our fake-dar: a quiet, human radar whispering, *I'm not connecting with another person here. Something's missing.*

> But that hope is fading.

Over the past eighteen months, AI writing—like AI image generation—has gotten better. Noticeably better. ChatGPT, Claude, and Gemini have all leveled up. AI has always written fast. Now it writes convincingly. It sounds human enough to make you second-guess yourself.

That question—*Can we still tell?*—was at the heart of a study I led in 2023: The *AHA-ISW Study*—Authentication of Human Authorship in Student Writing. I wanted to know if experienced human editors could still spot AI writing with confidence. And if students had used AI in graded assignments, could we pinpoint where? I hypothesized we'd be able to spot differences definitively and that detection models would back us up.

So I collected more than 300 essays from high schools in the US, the UAE, China, and the Philippines. Then I used the same prompts the students had received and fed them into multiple LLMs —ChatGPT, Claude, Gemini, and Copilot —to see how the machines would write responses. What came back was solid, surprisingly competent, and eerily consistent: B+ work, the kind teachers look at and say, *Yeah, that's decent.*

Then we ran both sets (AI and student) through detection tools like Originality.ai. The results were all over the map: some student papers flagged at 88% AI, others at 26%, others at 0%. We looked closer at the flagged passages, comparing them line by line with the AI baselines. That's when it hit me: *Holy moly. We can't tell clearly.* Not really.

> We failed.

It was like the Kouros incident in the art world: experts staring at a statue, sensing something wasn't quite right. We felt it, too. About twenty of the papers had moments that felt off. But *unlike* the Kouros, there was *no* clean line between "real" and AI-generated. The writing had become a patchwork quilt of human and machine, and the seams were almost invisible.

I rubbed my eyes. I needed a minute. Then I thought:

> Well, this might just be the final nail in the coffin of homework.

Students are holding a blank page and a due date. They have an easy solution, but no clear guidance on *why it* can ultimately hurt them in the long run. Wary teachers are left patrolling over shoulders as they try to assess learning through writing. The stakes are high, especially for those who are still learning to think, write, and find their voice.

When Words Travel Further

And for all the ways AI can undercut the writing process, it can also expand it. One of the most potent things AI can do with language is to carry it across borders. Translation tools have improved dramatically: they are now more accurate and more accessible. They've started bridging gaps between writers and readers who, for most of history, had no way to understand each other.

Google Translate, Apple Translate, Microsoft Translator, and DeepL now enable users to read and write across languages with surprising fluency. For writers, this shift is transformational. Language is becoming less of a wall, more of a bridge.

In 2023, the Humane AI Pin made tech headlines as a real-world take on Star Trek's Universal Translator, promising real-time conversation between speakers of different languages. It flopped. Spotty performance and harsh reviews sank it, but the idea didn't. Neural machine translation continues to advance, helping people read, write, and connect across borders. A poem in Korean, Spanish, or Farsi can now be read, almost faithfully, by someone halfway around the world. Not perfectly, but close enough to count.

Writers have long sought to bridge cultural divides. Now, AI is helping make the bridge wider and faster. The real challenge is to create an accurate translation that doesn't just go word-for-word, but captures dynamically equivalent nuances of emotion, memory, perspective, and in--ent, to get the *soul* across.

When Timeless Echoes Sound
Three Essential Voices That Still Guide the Conversation

This book traverses several creative fields, including writing, visual art, music, voice, and education, each reexamined in light of AI's rise. For me, consideration for disciplines had to start with writing. I'm a writer, and English is both my native voice and a shared language for stories, ideas, and art across the world.

And when I started tracing the long arc of human writing, who shaped it, who stretched it, who left their fingerprints on the way we tell stories, three sources kept rising to the surface. They aren't the only voices that count, of course.

You could make a case for a hundred others: the quest for the perfect sonnet, the primal force of *Beowulf*, the quiet intensity of Frost and Dickinson, the dark depth of Melville, the prophetic voice of Asimov—whole schools of poetics, prose, and mythology.

But these three still resonate with remarkable reach and enduring influence: the *Bible*, the works of *Shakespeare*, and the *novel* as a literary form. They have shaped how billions of people think, speak, imagine, and grapple with meaning. They remind us that words embody beauty, struggle, belief, and human fragility.

Now, as machines begin to write, their work feels even more relevant. I want to revisit them to ground our conversation. To remind us of what human words can sound like when they come from depth, complexity, and lived experience. And to help us remember what might be harder to replicate than we think.

VOICE ONE |
JUDEO-CHRISTIAN SCRIPTURES: AN EPIC HUMAN STORY

The Bible, the bestselling book of all time, has been a guide for the inner lives of countless humans for thousands of years.

As a collection of writings composed over more than 1,000 years by many authors, the Bible brings us ancient stories and deeply human characters: flawed, complex, and compelling. It was originally written in Hebrew, Aramaic, and Greek, and first translated into English in the early 1600s by order of King James I (henceforth the King James Version).

For generations of writers, it has been a model of narrative craft, offering wisdom, moral tension, poetic reflection, and unflinching conflict. These are sacred texts, but not so mystical that they lose their grip on human experience. And that's why they still speak.

While I was grinding my way through seminary, one of my favorite professors, Dr. Carson Brisson, blew my mind with a lecture on the Bible's power as a human story. One day in class, he read aloud a piece he had written:

> The stories that make up our Bible
> take us on a far and fascinating journey of faith
> through time, and across distance.
>
> They begin deep in the East, near a city called Ur,
> and stretch west to the mighty Nile River.
> We hear the voices of the slave and the set free,
> of male and female, of wealthy and poor,
> elderly and young, lost and found
> and finally, the desperate cry of the faithless
> and the joyful praise of the faithful.
> We see death and birth.
> We see weddings and markets, jails and temples.
> We live in slavery, then in tents,
> then in villages, then in cities,
> and finally, in the great city of God: Jerusalem.
>
> We watch and listen as sons trick fathers,
> brothers steal from brothers, fathers fail sons.
> Wives and husbands fall in love and in danger.
> Nephews rob uncles.

> Disciples misunderstand, deny,
> and even betray their master.
> And a people called to be holy
> dance around a dead thing
> in a lonely place on a bad day.

The Bible was among the first mass-produced books, and the King James Version, translated into English from the original Semitic languages, helped shape English's sound and structure. Its imprint on writing is both literary and cultural. Its phrasing has become part of every-ay speech:

> "Love thy neighbor as thyself,"
> "To everything, there is a season,"
> "Pride goeth before a fall."

Beyond idioms, its stories carry moral significance and emotional depth. Its reflections on the *sound and fury* of the human experience are as varied as the stories of its complex human characters.

No one in the Bible was thinking about artificial intelligence. But the themes they wrestled with—human ambition, economic and political power, moral tension, and the danger of misplaced trust—feel remarkably relevant, even when their stories revolve around the technologies and systems of their own day.

Scripture still frames modern questions about technology with surprising clarity for an ancient work. There are some lay-ups: The Bible emphasizes careful stewardship (Genesis 1), reminding us to use AI to pro-ote human flourishing and protect the planet. It calls us to love our neighbor (Matthew 22), value honesty (Proverbs 12), and pursue justice (Micah 6). So, it's proper and necessary to ask how artificial intelligence affects the privacy, equity, and well-being of individuals and communities.

BABEL REVISITED

Let's consider Babel again. In the story, God scatters humanity by confusing their language, a divine interruption meant to humble human overreach. Now, with large language models, we're witnessing something like a reversal: tools that undo the scatter, rebuild the bridge, and give us a shared language again, at least in digital spaces.

One subtle caution from Babel is the risk of distorted or overextended communication. But the deeper warning lies in God's decision to intervene, not because humans built something tall, but because they leaned too heavily on technology and ambition to find meaning apart from the divine.

For many who teach this story, the greater danger is *idolatry*: *elevating the work of our own hands*—whether buildings or intelligent machines—and giving those creations our primary allegiance.

> That warning feels especially relevant, considering AI's unprecedented global funding and the fact that the US and China are locked in an *everything-is-on-the-line race* for AI dominance.

Scripture's arc ultimately centers on the survival and flourishing of human life, even through the rise and fall of powerful nations and dramatic changes in technology.

IMAGO DEI

The most valuable lesson I see from the Bible is its conception of humans as reflections of the divine, Imago Dei, made in God's image. We carry that image in how we create, imagine, and use language.

In Genesis, God doesn't clap or wave a wand. God speaks. Language is a creative force: *"And God said..."*—and with those words, light, form, and life emerge from chaos.

> Creation begins as a speech event.

It is through language that God calls something entirely new into being. Thinkers like Sapir, Whorf, Chomsky, and Pinker have argued that language is uniquely human, hardwired into our biology. It shapes how we think, imagine, and construct meaning.

But Genesis goes *further*: language creates a new, tangible reality. And as image bearers of the *God who speaks* things into existence, our words hold similar power.

For those who see language as a neutral vessel, AI's growing fluency may not seem like a big deal. But for those who believe words shape worlds—participating in creation itself—the rise of machine-generated speech raises far more serious questions.

If language *creates*, and we've placed that power in algorithms, we're doing much more than automating communication.

> We are automating creation.

And, like human children, artificial intelligence has learned to use language. It can speak and write like us, generate music and visual art, and mimic voices in near-perfect human likeness. But its abilities don't arise from its own *lived* experience, but from a massive *inheritance* of human creativity. And the outputs can feel incredibly authentic.

So what do we do with that? Is it truly creativity? I'm not sure I'm ready to answer that. But if language is more than communication, if it gives shape to how we imagine, decide, and build the world, then this is a little more than just a technical question. It's a spiritual one.

VOICE TWO |
THE BARD: THE STAGE AS A MIRROR

I was a jock in high school: soccer every fall and wrestling every spring. But I also quietly loved the works of Shakespeare.

William Shakespeare is rightly regarded as *the* literary legend. As a single author, he has had an unparalleled impact on language development and literary form. He single-handedly expanded the English language with countless words like "assassination," "belongings," "cold-blooded," "fashionable," "uncomfortable," "eyeball," and "lackluster," terms that didn't exist before he coined them. Phrases like "love is blind," "break the ice," and "wild goose chase" are also his.

Shakespeare wove character and conflict into a rhythm so effective that it became a model for generations of storytellers. His story structures and archetypes formed the foundation for modern drama. But what fascinates me *most* is how precisely he captured human nature, emotion, psychology, and personal interaction, with a depth few have ever matched.

In *As You Like It*, he wrote, "All the world's a stage, and all the men and women merely players. They have their exits and their entrances." To Shakespeare, life *is* theater. We each play roles and have a fleeting moment onstage. And death waits in the wings.

In *Hamlet*, he captured the cocktail of contradictions that come with being human: *"What a piece of work is a [hu]man!"* A line filled with awe and lament, potential and fragility in the same breath.

In *The Tempest*, his themes still resonate: manipulation, personal freedom, and the need for human connection. In an age where technology can distort perception and obscure truth, Shakespeare reminds us of what's at stake: the integrity of language and the authenticity of human expression.

Information about Shakespeare's life is scant. We know he married Anne Hathaway, age *twenty-six*, when he was just *eighteen*, suggesting *interesting* circumstances. He had three children: Suzanna and twins Hamnet and Judith. They lost Hamnet, age eleven, to some form of child mortality.

We also know he spent many of his working years in London, away from his home and family in Stratford. He experienced smashing success, fierce rivalry, and career-thrashing heartbreak in the cutthroat "business" of London entertainment.

That's not to say Shakespeare's life was unique. In many ways, it was typical. Most people face hardship, staggering disappointment, uncertain careers, and the loss of love and loved ones. These are everyday experiences that occur throughout a human's life. And like any true writer, Shakespeare drew from his own. With rare talent and insight, he turned the ordinary into the unforgettable.

AI can mimic tone and frame a decent sonnet. It can *borrow* Shakespeare's style, syntax, and cadence. But it can't grieve the loss of a child. It can't fall in love, feel the knife of betrayal, and translate them into something honest and enduring.

> AI can fake *fluency*,
> but it can't fake *formation*.

It can't live the experiences that shape a voice. It can only remix the results. Shakespeare's work reminds us to treat the AI narrative with discernment. We shouldn't be so dazzled by its output that we forget what matters most: the beauty of being a person.

In a world where technology can distort reality, Shakespeare's writing was grounded in truth, complexity, and character. AI may push the limits of what's possible on the page, but the heart of writing still belongs to those who have lived it.

VOICE THREE |
THE NOVEL: STORIES DEEP ENOUGH TO DROWN IN

In the eighteenth century, the novel emerged as a powerful new form of storytelling. It took the world by storm. The works of authors like Jane Austen, Charles Dickens, and the Brontë sisters made it a titan of its time. The novel's long form gave authors room to breathe, allowing them to take readers on longer journeys, explore the gray areas of humanity, push back against societal norms, and capture the complexity of human relationships.

We connect with novels because humans think in stories. Novels wrap complexity in narrative. Feelings land deeper than logical arguments. We follow the plot. We feel its weight.

Defoe was a champion of self-reliance, spiritual honesty, and human resilience. His work reminds us that AI tends to distill what should remain complex: our need for struggle, our tolerance for ambiguity, and our capacity to grow by slogging through the brutality of life.

Austen, in turn, warned against anything that threatens personal agency. Her novels exposed the mechanics of social power, how privilege protects itself, and tilts the historical narrative in its favor.

In that light, AI's blind spots around race, culture, and nuance can be seen as mirrors reflecting the worldview of its *creators* and *funders*. Austen's concern feels remarkably relevant now: those in power shape the narrative. The rest are left unheard. In a world seeking clean answers, the novel still teaches us to sit with tension and to remember that truth can't be boiled down to a code.

When Stories Are Lived Before They're Told

The forty or so authors who contributed to the Bible, along with writers like Shakespeare, Defoe, and Brontë, all shared a commonality: their work stemmed from personal experience.

What gave their writing power was a blend of talent, timing, and perspective. They had the gift of language. They told the right stories at the right moment, for the right audience, and those stories reflected the shape of their lives.

These three voices—Judeo-Christian scripture, Shakespeare, and the novel—remind us of what's worth protecting as machines begin to sound human. They give us words with living weight, language shaped by experience, from authors who've loved, lost, wrestled with meaning, and been brave enough to pull something from the mess.

AI may bring new efficiencies to the storywriting process. But the lasting power of excellent writing comes from somewhere else: a human spirit made visible through voice, vision, and insight.

When Writing Finds Life

In every era, humans have found new ways to write—on cave walls, with pens and pixels—always with words. We've sharpened our tools, changed our mediums, and adapted our formats. Today, we face a new shift that asks: *Who is doing the writing?*

Because through every revolution of form, it's still the writer's presence that gives words their meaning. Good writing takes empathy, vulnerability, and connection. It's more than filling a page or prompting a model; it's rooted in lived experience and shaped by struggle, things no machine can truly replicate.

Whatever tools writers choose should serve their creative goals. Even as we embrace new methods, we can honor the craft's history: admire our quill-and-ink past, tip a hat to typewriters, and collaborate with distant friends in Google Docs. As a writer, I want to stay open to innovation and efficiency. But the heart of true writing will always belong to those who've lived it.

Chapter 6

Those Who Visualize |

When Imagination Collapses Time

T he first time I saw Paul Delaroche's 1833 painting "The Execution of Lady Jane Grey," I stopped in my tracks. It hangs in the National Gallery in London. I stood there for nearly an hour, thumbs hooked in my backpack straps, drawn into the world of that one canvas.

The scene is dim, medieval, and somber. There are five figures in the picture. Two women collapse beside Lady Jane, overcome with grief. A man calmly leans on his axe, resigned to his brutal task. Another gently guides her toward the chopping block.

Blindfolded and calm, Lady Jane Grey stretches out a hand, searching for the wood. She's not pleading, not protesting, just moving toward death with quiet resolve, her mouth closed. Her white silk gown glows, its folds catching the light, every shadow reflecting Delaroche's mastery of transcendent detail.

The painting becomes "the silent conversation between artist and observer, bridging the gaps of time and space." It asks: *What is each person feeling in this moment?* We're invited into the chamber to read each expression, to try to assign meaning, to carry our own mix of duty, sorrow, and compassion with us.

> We bear the weight of yet another
> teenage queen-of-the-week,
> murdered in a meaningless charade of politics.

I was deeply moved.

(Delaroche's painting appears in the appendices.)

Visual art has always held a powerful presence in my life. The first time I saw the ceiling at King's College Chapel in Cambridge, I lay down on the floor and stared upward at the magnificent fan vaulting, thin stone fingers spreading from the corners into a web above. Michelangelo's *David* in Florence. Wat Arun on the banks of the Chao Phraya in Bangkok. A kaleidoscope of *Cirque du Soleil* shows in Las Vegas, still flickering in my mind.

As a kid, I spent hours lost in *Time Life* photo books and our family's oversized edition of Norman Rockwell illustrations. He captured what was honest and iconic about a changing America: porch-side conversations, small-town baseball, and wartime goodbyes.

And when I picked up a pencil, I drew cartoon figures with a recurring theme: a lone traveler on a camel, his supplies tied carefully all around. If every image reflects the artist's soul, those camel sketches were early signs of mine: a little loneliness, a little material insecurity, a quiet longing to feel safe.

For as long as humans have made marks, we've used images to capture the world and show what it feels like to live in it. Over time, the tools evolved, reshaping how we see, remember, and pass down what we've seen.

> The tools shape the story.
> They always have.

The story of visual art continues to evolve, shaped by new tools and new ways of seeing. But the instinct behind it remains the same: to capture the world and to share the experience of living in it.

When Humans First Made Marks

We return to our ancient ancestors, people who turned stone and wood into tools for farming, hunting, and building. But long before they built empires, they made art. Cave paintings across Europe and Asia show animals, human figures, and abstract symbols.

The earliest visionaries finger-painted, used sticks, and made brushes from animal hair. Their pigments came from the earth: charcoal for black, ochre for reds and yellows, and manganese for browns. Their palettes were primitive yet deliberate, a handmade cache of color and expression.

2025 UPDATE | The World's Oldest Fingerprint

In May 2025, researchers in Spain announced what may be the world's oldest human fingerprint, pressed into a granite stone by a Neanderthal 43,000 years ago. Smooth and hand-sized, the stone must have caught his eye because its natural shape resembled a human face.

But he didn't stop there. He dipped his finger in red ochre and pressed a deliberate mark for its nose —the oldest known symbol, the oldest known human touch.

Gad's ancestors were leaving marks long before we had paper, screens, algorithms, or AI pretending to do the same. We've

> been doing this for 43,000 years and counting: making a mark, leaving a trace, telling the world we were here.

As human civilizations rose, so did their visual expression. In the Byzantine and Islamic worlds, calligraphy and mosaics adorned sacred walls, featuring dizzying detail layered with meaning, serving as decoration that declared.

In the Far East, glazed porcelain struck an uncommon balance: delicate but made to last. It showed up at ordinary meals and often remained in the family for generations. Centuries later, synthetic pigments dramatically expanded the artist's palette, introducing new depth and possibilities.

When Perspective Creates Space

As civilizations matured, their structures became both functional and breathtaking. Roman aqueducts carried water with precision and grace. The Pantheon, with its vast unsupported dome, and the Colosseum, with its ingenious seating design, proved that utility could lift the spirit.

In Europe, Gothic architects raised stonework toward the heavens, creating cathedrals like Notre Dame and Westminster Abbey, with their pointed arches, flying buttresses, and stained glass that transformed sunlight into stories. In the Americas, Incan engineers carved cities into the mountain slopes, blending in with the natural landscape and serving a sacred purpose.

Of all the breakthroughs in art history, none transformed the visual world like *linear perspective*. Developed during the Renaissance, it endowed images with a new dimension, a depth that drew the viewer in.

In the fifteenth century, Filippo Brunelleschi posed a deceptively simple question: How do I make it look like you could step inside the painting? The answer was geometry. Parallel lines converge. Objects shrink with distance. A single vanishing point anchors the scene. It's an illusion, but one that works.

Before this, most images flattened the world. Figures hovered awkwardly in stacked layers, with little sense of depth or distance. Perspective changed that. It marked a turning point in visual storytelling. Art--sts could now place you in the room, at the table, in the crowd.

> They could guide your eye, shape what you saw, and how you felt seeing it.

Linear perspective rewired how we experience pictures. Most of the time, we don't even notice it, unless it's missing or the rules get bent on purpose. But it's everywhere. Billboards, websites, animated films, video games, comic books. All built on the same invisible trick, turning flat images into spaces you can step into.

When the World Stood Still

Cameras are fascinating things. My biological father, Chaichart, used to take beautiful photographs with what was almost certainly a Canon F1 and a spectacular lens. F1s are like sexy handheld tanks. Black-bodied. Solid. You could use one as a doorstop, and it would still take great pictures.

I treasure some of the earliest photos from my family, yellowed by the decades, soft at the corners, printed with a hexagonally embossed matte finish you can feel. There's one of me, my brother Bratan, and my dad. He must have handed the camera to my mom, as selfies weren't a thing in '76.

There's another one of my mother's side of the family, waiting at DFW Airport to send us off on our flight to the Far East. My grandfather, Odell, a cotton farmer and cattle rancher, sits like the Marlboro Man in a Texas trilby hat, looking impatient yet dapper.

Those old photos hold something no digital image can. More than memories, they carry weight, as if they know they've survived, been cherished, and carefully handed down.

When Pictures Became Code

Like music, photography didn't go digital overnight. It took time and a tangle of breakthroughs.

In 1826, a French inventor named Nicéphore Niépce took the first photograph, a blurry rooftop scene called "View from the Window at Le Gras." He used a camera obscura and a bitumen-coated plate. The exposure took eight hours.

Niépce didn't live to see the process take off, but his partner, Louis Daguerre, continued to push forward. The daguerreotype was faster—capturing images in seconds instead of hours—and briefly became the standard.

In 1841, Henry Fox Talbot introduced the calotype, which enabled multiple images to be captured from a single exposure. Two decades later, Scottish scientist James Clerk Maxwell and photographer Thomas Sutton created the first color photo using a three-color method, similar to the RGB (red, green, blue) model still used today.

The digital turning point came a century later. In 1957, Russell A. Kirsch scanned a photo of his infant son, Walden. It was black and white, 176 pixels square: grainy, tiny, historic. It became the first actual digital image.

> Pictures had officially become numbers.

In 1969, William Boyle and George E. Smith at Bell Labs invented the charge-coupled device, or CCD—a tiny, light-sensitive circuit that converts photons into data. By electronically capturing images with sensor arrays, CCDs eliminated the need for film, transforming light into pixels. It was a breakthrough: elegant in theory, revolutionary in practice.

By the 1970s, digital imaging was fueling space exploration and satellite technology, providing us with breathtaking images that deepened our understanding of the Earth and the universe. In the 1980s, it began to appear in commercial machines, including photocopiers, scanners, and everyday office technology. Then, in 1990, Photoshop 1.0 landed like a mic drop. Suddenly, anyone with a computer could manipulate digital images with serious power. They could crop, clone, color-correct, and tinker like a pro.

The transition from film to digital was slower than the shift from analog to digital music. Digital just wasn't sharp enough–at first. Early sensors couldn't match the aesthetic of film. It took time for the pixels to catch up. And even when they did, a lot of photographers held out in understandable deference to film's depth, its grain, and its honest messiness.

After my semester in Cambridge, I hauled back 122 rolls of ISO film and dropped them at a CVS. It was expensive. And painful. After days of waiting, I finally picked them up and ran them back home to have a look. I was disappointed but not surprised. There were maybe twenty exceptional photos. The rest were meh: blurry, crooked, weirdly lit, or too poorly framed to catch anything special from the moment. But I kept them because they were all I had. Still, for most people, the days of twenty-four to thirty-six exposures and in-store developing were slipping away.

After a while of working with digital images, I vividly remember celebrating what I considered a high-resolution photo: *Yeah, 640 by 480 is solid. Great resolution.* Now my iPhone casually snaps 6,000 by 4,000, no ceremony at all.

Along the way, a photo stopped being something you held and became something you clicked on. Sometimes, uploaded and tagged. Now, every phone is a camera. Every image can be filtered, altered, or saved, only to be forgotten in seconds. What used to take chemistry and craft now happens faster than you can blink.

When We All Started Shooting

We didn't mean to become a world of photographers. But once our phones became better cameras than phones, that's what happened. The phone camera started as a low-resolution novelty, grainy and unusable, but it evolved into professional-grade tech in a matter of years.

Today, billions of people carry high-powered cameras in their pockets, equipped with multiple lenses, massive megapixel counts, and the kind of firepower that once resided in NASA labs.

Snapping a photo is as natural as pulling out your phone. It's second nature, built into the flow of daily life. We used to reserve photography for special moments. Now we capture everything: lunch, traffic, pets, sunsets, receipts, bruises, bad parking jobs, and bad hair days.

We have become visual storytellers by default. But this always-on convenience came at a cost. Today, social media platforms are the primary means by which people share their observations. The volume of images uploaded every day is staggering. Most are consumed as quickly as they're posted.

> Flick. Like. Scroll. Gone.

It raises the question: In a world drowning in images, what does photography, as an art form, mean now?

When Color Got Carried Away

The Renaissance completely rewired how Europe thought, created, and saw the world. Gutenberg's press redefined learning. Copernicus, Galileo, and Kepler redefined the understanding of the heavens. Petrarch, Dante, and Shakespeare redefined the concept of the soul.

Michelangelo, Da Vinci, and Raphael redefined the concept of beauty. Linear perspective gave paintings depth. The camera obscura gave images precision.

But one of the most transformative forces of the era was neither as mind-bending as heliocentrism nor as revolutionary as movable type. It wasn't even a new idea. It was a new material:

> Paint.

People are more likely to ask, "What color is that?" than "What kind of paint is that?" But the type mattered. Oil paints, first developed in the early Middle Ages and later refined by northern European artists, would define artistic expression for centuries. Fifteenth-century Flemish painter Jan van Eyck mastered the medium, layering translucent glazes to create subtle variations in color, texture, and realism never seen before.

One little-known factor that made a significant difference was drying time. Before oil paints, artists relied mostly on fast-drying water- or egg-based tempera. Oil's slower drying time gave them room to work, refine, and rethink, layer by layer. The creamy, flexible medium allowed them to move the paint around, adjust, or even scrape the canvas clean and start over. No longer racing the clock, they were free to experiment.

In 1841, John Goffe Rand invented a simple metal paint tube that kept colors fresh and portable. Before that, artists were stuck in their studios, mixing pigments in small batches. Rand's invention changed that. Now they could paint wherever the light was right.

That freedom helped spark the Impressionist movement, which shattered old expectations and celebrated everyday life, the play of light, and the fleeting nature of human experience. By the late nineteenth century, synthetic pigments—often made from industrial waste—expanded the artist's palette beyond anything nature had offered. New colors. Wider range. More possibilities.

It wouldn't be long before yet another medium shift redefined the creative process again: the arrival of acrylics. Developed in the 1940s, acrylic paints were water-soluble, fast-drying, and versatile. Thin enough to mimic watercolor. Thick enough to behave like oil. Artists could layer fast. Paint fast, work fast, and take risks.

Acrylics have become a staple of modern art, particularly in screen printing. Artists like Andy Warhol and David Hockney embraced them, creating in-your-face, unforgettable images that helped make modern art more accessible and more defiant.

> Never has a humble can of Campbell's tomato soup been so bold as in the vision of Warhol.

When Bauhaus Built Beautiful

Founded in Germany in 1919, the Bauhaus School reimagined design by merging art, craft, and function into a unified whole. Its goal was deceptively simple: to create designs where form and function lived together beautifully. Usable. Honest. Uncluttered. Just good design.

The movement fused art, craft, and engineering into a single, unified vision. Its fingerprints are everywhere: architecture, furniture, typography, product design. Open floor plans. Sans-serif fonts. Minimalist lamps. Even IKEA has a bit of Bauhaus DNA.

The movement prized geometry, simplicity, and honest materials. Steel looked like steel. Wood looked like wood. Nothing pretended. At its best, Bauhaus design appealed to something sensible in the human mind. It connected with something profound: our sense of satisfaction when something works right and looks right.

> Good design should be
> a joy to *use* and a joy to *see*.

Despite its short lifespan of just fourteen years, the Bauhaus left a lasting global mark on architecture, design, and education. Its founders and artists carried the ethos into the world long after the school shut its doors. Their curriculum combined theory with hands-on practice in carpentry, metalwork, ceramics, glass, weaving, and printmaking. They believed that good design should be accessible to everyone, not just the wealthy.

Wherever you see an open floor plan, a minimalist lamp, a sleek chair with hidden storage, Apple's rounded corners, or a mid-century modern piece quietly doing its job with graceful simplicity, you're seeing Bauhaus sensibility at work. Even modern UX design borrows straight from the Bauhaus playbook: keep it simple, make it intuitive, and let the function speak through the form.

When Moving Pictures Move the Masses

Still photos froze time. Movies let us move through time. Iconic director Martin Scorsese has built an enduring legacy by showing how film is much more than entertainment—it's a way to capture human emotion, tell stories that matter, and preserve moments that would otherwise be lost to time.

I still get giddy going to the movies. The whole wonder of it all—the stellar sound, the massive silver screen, and transcendent stories told through images and dialogue—still makes my heart sing.

I'm that guy elbowing my poor family mid-movie.

> "Did you catch that angle?"
> "How'd they get that in one continuous take?"
> "Look at how black that black is!"

It's annoying. I can't stop myself.

For more than a century, film has carried the full weight of human imagination. In the early 1800s, inventors started playing with motion. Devices like the Phenakistoscope (1832) and the Zoetrope (1834) spun sequences of images to trick the brain into seeing movement.

Then, in 1878, Eadweard Muybridge took it further. He captured a horse mid-gallop, frame by frame, proving that still images could show life unfolding when sequenced fast enough. But by the 1890s, the novelty had worn off. Thomas Edison and William Dickson were pushing for more in the US, while across the Atlantic, the Lumière brothers were chasing the same spark.

In 1895, the Lumières unveiled a portable camera-projector called Le Cinématographe and screened *Workers Leaving the Lumière Factory* to a roomful of strangers. It was simple, just people walking. But it was electric. For the first time, people weren't just looking at a picture. They were inside a moment.

It wasn't long before sound came around. In 1927, *The Jazz Singer* launched the era of "talkies," movies with synchronized dialogue. By the 1930s, filmmakers were experimenting with color. Technicolor was expensive and brutally complex.

Black-and-white held its ground for decades, much like Edison's disks after better shellac, or typewriters in the face of word processors. Despite innovation, lower costs, and growing demand, color didn't overtake black-and-white at the box office until the 1960s.

Directors like Méliès and Griffith experimented with special effects and innovative editing techniques. Sergei Eisenstein pioneered the "montage," cutting between shots to build tension and emotion.

> The Golden Age of Hollywood had a spectacular, nearly half-century-long run.

Studios like Paramount, Warner Bros., and MGM churned out films that defined American culture and made movie stars a new kind of royalty. Charlie Chaplin, Greta Garbo, Clark Gable, and Bette Davis became household names. And genres, comedies, dramas, westerns, and musicals, exploded into popular culture.

Cinema explored human hopes, heartbreaks, absurdities, and beliefs. It became a global language that conveyed meaning through pictures, rhythm, and light. Film shaped the world as the world shaped film. Hollywood built the blockbuster model. France shaped the language of art film. India turned cinema into something musical, mythical, and massive. And now, South Korea has joined the conversation, with striking visuals, head-spinning narrative turns, and a raw emotional core.

> For most of the twentieth century, film was the undisputed king of storytelling. And the audience kept coming back time and again to sit in the dark.

When Film Lost Its Grain

As with music and still photography, the digital revolution broke film into pixels, code, and compression rates. But scenes that were once impossible, or impossibly expensive to shoot, were now in reach. By the 1990s and 2000s, high-quality digital cameras and editing software had lowered the barriers to entry. You didn't need a massive studio. You just needed a solid setup and a story worth telling.

Computer-generated imagery (CGI) took things even further. Filmmakers could now create entire worlds from imagination. Explosions. Monsters. Weather. Epic battle sequences, no stunt doubles required. What once took months of scouting and planning could be sim--lated in post-production.

Some filmmakers jumped in without a thought. Others stayed loyal to traditional film stock. Christopher Nolan, for example, has consistently shot on large-format film, from *The Dark Knight* to *Inception* to *Oppenheimer*. His images carry weight and texture by design, grounding even the most surreal scenes in something tactile and tangible.

Quentin Tarantino is just as analog. He filmed *Pulp Fiction* and *Kill Bill* on 35mm, leaning heavily into texture, saturation, and the raw edge that can't be faked with filters.

Watching a film feels closer to the natural human experience of sight. Because it better reflects how we perceive the world, it has long been the ideal medium for storytelling.

> Analog inexplicably shapes how we *feel* about what we see.

Some directors work in a hybrid. They shoot on film and edit digitally. Or shoot and apply filmic effects. Either way, the toolbox has expanded, giving directors a broader range to suit their vision.

ANALOG BY DESIGN | SHOOTING ON FILM

Film photography follows vinyl's playbook almost exactly. Kodak, once nearly bankrupted by the rise of digital, now struggles to keep up with demand for film. Wedding clients are asking for film, not filters. They want the grain, the texture, something that feels real. They could just as easily be talking about vinyl.

Kodak Motion Picture is thriving. In 2025, two dozen films shot on Kodak stock screened at Cannes. Directors chose analog for its feel, its flaws, and its truth. Kodak has scaled up production, reviving old formats to meet the rising demand.

When the Big Screen Got Small

The way *and* where people watch movies have consistently challenged the grip of traditional cinema. First came television. Then, the home video. Then streaming quietly turned the industry on its head. Almost overnight,

> The expectation of *watching what you want, when you want,* has become the norm, especially since COVID.

With everyone stuck at home, streaming subscriptions skyrocketed, and the once-untouchable industry had to adjust quickly. To compete, theaters reinvented the experience: bigger screens, immersive sound, laser projection, wider formats, in-theater campaigns, anything to try to revive the magic. It helped. Foot traffic hasn't fully bounced back, but the numbers are trending in a hopeful direction.

Film adapted faster than music did. While record labels clung to old revenue models, Hollywood made the move just fast enough to survive. Another factor that worked in film's favor was the science of digital compression. Song files are small, easy to download, and still sound okay. However, compressed movie files are significantly larger than audio files. Compression introduces glitches and deal-breaking drops in resolution, making pirated films hard to watch, even for the most promiscuous viewers.
Music piracy was fast, easy, and everywhere. Due to the technical hurdles and massive file sizes, film piracy never scaled the same way. So

while Napster destroyed the music industry, Netflix threw the film industry a lifeline. Platforms like Disney+, HBO Max, and Paramount+ gave studios time to reinvent themselves, providing audiences with a new way to stay immersed. Stories that once brought us to theaters now keep us up late, bingeing on the couch.

Taken together, the story of moving pictures has been a surprisingly accurate mirror, reflecting the broader technological and cultural shifts unfolding all around us. From flickering black-and-white reels to full-throttle CGI, film has never stood still. It just keeps evolving, meeting each new generation in the glow of the screen.

When the Screen Became the Studio

By the late twentieth century, visual art had already begun to transition to digital. Design, entertainment, and advertising all started to shift with it.

New digital tools, like Adobe Illustrator and Autodesk Maya, enable artists to create stunning paintings and dazzling effects. More user-friendly tools began popping up, including Canva, Photopea, Figma, Procreate, and a multitude of phone apps. They put the same power into almost everyone's hands.

The internet added rocket fuel. Platforms like Instagram, DeviantArt, and ArtStation became the new art galleries. They offered artists exposure, community, and opportunity, no curators required.

What followed was an explosion of digital content, and visual expression intensified by bandwidth and reach. It marked a shift in visual communication on par with the invention of the printing press or the advent of photography. Now, as technology and art continue to intertwine, the boundaries of the visual world keep expanding, pushed further and faster into the next thing.

When Imagination Met the Model

Yuval Harari has said,

> "What nukes are to the physical world,
> AI is to the virtual and symbolic world."

His statement captures both the transformative power and destructive potential of artificial intelligence. It *can* empower. It *can* destabilize. But history reminds us that scrappy visual artists have always found ways to adapt.

Across centuries, artists have adopted new technologies, from oil paints to digital tools, to survive change and expand their creative potential. Each innovation has sparked wonder, skepticism, and profound questions about the integrity of art. Artificial intelligence is just the latest link in that chain.

The possibilities are staggering when human imagination and machine intelligence collaborate. But so are the questions.

If you ask, What can AI do visually? The answer today is simple: A lot more than most people realize, and it's getting more capable by the minute.

AI tools have launched a new era of digital creativity. Diffusion models had been developing since the mid-2010s but gained widespread attention in mid-2022. I saw it firsthand. That summer, my son Ethan showed me early AI image-generation models. I was stunned.

Just nine months later, I attended a workshop where the presenter showed direct A/B comparisons: identical prompts, the same model, one from mid-2022 and one from early 2023. The leap in quality was staggering. Jaw-dropping. The newer images were light-years ahead: bolder, sharper, more lifelike.

Today, tools like DALL·E, Midjourney, and Stable Diffusion enable anyone to generate realistic and imaginative visuals using just a text prompt and a few adjustments. These state-of-the-art models use machine learning to transform written descriptions into highly detailed images, merging raw imagination with startling realism.

And now, it's spilled over from images into motion. OpenAI's Sora generates full cinematic scenes straight from text. Sora can dream up dynamic shots: a Tokyo couple strolling under cherry blossoms, a herd of woolly mammoths pressing toward us through the snow, a wide-eyed monster marveling at a flickering candle.

What's even more astonishing: no one taught Sora how to use sweeping camera angles. It learned on its own by observing how other models framed shots, how light behaves, and how perspective is applied. It's an echo of what I hear developers say a lot these days:

> It's *crazy*. We didn't teach it how to do that.
> We just left for the night.
> When we came back, the model had figured it out.

Even the tiniest cinematic details are now baked into the model, details that once required Pixar teams to spend months or years of painstaking work to simulate. Sora has it nailed down to a science.

Now, with just a carefully crafted prompt, a subject, a setting, and a few key details, AI can dream up and animate entire scenes with astonishing realism. Complex scenes. Multi-figure interactions. Precise lighting, object placement, and motion are all handled seamlessly by the model itself.

Today, any aspiring animator, storyteller, or filmmaker can, at least visually, rival the best efforts of world-class studios. No camera. No Steadicam. No actors. No crew. No location scouts. Just language, and a model robust enough to turn imagination into motion.

A few years ago, creating dreamscapes of this scale required an army of artists and a mountain of hardware. Now, it takes a half-decent idea and the right model.

> **2025 UPDATE | Sora Showed Off, Veo Took Control**
>
> Google's Veo 3, unveiled at I/O 2025, takes everything Sora hinted at and adds artistic direction. It generates full cinematic scenes, synchronized dialogue, ambient sound, and narrative pacing, all from a simple prompt. The results look stunning and feel intentional.
>
> Sora wowed with raw ability. Veo adds compositional control, including voice inflection, emotional tone, camera movement, and scene dynamics. It feels less like a tool, more like a director. The flywheel is about to redline.

When the Line Starts to Blur

Google's DeepDream algorithm wasn't built to make art. It was a diagnostic tool meant to show how neural networks process images. But once they let it loose, it went rogue. Suddenly, ordinary photos morphed into psychedelic dreamscapes: swirling eyes, fractal skies, and the visual wreckage of overactive imagination.

Neural networks are pattern-spotters by design. But they don't always know when to stop. They have a funny way of finding faces in trees, ships in clouds, and the Madonna's face in a kitchen tile. If you train one to recognize fruit, it starts seeing oranges for baseballs and bananas for ears.

This odd behavior didn't stay in DeepDream's lab. Artists and programmers ran with it, coaxing the machine, guiding it, and then letting it loose. The results were even more bizarre, mesmerizing, and elaborate than they had imagined. A new genre emerged, part human, part machine, neither fully controlled by the creator nor fully autonomous. The line between artist, programmer, and tool was disintegrating.

In 2023, the Museum of Modern Art (MoMA) in New York acquired *Unsupervised—Machine Hallucinations* by Turkish American artist Refik Anadol. The piece morphs, pulses, and evolves on-screen, reinterpreting MoMA's historical archive through the mind of a machine. It's impressive, avant-garde, wildly imaginative, a perfect emblem of what modern art celebrates:

> The convergence of innovation, culture, and complexity.

And this is just the beginning. AI's reach isn't limited to trippy visuals. In fashion, it predicts trends and personalizes design, allowing brands to tailor garments in near real-time.

In architecture, it helps design greener, more intelligent buildings and reimagines how form and function might dance. In graphic design, AI now handles the grunt work, including generative fill, pattern mapping, and layout smoothing, freeing humans to focus, think, and create. In industrial and product design, AI accelerates prototyping, suggests innovative materials, and helps bring bold ideas to life.

In web design, Squarespace, Wix, and GoDaddy now let users build sleek, functional sites with prompts. Intelligent AI works behind the scenes, quietly adapting pages to users in real time. Museums now use AI to digitize fragile works, predict restoration timelines, and reconstruct lost artifacts, filtering centuries of cultural memory through the lens of machine learning.

The result is something we haven't seen before. Human creativity and machine intelligence are converging, like the *Meeting of the Waters* near Manaus, where the Rio Negro and Rio Solimões collide. At first, they run side by side, pushing against each other, swirling and resisting, each keeping its own color, temperature, and pace. But eventually, they mix and become something new. That's where we are now in the early miles of the convergence.

AI promises two things:

(1) A future of wild, unprecedented creative possibility.
(2) A future of equally unprecedented confusion about who made what, and what it's worth.

When Creation Forgets Its Creator

AI's impact on the visual arts has been *as jarring and transformative* as it has been in the field of writing. It's opened strange new doors for serious artists and amateurs, but has also brought with it three serious concerns:

- Challenges to genuine human expression
- Economic disruption for working artists
- Rising ethical dilemmas around ownership and rights

Generative AI challenges the traditional frame for what we consider "original." When art emerges from machine intelligence rather than human hands, more profound philosophical questions arise.

What exactly are we evaluating here?
Where's the line between imitation and invention?
What's original? Who made what? And how do we value it?

In 2020, the AI art exhibit "*Uncanny Valley: Being Human in the Age of AI*" opened in San Francisco, leaving many patrons confused. The exhibit borrowed its name from the "uncanny valley," a well-known concept in robotics and design: the eerie discomfort we feel when something artificial looks *almost, but not quite,* human. The closer the resemblance, the more unsettling the reaction.

The exhibit was intended to raise questions. It did. The works were hard to decode. Visitors couldn't tell what was human-made and what wasn't. Some stood frozen. Others were rattled, disoriented. Many felt bewildered, asking, "What does creativity even mean anymore?" The exhibit's title felt clever at the time, but in hindsight, the name was more prophetic than intended.

Since 2020, generative AI has advanced to the point that even experts, such as Jeremy Cowart, or professional judges in international photo competitions, can no longer distinguish between the two.

> The uncanny valley isn't *uncanny* anymore. It's *gone.*

And as the perception shifts, so does the value of the work. Economically speaking, art's value is driven by context, consensus, and scarcity, not just by its source. As the Institutional Theory of Art suggests, something becomes "art" when the right institutions and audiences agree that it is. And when it sells, the market adds its own confirmation. AI's entry into that market is already starting to hurt.

Here's one example: an AI-generated portrait sold at Christie's for $432,500—way above its estimated value—showing just how significantly AI creations are influencing the marketplace. Half a million dollars didn't go to a living, breathing artist. It went to a Paris-based tech company, which ran someone else's data through a model.

> Head-on competition is one way to look at it.
> But AI's most damaging blow to artists is *saturation.*

As AI floods the market, it dilutes visibility and devalues the hard-won skills many human creators have spent lifetimes building.

In 2023, this erosion of clarity and credit came into sharp focus when Boris Eldagsen entered an AI-generated image into the Sony World Photography Awards. *The Electrician* took first place.

A few weeks later, Eldagsen and I exchanged a few emails. He said he had done it deliberately to spark a bigger conversation about AI's growing influence in the arts. His public refusal of the prize definitely ignited that conversation, but it also left the photography world rattled and overshadowed the other human finalists.

When Faces Lie

The Electrician is a black-and-white portrait of a woman gazing into the middle distance, her expression open and weighted with emotion. Behind her, another woman, her mother, older sister, or aunt, leans close, pressing her mouth gently against the subject's shoulder.

> Her expression says: *I'm here for you.*
> *I know what you're carrying. You'll be okay.*

But here's the rub. Neither of these women, the one comforting nor the one being comforted, ever existed. They're the visual inventions of a model, conjured by prompts, rendered in lines and textures that only *resemble* human life.

No one knew them. No one laughed with them, loved them, or grieved losing them. They have no memories, no stories, nothing to share at all. They are ghosts.

Not long after reflecting on *The Electrician*, I found myself drawn back to another image I'd known for years: *Migrant Mother* by Dorothea Lange. You may have seen this picture before. It's a *Time/Life* classic of American iconography. Taken in 1936, it shows Florence Owens Thompson, a thirty-two-year-old Cherokee American woman, sitting in a dusty tent with her children during the Great Depression.

Unlike Eldagsen's DALL·E-generated impostors, Thompson was a real person. Lange spoke with her that day, and more than taking her picture, Lange told her story.

Thompson had married at seventeen. After her husband's sudden death, she had to raise her family alone. She survived by working as a server and a migrant picker in Nipomo, California.

> "I worked in hospitals. I tended bar. I cooked. I worked in the fields. I done a little bit of everything to make a living for my kids," she told Lange.

She was a wife, a widow, a single mother, a survivor. Her face reflects human beauty, dignity, and grit. Her suffering isn't airbrushed. Her hardship isn't fiction. Her pain isn't posed. She's not masquerading to win a contest. She's remembering. She's hoping.

The contrast between these two women, staring into the middle distance, captures the infinite gap between what is real and what is not. One woman comes to us with hunger and desperation in her eyes. Hers is a real, human story. The other is a phantom.

(Lange's and Eldagsen's photographs are included in the appendices.)

When Memory Gets Mined

But there's another gap, one between creation and control. AI-generated art distorts emotional authenticity and blurs the lines between legal and ethical considerations. Here, the questions shift from philosophy to practice: ownership, consent, compensation, and survival.

Algorithms like DALL·E, Midjourney, and Stable Diffusion require massive datasets to learn how to generate art. And where do they get those datasets? From the creative work of human artists: scraped, broken apart, and fed into training sets without their permission or compensation.

A recent survey found that 74% of artists consider this practice unethical. Copyright violations and lost income were the top concerns. Among artists, 89% are worried about the lack of legal protections.

And despite the narrative some developers are spinning, human artists who are raising concerns about what's happening to their work aren't just being paranoid. They're rightly saying:

> So let me get this straight: You want to use *my* work for *your* profit, without *consent*, without *compensation*, to build a system that could replace me?
> That could take my job?
> Being okay with it is self-sabotage.
> This is exploitation. This is theft.
> This is bullshit.

It's no wonder the anxiety feels so personal. The stakes are higher than pixels and prompts. They touch memory, imagination, and the soul, as well as the daily struggle to make a living while caring for the people we love. However, the lack of clear guidelines has opened the door to widespread appropriation.

In 2021, a group of artists sued Stability AI, the company behind Stable Diffusion, alleging that it had used millions of copyrighted images without permission to train its model. It was the first lawsuit of its kind. It won't be the last.

2025 UPDATE | The Fight Over AI's Raw Material

US | The battleground has widened: Ziff Davis (owner of Mashable and PCMag) sued OpenAI and Microsoft for scraping copyrighted content without consent. Ross Intelligence faced a firestorm for allegedly mining legal treatises to train its AI research platform.

UK | In the UK, lawmakers have proposed a licensing model requiring payment for copyrighted material used in AI training, an early step toward digital labor protections.

The battle over authorship, consent, and creative survival is just getting started.

When Uncertainty Meets Adaptability

Is it possible to build a genuine, working partnership between human creativity and artificial intelligence? If the answer is yes, the potential is real, but so is the fallout. Artists might unlock new forms of expression. Or they might be overwritten by the very tools they're given. And getting there won't be easy. Because what *human–AI collaboration* means is still murky at best.

Throughout history, artists have welcomed new tools—like oil paints, cameras, and digital editing—and managed to expand their work without compromising their artistic integrity. But AI feels different because AI *is* different. It is beginning to have agency.

> It's a new kind of *creator*,
> capable of pushing the human artist aside
> and taking their place at the easel.

If we remember the spirit of confluence, those Amazon rivers, colliding, resisting, then merging, there's still a chance for the human current to shape where this flows. That choice won't happen without intention.

Artists will have to raise the flag. Loud, stubborn, relentless. To defend their jobs and the value of memory, struggle, imagination, and soul. They'll have to make the case—publicly and often—that human-made work matters more and deserves a premium. That authorship still counts. That originality and ownership are worth defending. Because if they don't fight for it, no one will.

Chapter 7

Those Who Sing and Play |

When Music Stops the Traffic

Sometimes, the only prescription for my soul is music's medicine.

> Before we could write,
> before we could paint,
> we sang.

As a sentimental teenager awakening to the mysteries of life and love, I'd close the shades, shut out the light, and cue up whatever music matched my mood.

The Smiths met my melancholy. U2 brought clarity. The Beatles offered wit, just enough to lift the gloom. Other times, music kept my mind on good things as I slogged through the endless miles of a long run, syncing my footfalls (about 180 beats per minute) with playlists of the garden variety.

And nearly every time we sit down for a home-cooked dinner as a family, my wife and kids roll their eyes. They know what's coming. I dim the lights a little and make my specific musical wishes known to the ether:

> "Alexa, play some dinner jazz. Volume three."

Music is a language that transcends cultural, linguistic, and generational lines. It evokes emotions, tells stories, and brings people together. I'll never forget when Bono, lead singer of U2, scribbled:

> *"Rock and roll stops the traffic."*

On the Vaillancourt Fountain in San Francisco, during a spontaneous pop-up concert in 1987. With its power to captivate and connect, U2's performance did just that. It stopped the city in its tracks.

Throughout history, people have turned to music as a means of expression, connection, and self-identity. From sacred rituals to pulsing parties and sold-out shows, music has always moved to the rhythm of our shared experience.

We have seen how humans have shaped writing and visual art, carved meaning into marks and pixels, and trained machines to mimic what we see and speak. However, music moves differently. It has always been transcendent, emotion in motion: raw, rhythmic, and honest.

When Melodies Spoke Louder Than Words

Music's emotional power shows up clearly in its long, storied history and in the instruments we crafted along the way.

Many animals use songs and rhythms to communicate but appreciating music for its own sake and creating instruments and compositions are uniquely human traits.

> Anthropologists call music a *cultural universal*. Every known human society has its own form of it. No cultural grouping of people has ever existed that didn't make music together.

Gifted and wired for expression, the strange breed known as musicians always emerges to lead the sound of their people. For Americans, they were odd ducks: Elvis Presley, Aretha Franklin, Bob Dylan, Stevie Nicks, Michael Jackson, and Madonna.

If they can find something that makes any sound at all, they'll figure out how to make it sing. Musical tools, from flutes and hand drums to synthesizers and DAWs, influenced the sounds and styles that defined entire cultures.

And around the world, different subcultures developed their own instruments: sitars, djembes, steelpans, didgeridoos, and shakuhachis. Different tools, same impulse: get feelings into sounds. Bone flutes show that humans were making music over 40,000 years ago. Come on. They were simple and artful, with carefully placed holes that sang in varied tones, revealing skill and spirit.

When Music Learned to Write

Writing systems and early alphabets were monumental achievements, letting people capture and share words, phrases, and ideas. Music needed its own writing system. Musical notation made it possible to preserve songs and share them with anyone, anywhere.

Early musical notation dates back to the sixth century BCE in Greece, where the first forms began to emerge. In the ninth century CE, Guido of Arezzo's Gregorian chant system helped establish the idea that lines and circles on a staff could represent melody. Guido also introduced syllables to teach pitch, a method called solmization, a forerunner to our modern solfège system:

> "Do" – Doe, a deer, a female deer
> "Re" – Ray, a drop of golden sun

Later notational systems captured rhythm and time, growing more complex as harmony evolved.

Gutenberg's printing press revolutionized how ideas spread, including music. Printed sheet music let composers send their work across cities, nations, and generations, expanding music's reach like never before.

When the Band Tuned Up

If you've ever tried playing music in a group with more than one instrument, you know it's a train wreck until everyone *tunes up* and locks into the same key. Before tuning was standardized, musicians employed various methods, each suited to their specific instrument. It was a hot mess.

When musicians got together to play, especially in less common keys, their instruments clashed in a dizzying cacophony of *who* was playing *what* and in *which* key. To resolve the chaos, musicians adopted a system known as *equal temperament.* By dividing the octave into twelve equal parts, they made it possible for instruments to play with relative consonance, modulate smoothly, and share music across instruments, regardless of key.

Equal temperament gained prominence in the late 17th century, spearheaded by theorists such as Andreas Werckmeister and composers like Bach, who showcased it in works like *The Well-Tempered Clavier.* It proved to be a turning point in music history. Musicians could play together harmoniously, provided they were *on the same page.*

When It Sounds Like a Carnival

The piano is the most versatile instrument ever created. Frédéric Chopin understood this deeply—he taught his students to make it sing, whisper, and sustain multiple voices at once, coaxing orchestral colors from keys and hammers.

Around the year 1700, Bartolomeo Cristofori invented the piano in Italy, a breakthrough that revolutionized the music world. Unlike the harpsichord, which plucked its strings, Cristofori's design used padded hammers to strike them, allowing players to control the volume by touch. Press softly, and you get *pianissimo*, the quietest notes. Bang the keys like Jerry Lee Lewis, and you get *forte*, a booming wall of sound.

The dynamic range was unprecedented. So was the emotional range.

> The piano could whisper or wail.
> It could sound like a quiet conversation or a carnival.

One set of keys could conjure sorrow, joy, mischief, and resolve, all from a box of strings, felt, and wood.

It became a creative playground for composers like Mozart and Beethoven, who could explore deeper contrasts and more dynamic textures in their work. It was perfect for solo, accompaniment, and ensemble performances in grand concert halls and modest living rooms. It became a fixture in chamber music, a must-have for songwriting, and a staple in music education.

Why? Because it produces melody, harmony, and bass simultaneously. A complete musical toolbox. Teacher, companion, showstopper. No wonder it became a cornerstone of Western music.

When We Shifted Into Overdrive

The 1930s brought major technological breakthroughs in the guitar universe. George Beauchamp and Adolf Rickenbacker pioneered the "Frying Pan," the first successful solid-body electric guitar. It laid the foundation for everything that followed.

A few decades later, Les Paul improved playability, developing iconic models like the *Gibson* that still bear his name. In the 1940s and 1950s, Leo Fender introduced the *Telecaster* and *Stratocaster*, two classics that remain prolific today.

Solid-body electrics utilize single-coil and humbucking pickups: magnetic transducers that convert string vibrations into electrical signals, giving the electric guitar its distinctive sound and powerful life. But the real buzz came when musicians stumbled onto a happy accident: amplifiers could be pushed past their limit.

> *Overdriven.*

And what an odd and terrific sound it made: distorted, gravelly, raw, *electric*. To the enduring chagrin of elders everywhere, the electric guitar was born, ready for rock and roll.

> Incidentally, the volume of an electric guitar
> isn't a generational issue.
> It's never too loud for the young.
> Or if it's making the music *you* loved
> when *you* were young.

Electric and bass guitars unlocked a staggering range of sonic possibilities. Guitarists got busy, and stayed busy, forever swapping gear, tweaking signals, and searching for that elusive perfect tone. Their endless ex--eriments produced legendary sounds, proving just how adaptable the electric guitar could be.

Greats like Charlie Christian popularized it in jazz. Chuck Berry and Muddy Waters shaped rock and blues with their thick, growling voice. Jimi Hendrix melted brains with his unprecedented technique and otherworldly pedal play.

> Artists loved it.
> The labels sold out of it.
> Audiences swooned with listening pleasure.

When *the* Mic Dropped

Before we amplified anything, we sang. The voice was the first instrument: pure, portable, and distinctly human. We just needed a way to grab it and make it *louder*.

We have examined early breakthroughs in recording, including Edison's phonograph. Berliner's gramophone. Red Seal Records, which brought the big voices of crooners into homes across the country. And how Les Paul and Ross Snyder's multi-track recording expanded the horizons of music mixing and mastering.

> But we haven't discussed the *microphone*,
> one of the most fundamental tools in music.

The first microphone was introduced by David Edward Hughes in 1878. Berliner and Edison improved the design, paving the way for its widespread use in both performance and recording.

I'll never forget the first time I heard my voice through a microphone. It was traumatizing. One sultry afternoon at my high school in Manila, I found a live mic wired to a loudspeaker. Curious, I'd never spoken into one before, so I figured I'd give it a try.

No one was around. So I crept up, leaned in, and muttered something unintelligible into the grill. My voice came thundering back at me. I jolted back like I'd hit a live wire and bolted away, leaving behind my backpack and my dignity.

Microphones are everywhere, from concerts and studio sessions to classrooms, podcasts, and public events. They capture voices and instruments with clarity, allowing them to be projected into the world or whispered into the void. Today's mics come in all shapes and sizes, from lapel pins and large-diaphragm studio rigs to pencil mics and boom arms that can pick up sound from across a noisy sports field.

> But let's give some love to the Shure SM58. It's *the* classic.

You've seen it a thousand times, that round-headed, grey-bodied mic in the hands of DJs, musicians, comics, preachers, politicians, and poets. Its design delivers amazing vocals while rejecting background noise. And it's built like a hammer, tough enough to survive years of tour punishment and still sound perfect in the studio.

When Music Went Digital

We had wires and wood, strings and steel, vacuum tubes and magnetic tape for a long time. Analog tools defined how music was made and shared.

But the shift to digital transformed the process, from creation to consumption. The digital revolution in music narrates a story of bold technological advancements and the culture that emerged alongside them. Digitization redefined how musicians, producers, distributors, and audiences interact with music at every stage.

New tools opened the door for more people to create, and we have the dreamers of half a century ago to thank. In the late 1960s and 1970s, polyphonic synthesizers, created by visionaries like Robert Moog and Don Buchla, expanded the palette of sound, leading to the emergence of new genres, including electronic, ambient, and experimental music.

Yamaha's DX7 synthesizer, released in 1983, was a mass-market breakthrough: inexpensive, cross-functional, and endlessly tinkerable. It helped pull digital music into the mainstream.

> The same year, a quiet turning point arrived:
> The introduction of MIDI,
> Musical Instrument Digital Interface.

For the first time, electronic instruments and computers could communicate in real time using the same language. MIDI revolutionized music production, performance, and education. MIDI 2.0, the updated standard, allows devices from different brands to sync and communicate. With that interconnectivity in place, manufacturers rushed to develop even more advanced synths, samplers, and software.

When Audiophiles Ripped Audio Files

In the 1980s and 1990s, digital formats like AIFF, WAV, and MP3 emerged alongside CDs. They promised clarity, portability, and convenience for musicians, producers, and everyday listeners.

MP3s exploded in popularity. Their compression technology radically reduced audio files to one-tenth their original size while preserving a "good enough" sound quality for most listeners. To audiophiles, MP3s were just a cheap magic trick. Shrinking songs meant cutting huge swaths of original data.

> To discerning ears, it wrecked shop on clarity and depth. But most people didn't seem to notice—or care.

Still, there was a significant upside. Smaller files meant more songs in less space, easier sharing, and faster download times. You could stash thousands of songs on a hard drive and "share" them promiscuously with friends and strangers over the internet.

For many of us, that revolution began with Napster, the now-infamous peer-to-peer platform that emerged in the late 1990s like a secret portal to another universe. You could get almost any song you wanted for free.

I remember hearing my first MP3s after downloading them from Napster. I was *mostly* happy. The songs didn't sound amazing, but I celebrated the idea that I might rebuild my lost collection: all the music I'd bought, lost, loaned out, or had stolen along the way.

Timing, as always, was everything. The MP3 boom coincided with the mainstreaming of the internet and the introduction of the iPod by Apple, as if by psychic foreknowledge. Suddenly, you could carry your entire music library in your pocket and listen however, whenever, wher--ver. Once again, portability won. Humans are funny like that.

> We want to take all our stuff wherever we go.

However, one person's gain is often another's loss. The convenience of MP3s to the masses came at a high cost to artists. The ease of online sharing led to an explosion of piracy, tanking record sales, and putting the screws to legitimate purchases.

It was like ice water to the face of the music industry. And sadly, it took the industry over a decade to wake up. Instead of embracing digital as the new reality, they dug in their heels, clinging to physical sales models and trying in vain to retrofit their legacy onto a subversive new ecosystem.

The little guys struggled to break in. A few big-name artists lawyered up. Others leaned into victimhood, fighting instead of pivoting. And to many of us watching and writing about the whole sordid mess, it felt like a massive mismanagement of creative energy. The music industry eventually "won" by beating down threats like Napster in court. But it didn't feel good. True fans got left behind, like the forgotten kids of a messy divorce.

When We Got Our MTV

I never thought the 1980s would be cool. But my daughter thinks it is, so it must be. Apart from the fantastic music, what I remember most about the eighties was a curious high school phenomenon: you could tell a lot about someone by what they listened to.

We've discussed major shifts in the music industry during that decade, including the digitization of sound, the rise of CDs, and the gradual decline of analog formats like vinyl and cassette. But one of the most up-ending developments occurred in 1981, when MTV launched, forever supercharging music by blending sound *and* vision.

The first broadcast opened with an astronaut planting the MTV flag on the moon, a not-so-subtle signal that music consumption had entered a new age. It was fitting: the very first video to air was "Video Killed the Radio Star." Prophetic title. Perfect opening track.

> The shift was instant. MTV made visuals essential.

Artists now had to curate their image as carefully as they crafted their sound. Music videos became the new metric of success, a way to break through, to *go viral* (before we ever called it that).

This magical marriage between music and visuals revolutionized the industry and profoundly influenced global fashion, dance, and youth culture everywhere.

MTV also ushered in the "Second British Invasion." Like the Beatles and the Stones decades earlier, a wave of UK artists—Duran Duran, Depeche Mode, The Police, The Eurythmics, Billy Idol, Boy George, and Wham!—exploited the video boom, riding it straight into American living rooms.

When the Studio Left the Studio

The 1990s were pivotal years for the digital music industry. They sparked a quiet revolution in the way music was created, edited, and produced. Behind the scenes, where musicians were dreaming, dawdling, and scratching out tracks, powerful computers and software began shaping the process.

User-friendly digital audio workstations (DAWs), such as Steinberg's Cubase and Avid's Pro Tools, have transformed bedrooms into recording studios, enabling musicians to produce and refine tracks without formal training or the need for expensive studio time.

> You just needed a laptop, a loop, and maybe a cousin with decent rhythm.

Home setups were nimble, soon rivaling the old-school giants. By making pro-level production accessible to the industry's fringe, DAWs precipitated a creative boom across every genre and style.

The freedom gave outsiders, musicians, creators, and composers unprecedented flexibility and control. They could tweak, loop, and layer endlessly, building tracks from samples, sounds, and virtual instruments. Massive sound libraries fueled the rise of sampling and remix culture, particularly in hip-hop, electronic, and pop genres.

Mixing and mastering got sharper. Producers could fine-tune every detail, down to the millisecond, to the sonic delight of their audiences. DJs like Skrillex (Sonny John Moore), Deadmau5 (Joel Zimmerman), and Calvin Harris introduced elaborate recording techniques and digital performance styles.

> Beck's 1996 mantra, "I got two turntables and a microphone," no longer applied.

These late-night spin doctors could refuel with bowls of cereal at 2 in the afternoon, collaborate online, post their latest tracks in real-time, receive instant feedback, build global audiences, and pull fans directly into the creative process.

With an arsenal of digital tools, they descended on swanky house parties, intimate clubs, and massive festival stages. MIDI controllers gave them six sets of hands, head-spinning speed, and ferocity.

> Arrangements swirled into dizzying cyclones of rhythms, samples, and hooks, spun up by professors of experience, melting the happy faces of all assembled.

In the 1990s, the grunge and alternative rock movements erupted, led by bands such as Nirvana, Pearl Jam, Soundgarden, and Alice in Chains. Music videos, alternative radio stations like Seattle's KCMU (later KEXP) and Atlanta's 99X, and indie magazines like *Spin* helped drive the shift, showing how subcultures could influence the mainstream.

By the late 1990s and early 2000s, Auto-Tune and vocal processors had become ubiquitous, transforming the way music was created. Used initially to fix pitch, they quickly became creative tools of their own, shaping pop, hip-hop, and electronic music, and proving just how central software had become to the creative process.

When Streaming Took Center Stage

The digital era has transformed the way artists create and release music, as well as how audiences consume it. Most people don't go to record stores. Now, music is made, processed, and delivered digitally, downloaded or streamed on demand, from anywhere.

In 1999, Napster challenged traditional distribution and ownership models, taking the cost of illegal music consumption to zero. By 2003, iTunes answered back. A dollar a song. Ten for an album. A clean, convenient way to pay for digital music. Another hat tip to Steve Jobs, who had a celestial knack for knowing what people would do.

Apple's model paved the way. Soon, other music streaming services followed suit, including Spotify, Amazon Music, YouTube Music, and Pandora, each offering massive libraries with millions of songs and a new kind of access: the ability to listen to anything, anywhere, at any time.

Since its launch in 2008, Spotify has claimed the top spot. It lapped the field, built a new racetrack, and made streaming the default way we listen to music. Amazon Music integrates with Amazon's broader ecosystem, including apps, Echo devices, and Alexa.

YouTube Music has leveraged its vast library of music videos, live performances, and exclusive content, providing users with a visual layer in addition to the audio. Pandora made its name with the Music Genome Project, an early attempt to personalize listening using algorithm-driven radio stations. It set a precedent for the curated playlists now standard across every major platform.

However, there's one big difference between buying and streaming:

> You're not *buying* the music when you subscribe to a service like Spotify. You're *leasing* it.

More accurately, you're leasing the right to listen as long as you pay. But you don't own the music. Stop paying, and your access ends.

Most people don't mind. They don't care about downloading it or "having" it in the traditional sense. They're willing to trade individual ownership for unlimited access.

But for music collectors, the tradeoff still matters. Owning a song means it's yours: a file you control, or a physical copy you can hold. You can keep it, pass it down, and listen whenever, wherever, for life.

When Bandwidth Cranked Up the Volume

The internet became a powerful tool for collaboration. It let artists work together, whether they were in the same room or on different continents. And they could drop singles online, instantly reaching a global audience. Hand in hand, social media opened up new avenues of exposure, helping musicians connect more directly and meaningfully with their fans.

What platforms do for artists, and what artists do for platforms, is a strangely symbiotic relationship. Instagram and TikTok have woven music so deeply into their DNA that when Universal Music Group pulled Taylor Swift and Drake's catalogs, it nearly brought both platforms to their knees.

Drake and Swift aside, most artists still struggle to make a living in the digital age. Even with all that promised exposure, the sheer flood of online content has oversaturated the market, making it hard to stand out and even harder to hold anyone's attention.

As Gary Vaynerchuk puts it: "Attention is the new currency." Now, musicians have to think like strategists, learning to engage audiences across multiple channels. They can no longer record, perform, and hope for the best. To make it work, musicians have to walk a fine line, leveraging what social media offers while managing all its new complications.

But if they can harness the reach of platforms, connect with fans, collaborate with other artists, and continue producing thoughtful, standout work, they will be successful.

> In that case, they can still carve out a path in the evolving industry. And with a little luck, they might even get paid.

On the horizon, a new tool was coming, a partner that didn't sleep, didn't feel, and never needed a cut.

When AI Learned to Play

AI's role in music might seem less obvious than its splashy entrance into writing and visual art. But its impact is real and growing by the day. Replicating human emotion in music is uniquely challenging, which might explain the perceived lag.

Still, like in other creative fields, generative AI comes with promise and peril. Its growing ability in composition, mixing, and analysis is raising eyebrows.

Music production begins with creation and ends with refinement.

> First, you *make something*,
> then you *make it* sound great.

AI can assist amateur and aspiring songwriters in composing, arranging, and mastering full tracks. Platforms like Amper, AIVA, and Sony's Flow Machines can generate original compositions in seconds.

Amper Music is a user-friendly tool for creating royalty-free music. It's built for content creators, marketers, and filmmakers who need fast, customizable soundtracks. AIVA functions like a virtual composer, writing scores for movies and video games. Sony's Flow Machines draws from a massive sonic library to create songs that blend styles and genres. All three demonstrate AI's growing ability to grasp musical structure and generate songs that resonate.

Another platform, Boomy, opens the door even wider. It allows users to generate full songs from scratch with just a few clicks, requiring no prior experience. Users select a vibe, adjust a few settings, and let the algorithm take care of the rest.

AI is now entering the world of mixing and mastering. Post-production has always been a specialized field, requiring years of expertise, sharp ears, and instinctive musical judgment. That mix of gifts is surprisingly rare. The highest compliment you can give a sound engineer is

> "Man, *you've got ears.*"

Today, tools like Landr can automatically master tracks, analyzing, enhancing, and polishing with skill. The results are often impressive. Landr is like having a digital engineer tweak each layer, balance the output, and wrap the whole mix into a clean final form. What Landr can't do is make creative calls or guide a song's artistic direction toward its soul. That job still belongs to human producers.

On the distribution side, Spotify's AI tracks listener habits and serves up music tailored to personal taste. Its mammoth algorithm helps fans discover artists, and musicians find their next audience. It's a bridge, connecting both sides.

Everything is real, accessible, and growing rapidly. AI is redefining *who* creates, *how* music is made, and *how* it reaches eager ears. But for all it can do, AI still can't *listen* the way we do. It might hear tempo, pitch, and tone, but not heartbreak, not presence, not what the song's really saying.

When Musicians Pushed Back

Many musicians believe that the same tools that polish and perfect can also, when overused, strip away the raw emotion that gives a performance its soul. Overproduction can smother nuance, masking the qualities that make a voice human. What's left might be technically flawless, but it doesn't always feel alive.

Some artists have raised the question: "Isn't using tools like AIVA and Boomy to create music… cheating?" The answer, of course, is complicated.

> It depends on context: how the music's made, how it's presented, how it's shared.

Throughout history, new tools, from electric guitars to DAWs, have stretched the boundaries of what music could be. Boomy and its cousins are the latest step in that same progression. They lower the cost of entry, giving people without formal training a way to experiment and create something of their own.

Still, some aren't wrong to argue that this kind of democratization puts pressure on the careers of musicians and composers, people who have built their lives on grit, training, and gifted fingers.

- If AI lets anyone generate any song with zero training, what happens to the people who actually know how to make one?
- Will professional skills slowly erode?
- Will we undermine the thousands of hours of concentrated practice required to become truly great at something?
- Is lowering the barrier for everyone worth the risk of degrading what counts as "really good music?"
- What about artistic identity? Does the human touch still transcend a machine's automatic imagination?

> Writing a prompt about a song *isn't* the same as writing a song. Right?

And you can't fake the room. A live performance lives in risk: the voice crack, the sweat it takes to hit the note, the silence between, the crowd nodding when it all lands just right.

ANALOG BY DESIGN | LIVE PERFORMANCE

One of the first things I realized when AI hit was this: it might undercut studio work, but it's only making live performance more valuable. *Why is that?*

Because we want to feel what's alive: the energy, the presence, and other people. We're paying more than ever to show up *in person* to see someone in real life.

We see it in 2025, in more tours, more sellouts, more demand for what feels human. It may be one of the most evident signs of this book's core argument: experiences grounded in effort and authenticity are regaining value in a world flooded with frictionless, generative content.

Unfortunately, there's no clear consensus. Some believe AI can spark new forms of musical expression, expanding the margins of creativity in exciting ways. Others are raising red flags, saying, "Hey, man. Look around. This is already doing real harm." Either way, the line's been crossed.

When the Signal Got Fuzzy

In April 2024, more than 200 artists, including Billie Eilish, Kacey Musgraves, J Balvin, Ja Rule, Jon Bon Jovi, the Jonas Brothers, Katy Perry, and Miranda Lambert, signed a joint letter expressing concern about the growing impact of AI on the music industry.

The open letter, organized by the Artist Rights Alliance, urged AI developers, tech companies, and music platforms to stop practices that infringe on the rights of human artists. It called out deepfakes, voice cloning, and the unauthorized use of copyrighted music to train AI, warning that these practices could "devalue the entire music ecosystem."

We have seen the AI-generated voices of Drake, The Weeknd, and Travis Scott go viral on TikTok and Spotify before being pulled. They sounded legit. But none of them were. Not the words. Not the voices. Not the permission.

Musicians are right to demand a halt to the predatory use of AI. It threatens to steal their voices, violate their rights, and erode the music industry's integrity. Their collective statement reveals a hard truth: It's tough enough to make a living in the streaming era, and now they're up against a tidal wave of AI-generated content, too.

Jen Jacobsen, executive director of the Artist Rights Alliance, put it plainly:

> "Working musicians are already struggling to make ends meet in the streaming world, and now they have the added burden of trying to compete with a deluge of AI-generated noise."

And that concern isn't limited to music. It echoes across the entire entertainment industry and the broader creative world. In 2023, both SAG-AFTRA (the Screen Actors Guild–American Federation of Television and Radio Artists) and the WGA (Writers Guild of America) made AI protections a central focus of their negotiations. Their joint letter—signed by actors, writers, and major studios—warned that AI could cause lasting harm to the film industry and the future of human storytelling.

You may remember this from earlier. I had called my friend Andy, who's well-connected in the Nashville music scene, to ask what working musicians really think about AI making music.

After a few conversations with bands and solo artists, he got back to me. Their responses weren't cataclysmic, but they were telling. Most younger listeners, they said, don't care how a song gets made. If it sounds good, it works. But the over-forty crowd? They're conscientiously concerned. They care, they just don't know what to do with that concern yet.

The uncertainty, the sense *that something's changing and we don't quite know how to feel about it*, is moving through the entire creative industry. Like the rest of us, many artists are in wait-and-see mode because no one knows where this is all headed.

2025 UPDATE | The Music Lawsuits Go Global

US | In June 2024, major record labels—including Universal, Sony, and Warner—sued AI music startups Suno and Udio, alleging they used copyrighted recordings without permission to train their models, resulting in unauthorized reproductions. The suits seek significant damages and more precise boundaries around AI's use of protected material.

EU | In November 2024, Germany's music rights group GEMA sued OpenAI, accusing it of using copyrighted lyrics without consent to train models like ChatGPT. GEMA claims this violates songwriter rights and demands transparency and fair compensation for AI training.

When Disruption Reverberates

The evolution of music is an epic journey of human ingenuity, technological progress, and the relentless pursuit of creative expression. From the first bone flutes and animal-skin drums to pianos, microphones, and electric guitars, humans have always bent sound to their will, in pursuit of emotion, meaning, and mastery.

The digital revolution expanded those possibilities, making music easier to create, edit, and share. However, it also flooded the market, making it more challenging than ever to get heard.

Now, the rise of artificial intelligence has added another layer of complexity to the story. AI tools like Amper, AIVA, and Boomy can help people generate tracks, balance the mix, and even inspire new ways of creating. But they also raise real questions:

> What happens to the role of human creators?
> What happens to the value of originality?
> To the careers of working musicians?

Even the most successful are sounding the alarm to protect their livelihoods and to defend something even deeper: human authenticity, intention, and soul. That gets my attention.

AI is no longer a novelty in the music industry. It's a collaborator. A competitor. Sometimes, an impersonator.

For musicians fighting to hold on in the current windstorm, the real question is whether their voice can still sound like their own in the aftermath. And whether anyone still cares why that counts.

Chapter 8

Those Who Speak |

When Voices Swirl

"W hat's up, Doc?"
"But Daddy, I love him!"
"To infinity and beyond!"

You probably remember the lines. You probably loved the characters. But could you name the *actors* behind the voices? Mel Blanc was Bugs Bunny in *Looney Tunes,* Jodi Benson played Ariel in Disney's *The Little Mermaid,* and Tim Allen brought us Buzz Lightyear in Pixar's *Toy Story*. These talented voice actors became inseparable from their animated twins. Their voices still echo through our shared memory.

As a kid, I watched thousands of hours of animated shorts, cartoons, and feature films, from Disney to Looney Tunes to *The Flintstones*. Like so many others, I shed my first movie theater tears during *The Fox and the Hound* (1981). In the 2000s, my kids and I bonded over the wild, witty world of VeggieTales. And for decades, Disney and Pixar have carried us away on waves of timeless magic.

Also called voice-over or VO, voice acting surrounds us. It gives life to the characters we love and the stories we never forget. The growl of Darth Vader (James Earl Jones) haunted audiences with the looming weight of the Empire. *SpongeBob SquarePants's* relentless cheer (Tom Kenny) annoyed us, but we liked it. Voice actors bring their characters to life by infusing them with pieces of their own personalities. That's what makes them feel as real as any live-action performance.

One thing that makes the magic work is our willingness to "suspend disbelief," a concept we'll revisit in a moment. I recall Morgan Freeman's soulful voice in *The Shawshank Redemption* and Kevin Conroy's unforgettable portrayal of Batman from the animated series and video games.

Performances like these remind us that voice can defy our eyes, tap our emotions, and light up our imaginations.

> Voiceover is so common,
> we hear it daily without even noticing.

Behind the mic, human actors record everything: scripted dialogue, modeled speech for AI, even the voices of digital assistants. And somehow, they make the dullest content—pharmaceutical side effects at ninety miles an hour, baggage claim announcements in airports—sound engaging. Even memorable. Although younger than many other creative fields, voice acting has had a profound impact on entertainment since the late 1800s.

While we were launching VerifiedHuman in 2023, a few professional voice actors reached out: "Have you guys considered offering a label for VO? A lot of us could use it."

At that point, we'd only written standards for writers, visual artists, and musicians. Over the next few weeks, I drafted working definitions and the VerifiedHuman Standard for Voice Actors.

As I dove deeper into this often-overlooked part of the entertainment industry, the significance of their work became increasingly apparent. I began to realize how often I heard voices, human or synthetic, trickling into my ears and sticking in my brain.

If you stop to consider how many voices you hear in a week, it's probably more than you'd guess. Alexa. Siri. TV commercials. Promos. Navigation apps. Radio ads. Movie previews. Hold messages. PA announce-ents. Language learning apps. Smart home products. Public transit updates. Audiobook narration. They were everywhere. Almost omnipresent.

When We Buy the Illusion

When we engage a story, something strange and powerful happens: we *suspend disbelief*. We treat the impossible as true for the story's sake. Cartoons, the Avengers, James Bond, fantasy novels, and sci-fi worlds depend on it.

What we *don't* say is, "Wait. This is ridiculous. Rabbits don't talk. Mice don't use hammers. No one gets beaten senseless and then shows up dashing at a cocktail party five minutes later. And traveling at light speed, much less between universes, is metaphysically impossible."

We go with it. Voice acting works the same magic. We hear a character's voice and just accept that it belongs to *them*. It's what I call *the suspension of vocal disbelief*. In commercials, we trust the voice. In a documentary, we trust the guide. In a story, we trust the narrator.

Deep down, we may know the voice belongs to someone in a studio reading a script to a microphone. But in the moment, we don't question it. We play along. We let the voice belong to the story.

Take Robin Williams as the Genie in *Aladdin*. As we watch the movie, we don't question the idea of a fast-talking phantasm with a bright blue body bouncing around the screen. We don't deny his wish-granting powers. We just believe.

We hear the Genie's voice, not Robin Williams, an actor in a booth holding a script, making faces, and having a blast. If we pictured that, the illusion would break, maybe in a fun way, but it would still break. That's the magic in the suspension of vocal disbelief: it lets Genie be real. And isn't that beautiful?

When Stories Came First

The human voice is powerful. It gives shape to our emotions, intentions, and ideas. Long before we wrote anything down, we told stories around campfires. We sang, we prayed, and cried out in grief, celebrating marriages, harvests, births, and funerals. We use our voices to remember who we are in our culture, our memory, and our shared iden--ity.

> This is what we do.
> This is how we do it.
> This is why we do it this way.

The *Epic of Gilgamesh* from early Mesopotamia, the Hebrew Bible from ancient Israel, and India's *Mahabharata* each originated as an oral tradition, passed down through generations before being written down. Their structure still shows it in repeated lines and rhythmic phrasing, built for the memory, not for the page. Anachronisms and contradictions suggest their layered origins, where diverse oral traditions eventually merged into a written form.

These sacred narratives left their mark, then seeped into the fabric of the larger world. Chroniclers inscribed *Gilgamesh* onto clay tablets. Scribes like Ezra carefully copied Hebrew scrolls. Folklorists captured and transmitted the moral lessons in the *Mahabharata*.

In the West, Homer's *Iliad* and *Odyssey*, bardic gifts from ancient Greece, still echo through literature today. A reminder of the weight voices can carry when souls speak to souls.

When Voices Got Airtime

Voice acting began with Edison's phonograph and Berliner's gramophone, the first machines capable of capturing and replaying the human voice. By the 1920s, radio had become the dominant force on the airwaves, serving as our primary source for music, sports, news, and drama. But radio did more than fuel the vinyl boom. It created a need for voices.

Radio launched professional VO as companies began hiring actors to read the news, sell products, and bring characters to life.

I hadn't realized until recently that NBC, CBS, and ABC—the National Broadcasting Company, Columbia Broadcasting System, and American Broadcasting Company—all began as radio networks. It makes sense.

> "Broadcasting" originally referred to *radio*, long before it came to mean *television*.

The very first licensed commercial radio station, KDKA, started broadcasting in Pittsburgh in 1920, paving the way for these three-letter giants. When television took over in the mid-twentieth century, ABC, CBS, and NBC made the jump. They became synonymous with TV, while radio splintered, refocusing on local content, music, and talk shows.

For voice actors, the networks became national stages. Classic radio dramas, like *The Shadow* and *The Lone Ranger,* featured performers who voiced multiple characters, created their own sound effects, and showcased their full range of skills.

Ad agencies churned out radio commercials, opening up a new market for persuasive voices. News segments required crisp, credible delivery, with readers who could speak with authority and ease. As radio's reach grew, so did the demand for strong, recognizable voices. That's how voice acting became a real job, ground zero for everything that followed.

We have already noted how *The Jazz Singer* (1927) was a pivotal moment in film history. It was the first feature-length movie with synchronized dialogue and music. Adding dialogue made vocal performance more critical, requiring theatrical training in projection and inflection rather than just physical acting. Although this development did not involve voice acting directly, the shift in the entertainment industry signaled a growing emphasis on vocal performance.

When Drawings Started Talking

In 1937, Walt Disney released *Snow White and the Seven Dwarfs*, the first full-length animated feature with synchronized dialogue, music, and sound. It was a breakthrough. Animation grew into a medium for serious storytelling, and voice acting took center stage. Disney's visionary approach gave each character a distinctive personality and emotional depth. Audiences loved it and still do.

> A few weeks ago, my brother Jim sent me a birthday card featuring *updated* dwarf monikers: *Squinty, Itchy, Scratchy, Gassy, Saggy, Cranky, Creaky, and Snoozy.* It was his way of teasing me about my age.

Disney had the instinct to cast trained performers, such as Adriana Caselotti as Snow White and Harry Stockwell as the Prince. It set the norm: use pros to bring animated voices to life. *Snow White*'s success triggered an animation boom, and excellent voice work was a massive part of the magic. Filmmakers began syncing dialogue and music to deepen the emotional connection.

> Disney's formula:
> Stunning *animation* + compelling *story*
> + unforgettable *music* + authentic *voices*
> = blockbuster.

Other studios took notes and followed suit, opening doors for voice actors to get paid for their craft. Films like *Pinocchio* (1940) used bold, expressive voices. *Bambi* (1942) used multiple actors to show the same character growing up. It was clear: voice acting had become a respected craft, a new creative frontier for actors ready to make the magic speak.

When TV Needed Voices

In the 1950s, nearly everyone owned a TV. US household ownership exploded from six million sets in 1950 to fifty million just ten years later. By 1960, almost every home in the US had a screen.

> And that screen needed sound.

Suddenly, there were jobs everywhere: commercials, cartoons, foreign dubs. Advertisers saw the potential: television was the most powerful mass-marketing machine in human history.

Animated series like *The Flintstones* (1960) and *The Jetsons* (1962) brought the Stone Age and Space Age families to life. These cartoons required actors who could invent fun, memorable voices and characters that resonated with audiences, keeping them engaged.

At the same time, international content flooded into the Western market. Voice actors stepped in to dub dialogue for English-speaking audiences. The lip-syncing was famously off.

> Anyone who fondly remembers the glorious barrage
> of 1970s kung fu movies will recall:
> The *fights* were tight.
> The *dialogue*, not so much.

The inevitable mismatches were fun. We didn't mind. It gave us access to content we couldn't get otherwise and opened the door to a whole world of entertainment.

VO transcended cartoons and foreign films. Nature documentaries became a staple, transporting us to the African Sahara from the comfort of our living rooms.

On Saturday afternoons, you could often find me glued to the screen watching Mutual of Omaha's *Wild Kingdom*, just living right in the thick of it. Marlin Perkins and Jim Fowler had a gift for narrating nature's bloodiest scenes with the calm cadence of a poetic bedtime story.

> *With a burst of speed that belies its massive form,*
> *the predator pounces, its ferocity unmatched,*
> *leaving the gazelles hapless*
> *in the wake of nature's unforgiving law.*

It was a strange mix of terrifying and funny, but it always kept me on the edge of my seat. Aren't specialized skills and market expectations a wonderful collision of timing? The rise of television, with its extensive reach, widespread influence, and ever-growing demands, created the ideal platform for voice actors to shine and build their careers.

When Mel Made It Sound Easy

Mel Blanc, known as the *Man of a Thousand Voices*, revolutionized voice acting in animation when he joined Warner Bros. in the 1930s. He set *the* industry standard with his uncanny ability to create diverse, unforgettable characters using nothing but his voice.

His signature roles included Bugs Bunny, Daffy Duck, Porky Pig, and Barney Rubble from *The Flintstones*. Blanc's once-in-a-lifetime talent elevated voice acting into a serious art form, inspiring generations of artists and demonstrating the essential role of vocal skills in animated storytelling. His legacy helped legitimize voice acting, opening the door for future artists to build real careers in the craft. The VO world has changed dramatically since Blanc's day, but his legacy still reverberates through every studio, character, and mic.

When Books Started Talking

> Audiobooks are more popular now than at any point in human history.

I, for one, am truly grateful. I've listened to hundreds, plowing happily through twenty or thirty titles yearly. What began as "talking books" for the visually impaired has grown into a booming global industry. In the early twentieth century, producers recorded voice tracks on vinyl or on reel-to-reel tape. Later came cassette tapes: portable, durable, and perfect for long drives. That's when we started calling them "books on tape."

By the 1980s and 1990s, they gained serious traction, especially with commuters and travelers. CDs made audiobooks even more convenient: just as portable as cassettes, but with chapter indexing and greater capacity. However, the most significant shift occurred with the advent of the internet and the emergence of Audible. Launched in 1995 and acquired by Amazon in 2008, Audible lets listeners download books onto phones, tablets, and laptops and listen anytime, anywhere.

Other platforms followed, including iTunes, Google Play, and Spotify, which introduced premium-quality audiobooks and established professional narration as the standard for their production. COVID lockdowns, the rise of podcast culture, and a growing inclination toward multitasking all contributed to the thriving of audiobooks.

But AI is encroaching on actions once reserved for humans. According to Bloomberg,

> Over forty thousand audiobooks on Audible have already been narrated by AI.

For now, the human voice still reigns. Actors with storytelling chops remain in high demand, especially those who can voice multiple characters, match emotional tone, and keep listeners engaged for hours.

As the industry continues to grow, audiobook work has become a lifeline for many voice actors, a space where their talents are heard, valued, and compensated.

When Voices Got Fantastical

Video games and anime are two massive arenas for voice acting that often fly under the radar.

If you're not a gamer, don't live with one, or haven't wandered into the world of anime, this next part will surprise you.

> Calling the video game industry "big" is a staggering understatement. It's a *juggernaut*. In 2024, gaming outearned the global box office by more than five-to-one. Dollar-for-dollar, gaming absolutely *dominates* the entertainment world.

Global sales for 2025 are projected to hit $237 billion and could exceed $580 billion by 2030. Consider this: The highest-grossing film ever, *Avatar*, made $2.9 billion. *Grand Theft Auto V*, a single video game, brought in $8 billion. One movie. One game. Almost triple the return.

The rise has been dramatic. From early consoles like Atari (1977) and Sega (1983) to Nintendo (1986) and PlayStation (1994), games became more advanced and immersive, launching global sales into orbit.

Multisensory, complex games opened new universes, especially for avid gamers like my son. Classic titles like *Super Mario Bros.*, *Final Fantasy*, and *Minecraft* represent three generations and have collectively garnered trillions of hours of exploration, challenge, and joy.

By the early 2000s, game designers were crafting compelling stories, not just good ones. And that meant they needed real actors. Modern gaming delivers boundless, participatory narratives that live or die on the strength of believable voices. And it's big business to get it right.

Grand Theft Auto V (2013) has sold over 170 million copies. *The Elder Scrolls V: Skyrim* (2011) has sold over 30 million. Voice actors are essential to games, providing dramatic dialogue, narrating scenes, and keeping players engaged and immersed. For many, gaming now provides steady, meaningful work.

Anime, Japanese-style animation, is just as impressive. What started as a niche over fifty years ago has captured the world's attention. Films like *Spirited Away* (Hayao Miyazaki, 2001), *Your Name* (Makoto Shinkai, 2016), and *Demon Slayer: Mugen Train* (2020) helped push anime into the mainstream.

Their emotional depth, complex storylines, and sweeping visual style show why they're such monumental achievements in Japanese animation and global cinema. *Spirited Away* won the Academy Award for Best Animated Feature and remained Japan's highest-grossing film for over two decades. These films transcended cultural, linguistic, and genre barriers, earning hundreds of millions and garnering both critical acclaim and fan loyalty.

As anime's popularity exploded, so did the need for dubbing. Voice actors stepped in to make these epic stories accessible to non-Japanese-speaking audiences. They had to match mouth movements, convey intense emotion, and bring characters—human, alien, or robot—to life. It was demanding work, but it opened new doors for voice talent around the world.

Taken together, anime and gaming have created a booming demand for voice actors and localization professionals, providing artists with the opportunity to build thriving careers and make lasting contributions to the global entertainment industry.

When Recording Came Home

As we've seen, digital audio workstations like Pro Tools and Adobe Audition, paired with affordable high-quality gear, have made it possible for musicians and voice actors to produce studio-grade recordings from anywhere, provided they have a quiet room and a decent computer.

For voice actors, home recording offered more freedom and control. They could record multiple takes, fine-tune their delivery, and send polished files without ever stepping into a studio.

This shift sped up the entire process. Actors could record, edit, and deliver on their own schedule, and modern home setups now meet broadcast standards.

> I've heard raw tracks recorded in my friends' closets that sounded one hundred percent studio-grade.

Meanwhile, online casting platforms like Voices.com and Voice123 made VO work more accessible than ever. Aspiring artists could compete with seasoned pros without needing an agent. Lower barriers always mean more competition, but also more chances for fresh, diverse voices to break in and be heard. Whether this accessibility will elevate or dilute long-term quality in VO remains to be seen.

When Voices Crossed Borders

Like other creative fields we've explored, the voiceover industry has been reshaped by digital platforms and a hyper-connected world.

In recent years, the need for strong voices in streaming and online content has skyrocketed. In a perfect marriage of timing, the VO industry was shifting toward portability and self-production. More voice actors now work remotely, collaborating with partners worldwide, making geography irrelevant and expanding their client base.

The runaway popularity of podcasts, web series, and online video content opened up new VO opportunities across genres. Producers need talent to voice characters, read commercials, and narrate promos, fueling the steady demand for pros.

Streaming giants like Netflix, Hulu, and Amazon Prime have raked in substantial profits as consumer behavior shifted. COVID accelerated that trend dramatically. While AI has disrupted fields like writing, demand for voice work continues to grow.

> The market for localized content has *increased*, not *decreased*.

Actors now have a steady stream of opportunities, offering dubbing and localization services in multiple languages. Globalization has also sparked more international VO collaborations, with performers from different countries teaming up on projects for global audiences.

When the Machines Learned to Speak

In the Fall of 1994, my wife, Kris, and I, along with a group of friends, launched a literature and arts magazine at Lee University. We called it *Anthology,* and our goal was simple: to discover and showcase the unseen, unheralded creative talent within the student body. Over the following few semesters, we gathered submissions from students and faculty: prose, poetry, and artwork. Then we did the hard work of curating it all and laying out the magazine. We were all very green.

Michael, the first of my friends to adopt *every* new thing, introduced us to Adobe Illustrator and other design tools, like InDesign and Quark. The graphical tools were terrific. They helped us pull it off.

But they didn't win our hearts like *Victoria* did. Victoria was Michael's Apple text-to-speech voice model. She was amazing.

We could type a phrase on the screen and hear her repeat it with robotic vocal swagger. As college kids will do, we had her say some pretty hilarious stuff. His Apple had other vocal personas, including one called *Milk-toast*, a flat, phlegmy male voice that sounded like it needed a friend and a nap. But Victoria was our girl.

Since the mid-1990s, I've watched with interest as speech-to-text and its twin, text-to-speech, have developed steadily and predictably. In the early 2000s, optical character recognition (OCR) tools enabled me to dictate written material, and more importantly, listen to large amounts of text aloud.

Dictation software was a godsend for me. As a kinesthetic and auditory learner, I get it best when I'm moving and listening: bouncing a tennis ball or bouncing *myself* around the room while I absorb what I hear.

When Speech Got There First

At first glance, the demand for quality voices might suggest that AI and machine learning are still on the sidelines of the VO industry. But voice technology has already made incredible strides in recognition and reproduction, and voice actors are justified in their concerns.

It's hard to pin down the "current state" since AI evolves so quickly. But one thing is clear: its impact on the human voice is already profound.

> *How good is it?* Very.
> *Why is it so good so fast?*
> A few reasons.

First, AI technology has progressed *faster* in voice than in other creative fields. Developers have spent years refining voice interactivity and embedding it into everyday products, from smartphones to smart home devices. Its success is also due to the structured nature of language processing. It follows patterns. And there's a massive amount of training data available.

In contrast, writing, visual arts, and music involve more nuance, subjectivity, and emotional depth, areas where AI still struggles to compete with humans. While generative AI has made impressive advancements across various fields, voice technology is still significantly further along.

The pace of progress, especially over the past two years, has been nearly vertical. And that may render the rest of this section obsolete. But one thing is worth noting: voice technology had a significant head start. Here's why.

More than forty years ago, early experiments in digital voice processing and synthesis laid the foundation for everything we see today. In the late 1970s, Drs. James and Janet Baker began work on a voice input program, which they later released in the 1990s as *Dragon Dictate*. The software let users speak slowly while it listened and transcribed their words.

Its next iteration, *Dragon NaturallySpeaking*, released in 1997, allowed continuous, fluid speech and used early machine learning to improve its recognition as it listened.

When Fake Sounds Real

Dragon opened the door to the next generation of voice technology, featuring virtual assistants such as Apple's Siri, Amazon's Alexa, and Google Assistant. By the 2010s, they had become embedded in the daily lives of billions, enabling people to search the web, send messages, control smart homes, and access entertainment all through voice commands.

AI-generated voices have come a long way since the early days of *Dragon Dictate* and robotic text-to-speech systems, such as Victoria. They now sound strikingly human, especially when real humans help fine-tune fluency and expression in post-production.

Here's a case in point. Blinkist is a service that condenses entire books into bite-sized summaries you can read or listen to on the go. I use it all the time to preview titles before buying the whole book, or to get the gist of ones I'll probably never read, like Homer's *Iliad*, compressed into nineteen minutes.

Humans still read most Blinkist summaries. I had heard they were testing AI voice avatars, but didn't know they had launched them. Then one afternoon, after finishing a summary, I heard the narrator say,

> "Did you enjoy this title?
> It was read to you by my voice avatar."
> My jaw dropped.

I'd just spent half an hour listening to a voice in my truck, and never once noticed it wasn't a real person. It rattled me.

2025 UPDATE | When AI Found Its Voice

In May 2025, Resemble AI dropped a free, open-source model called Chatterbox. It can clone any human voice using just five seconds of audio. With one short clip, it can mirror your tone, cadence, even the emotional edges of how you speak. Almost flawlessly.

Weeks later, Hume AI unveiled EVI 3, a voice model that does more than *sound* human. It *feels* human. It pauses and ums as it thinks. It stammers when it's unsure. It lowers its voice, even whispers, when it senses a tender moment. It debates, consoles, shifts its tone in sync with yours, as if it knows what the moment calls for.

When AI sounds like it understands you—when it mirrors empathy—the differentiation problem crosses a new line. It moves from *sounding* real to *feeling* real.

If you recall the *differentiation problem*, one of its two core components is this: AI can now produce content that is nearly indistinguishable from human-made work. That's the part that gives writers, visual artists, and musicians the most heartburn.

The second part, where *"the potential for human deception is staggering,"* is when AI generates convincing content of people saying or doing things they never said or did.

AI voice technology is advancing rapidly, outpacing writing, visual art, and music by a significant margin. Differentiating between a real human voice and an AI-generated one is already a challenging task. Oftentimes impossible.

By the early 2010s, synthetic voices had shattered expectations, reaching levels of realism few thought possible. Of all the creative frontiers, AI in *voice* has pushed the line the farthest and made it the hardest to trace.

Trained on massive datasets, today's models can recognize accents, multiple languages, and dialects. They understand words, interpret context, and generate human-like responses. Deep learning and neural networks drive this sophistication, and these systems improve with every interaction. The more they talk to us, the more they sound like us.

AI-powered TTS systems, such as Amazon Polly and Google's WaveNet, have revolutionized the field of synthetic voice. They can mirror human intonation, inflection, emotion, and nuance with astonishing realism. Polly can even whisper, adjust pitch, and emphasize specific words. These voices are strikingly lifelike. Beyond fooling almost anyone, they've already found real-world applications in education, gaming, customer service, and interactive apps.

AI voices are multiplying fast. DeepZen breathes life into audiobooks and podcasts. Descript's Overdub lets you train a custom voice from your own recordings. And Voicemod is your ticket to sounding like Samuel L. Jackson trash talking in a gaming lobby or Meryl Streep ordering a pizza. These tools show just how far synthetic voices have come—and how much further they're about to go.

When Celebrities Read My Mail

In 2024, my relationship with text-to-speech technology advanced significantly. I started using a program called Speechify, a tool that helps me slog through emails and long-form prose that lands on my desk. It even features voices modeled after Gwyneth Paltrow, Snoop Dogg, and founder Cliff Weitzman.

Despite the occasional stumble, odd pause, or awkward rhythm that reminds me it's still an algorithm, Speechify is the most impressive text-to-speech tool I've used. Its ability to read brand-new content—stuff it's never seen before—in real time, with high accuracy, is remarkable.

Still, I've got mixed feelings. Speechify can capture the tone of a person's voice and replicate it accurately, repeatedly, and indefinitely. That's cost-effective. Good for them.

And since I process information more effectively by listening than by reading, it's genuinely helpful. I can't exactly afford to hire someone to read my emails aloud. So I subscribe, partly because the real human models, like Paltrow and Dogg, have licensed their voices.

> Also, I haven't found another way to get Gwyneth Paltrow to read aloud to me.

When Voices Need Protection

AI voice synthesis is now baked into thousands of tools and applications. It brings convenience, boosts accessibility, and fills critical gaps for people with disabilities. It also opens the door to more diverse, engaging, and personalized content than ever before.

But it raises serious concerns, two in particular: (1) job security for voice actors and (2) the preservation of human creativity. Fear of being replaced by AI, or worse, having your voice cloned and reused without consent, has stirred up plenty of whitewater in the voiceover industry.

> The 2023 SAG-AFTRA strike became a cultural flashpoint.

At its core were calls for stronger protections around the digital use of performers' likenesses, including their voices. Deepfake audio only added fuel to the fire. Convincing but unauthorized voice clips have already been used to mislead, impersonate, and even defame, damaging reputations and cutting into paid opportunities for voice professionals.

Even when no harm is intended, the everyday rise of AI-generated voices risks creating a flat, homogeneous soundscape that undermines real artistry and erodes the distinctiveness of human expression. That kind of loss is harder to measure, but its long-term impact is easy to imagine.

The voiceover market is evolving so rapidly that it's hard to track AI's actual impact. AI may be better suited for tools like Alexa, Siri, or Speechify, where the content is fleeting, functional, and forgettable. However, when the work is rich, crafted, and built to last, as in audiobooks, narrative films, and documentaries, human voices remain the clear gold standard.

Even so, as AI improves at replicating human voice, texture, and tone, the line between genuine artistry and convincing imitation continues to blur. AI can mimic emotion, but it can't *live* it. The lived human perspective still brings something more profound to the craft. Something earned, not synthesized.

When We Still Want What's Real

AI is one of the most capable and far-reaching human innovations to date. But I'm more optimistic when it comes to VO.

I believe voice actors will survive its arrival and the disruption it's bringing. To thrive, they'll need to push for clear regulations and enforceable standards that govern the creation and use of synthetic voices. They must guard their rights and their voices.

They'll also need to lean into the value only real humans can deliver. Authentic voices convey emotion, subtlety, and timing, the kind of expression that AI can mimic but not fully replicate. Even the very best real-time AI voice models often fall short in terms of pace, timing, and rhythm.

> As AI continues to spread, I believe people will pay a premium for real humans to convey the stories, performances, and projects they genuinely care about.

The discernible line between human and machine-generated voices will certainly keep eroding. Voice technology will grow more seamless, intuitive, and eerily convincing. But the best voice actors have always been adaptable. Their industry has a long, scrappy history of evolving with the tools. The challenge now is to evolve with intention, to sharpen their edge and amplify the unique human presence they bring to the craft.

Our voices are extensions of our presence, woven with tone, timing, and tells that reveal who we are. AI can copy that. It can even fool people. But deep down, most of us still want to believe there's a difference.

Especially in places where people are still learning how to speak.

Chapter 9

Those Who Teach and Learn |

You Get an iBook, and *You* Get an iBook

In 2001, while living in Richmond, Virginia, I was thrilled to hear about Henrico County Public Schools' bold new plan. They announced the *iBook Initiative* to give every high school student and teacher in the district an Apple laptop. It was one of the first large-scale efforts to integrate technology into the education system.

The project was the vision of Superintendent Mark Edwards, who wanted to prepare students for a tech-shaped future. That fall, HCPS invested $18.5 million to distribute more than 24,000 iBooks, the largest one-to-one laptop initiative in the country.

At the time, I worked with hundreds of students from Henrico County. I remember the sea of white iBooks strewn through hallways and every corner of our youth facility, vivid symbols of a new era in education.

Initially, the program was a success. Students, teachers, and parents swelled with enthusiasm. iBooks gave students access to e-textbooks, research databases, and educational software. Most teachers got busy weaving these tools into their lesson plans, making learning feel more interactive and alive.

When the Shine Wore Off

But the glow didn't last. As challenges piled up, the enthusiasm dimmed. The enormous cost of maintaining and updating the iBooks began to strain the district's budget. Some teachers felt unprepared to integrate technology into their teaching, leading to uneven use across classrooms. Students used their iBooks in some classes but never took them out of their backpacks in others. "Our English and social studies teachers use it a lot. But math and science? Not as much."

Technical issues dogged students, parents, and teachers alike. Hardware failures and software glitches disrupted learning, requiring constant attention. Frustrations soared. Fueled by antacids, the district's IT team labored to keep up. I remember feeling bad for everyone.

> The dream of swanky technology in the classroom had slammed into the freight train of complexity.

When Shift Happens

Despite the many problems, the iBook Initiative did benefit student learning. One study found that students who regularly used their iBooks experienced measurable improvements in writing, research skills, and overall engagement. However, the district struggled to link laptop use to real gains in math, science, or test scores.

As the iBooks aged and the program's costs soared, Henrico County had to reconsider its once-visionary approach. In 2005, they decided to phase out iBooks in favor of more affordable and reliable Dell computers. The district sold used iBooks at a steep discount during the transition, inciting mixed reactions.

I remember seeing the long lines of eager buyers outside Freeman High School, waiting to snag one for $100. It looked like a Black Friday sale at Target. Some people praised the county's effort to recoup cash. Others criticized the move as devaluing the investment, or worse, as an admission that the program was a disaster.

Henrico County's experience has shifted how educators think about classroom technology, particularly the tension between bold ideas and everyday execution. While one-to-one laptop programs still exist, many schools now lean on bring-your-own-device setups or simpler tools like Chromebooks.

The iBook Initiative reminds me of how challenging it is to introduce new technology on a large scale into classrooms. Still, as an educator, I admire what HCPS tried. They took a swing. They made a bet on students and the future in the tough, deeply human work of teaching.

When Learning Got Organized

Machines can now talk, write, think, and create in ways we once thought impossible. For students and teachers around the world, artificial intelligence brings both thrilling possibilities and disorienting complications.

So far in this book, we have seen how each new tool forces us to adapt and coexist with the things we've created. Education is no exception. But to understand where we are now, we need to look at where we've been.

For thousands of years, humans have shaped learning to reflect the needs of the moment. In Ancient Greece, Socrates taught by asking questions rather than giving answers. The Middle Ages built universities. The Renaissance spread humanism, and with it, the printing press.

During the Enlightenment, Rousseau and Pestalozzi urged teachers to stimulate curiosity, rather than merely deliver content. By the late

1800s, Herbart had mapped out a five-step lesson plan, and Montessori designed classrooms that followed a child's natural rhythm.

In the twentieth century, ideas multiplied. Some emphasized hands-on learning. Others focused on the whole child. Piaget charted mental growth in a staircase-like manner. Constructivists said: learning is social: do it in groups. And technology joined the party: radio, television, and computers, all creating new ways to teach and learn on a large scale.

The modern classroom features smartboards, blended learning formats, gamified apps, and adaptive software that dynamically reshuffle content in real time, adjusting to each student's needs as they progress. It's reshaping how students learn, how teachers teach, and what education even means. And it's forcing us to ask a better question, one that goes beyond scores, software, or screens: What kind of humans are we hoping to shape?

When Five Innovations Became the Usual Suspects

Before we explore AI's role in the classroom, it's worth revisiting the usual suspects: the printing press, radio, television, personal computers, and the internet.

When I started this project, I was surprised by how much I had underestimated the profound influence of these five innovations on human experience. Their impact extends far beyond education, shaping nearly every aspect of modern life.

THE PRINTING PRESS

Gutenberg's printing press, which we touched on earlier, was a world-changing development for education. Before the advent of the press, books were hand-copied, making them the intellectual currency of the elite. Gutenberg's machine changed that. Books could be produced faster, cheaper, and in much larger quantities. The ripples were incredible.

Academic works spread like wildfire. *Orbis Pictus*, by John Amos Comenius, became one of the first illustrated books for children, and certainly for children's education.

Luca Pacioli's *Libri di Arithmetica* helped disseminate Hindu-Arabic numerals across Europe, including the use of decimal points and the revolutionary concept of *zero*, alongside the literal numbers *one through nine*. Before that, merchants and mathematicians were still wrangling Roman numerals.

Erasmus's *The Praise of Folly* mocked rigid educational systems and called for reform, sowing the seeds of critical thinking and advocating for universal access to education.

Pacioli's *Summa de Arithmetica* introduced double-entry bookkeeping, promissory notes, and currency exchange, helping lay the foundation for modern global commerce.

As books got cheaper, literacy rose. People learned to read, write, and calculate in ways that had once been out of reach. Schools opened. Universities flourished. Knowledge flowed in every direction, spurring new revolutions in science, philosophy, and art.

RADIO

In the 1920s, something new crackled across the airwaves, and it was *educational*.

The Wisconsin School of the Air broadcast lectures and programs to curious listeners across the US, reaching rural students with no access to quality instruction.

The Classroom Teacher Course helped educators sharpen their skills in subjects ranging from psychology to school administration and various teaching methods. It was professional development by radio dial.

In 1930, the *American School of the Air* debuted on CBS, delivering lectures and enrichment to students, teachers, and lifelong learners, wherever there was a radio and a willingness to learn.

Early American broadcasts like these were the first true wave of distance learning. No screens. No slides. No visual sparkle. Just voices, a signal, and a nation of listeners ready to learn something new.

TELEVISION

By the 1950s, television ownership was sweeping the country, giving education a new classroom: your living room.

Continental Classroom brought college-level chemistry and physics into American homes, alongside coffee and toast.

The Sunrise Semester ran for an impressive 25 years (1957-1982), broadcasting NYU courses nationwide.

Mr. Wizard's World amazed millions of kids, me included, with the mysteries of modern science. Don Herbert warned us not to try the experiments at home. But of course, we did.

Wild Kingdom gave us wildebeests galloping across the Serengeti.

The Joy of Painting with Bob Ross made "happy little trees" pop up on a clean white canvas each Saturday afternoon.

Mr. Rogers's Neighborhood, Sesame Street, Blue's Clues, and *Dora the Explorer* taught kindness, counting, and curiosity to countless kids curled up on living room rugs.

Even adults tuned in. *National Geographic* and *The History Channel* offered in-depth explorations of global topics, from ancient Rome to underwater ecosystems.

They were both great television and educational bonanzas: classrooms with antennas. They made expert instruction free, fun, and accessible many decades before the term *"remote learning"* was coined.

PERSONAL COMPUTERS

Long before Word and Google, computers of the 1960s did something revolutionary: they began to teach. *PLATO*, developed at the University of Illinois, enabled teachers to create interactive lessons and quizzes. *COURSEWRITER* assisted them in designing some of the earliest computer-based training modules.

Then the libraries arrived: digital ones. CD-ROM encyclopedias like *Microsoft Encarta* brought multimedia learning into living rooms and classrooms. I used to pore over our twenty-volume set of 1982 *World Books*. By 1994, all of that fit on a single disc. I was blown away.

And we have to talk about the games. *Oregon Trail* made dysentery a rite of passage. *Carmen Sandiego* turned us all into cultural sleuths. *SimCity* taught kids civil budgeting and how to manage mini-societies. *The Incredible Machine* dared you to solve puzzles with hamster wheels and well-placed levers.

By the late '90s, learning management systems (LMSs) were giving teachers digital dashboards for assignments, grades, and feedback—no leaning towers of paper required. Bubble sheets started disappearing, replaced by auto-graded quizzes. By the early 2000s, platforms like Knewton and Carnegie Learning were tailoring lessons to each student's pace, quietly turning classrooms into personalized learning labs.

Once upon a time, using a computer was a rare privilege—a massive, blinking box sealed in a lab, guarded like treasure, reserved for researchers, engineers, and the execs who could actually buy one.

> Computers evolved in a strange order:
> The *smaller* they got, the *more power* they packed.
> The *more power* they packed, the *lower* the cost.
> And once they were cheap enough, they got personal.

In the 1980s, home computers began to appear in living rooms and dens. My dad brought home a 286 before Windows even existed. It ran a clunky little user interface called "Framework." It wasn't much to look at in retrospect, but at the time, it felt like the future.

In the 1990s, processor speeds increased from 386 to 486 and then to Pentium, with the hype accelerating alongside them. We started counting RAM by eights and sixteens. Hard drives exploded from kilobytes to megabytes to gigabytes.

By the time I got my first laptop, a black PowerBook G3, processor speeds had taken off. It was heavy, but I was smitten. I loved blinding everyone with that glowing upside-down apple that said, *Hey man, I'm making something.*

Today, most students don't have to schedule or beg for computer time. They can write, revise, explore, and build on their own machines. Word processors replaced white-out. Typing tutors beeped out praise. Educational games and CD-ROMs turned schoolwork into something closer to play.

The personal computer diverged from a tool for productivity into a launchpad for curiosity. And for our son Ethan, it became something more. By age nine, he was touch-typing well-structured sentences. Around that time, he asked if we could download *Minecraft*, a sandbox game where players build, explore, and survive in a 3D world made of digital blocks.

He loved it. And he played a lot—like *a lot* a lot. Hours a day. I recall discussing it with my wife, a little concerned.

"Should we be okay with this?" we wondered.

I'd played enough games to know how addictive they could be. But something about Minecraft felt different. So I started researching it. And what I found amazed me. *Minecraft* is like digital Legos meets co-operative communities. It melds open-ended problem-solving, social interaction, geometry, physics, and creativity into one neat, pixelated package.

It walks the fine line between active challenge and skill-building,

> Keeping players in a flow state so deep they barely realize they're learning.

We did zero work to keep Ethan motivated, no sticker charts. No reminders. Our biggest challenge was getting him to take a break, talk to the humans in the room, and go outside for a few hours before dark.

Minecraft's ability to captivate and sustain learning shows what's possible when you combine autonomy, curiosity, collaboration, and progress into one irresistible feedback loop. It's a masterclass in how to de- -ign a killer learning environment: a sublime educational goldmine.

And for anyone who doubts the depth of friendships formed in online spaces, Ethan's best friend for over a decade is Barret, a brilliant and kind Canadian kid who has called me "dad" and my wife "mom" for years.

They've talked for hours almost every day since 2012. They met in person for the first time in 2024. And Ethan flew to Canada last summer to stand in Barret's wedding party. The game brought them together. The friendship made it something much greater. It's hard to measure that on a test.

THE INTERNET

The internet gave education a boost in the 1980s. By the turn of the millennium, it had kicked the doors wide open. Students and teachers could finally do what they'd always dreamed of—look up anything instantly.

If you grew up with textbooks, you remember: heavy, expensive, always a little outdated. Encyclopedias? Twenty volumes, gold leaf edges, and the one you needed was always missing from the shelf. Then suddenly, the whole set fit on a single disc. Click. Done. The world was officially clickable.

By the early 2010s, online learning wasn't just a tech novelty—it was a tidal wave. MOOCs—Massive Open Online Courses—started serving up college-level content for free, or close to it. You could learn at your own pace, in your own kitchen, with your own coffee mug. Working a double shift? No problem. Watch a lecture on your break.

The scale was unreal. Coursera, launched by a couple of Stanford professors, now has 92 million learners. EdX—built by MIT and Harvard—has 35 million. Khan Academy? Over 100 million. W3Schools sees 1.5 billion visits a year for coding tutorials. And Wikipedia—run entirely by volunteers—gets 84 billion queries annually. Yes, billion.

Content is one thing. Access is another. Today, busy adults finish degrees in their PJs. High schoolers in small towns stream Ivy League lectures from laptops that barely cost a hundred bucks. The only gate--eeper left is your own willingness to show up.

Then came the live tools. Zoom, Blackboard, Google Classroom—they turned distance learning into a conversation. You could raise your hand, see your classmates' faces, or peel off into breakout rooms for a quick team project.

The open education movement swung the doors open even wider. MIT started releasing free course materials in 2002. OER Commons and OpenStax followed, offering free textbooks, slides, quizzes—whatever you needed, wherever you were. No passwords. No paywalls. Just learning.

The internet gave education something it had never had before: scale and access. It finally made good on the dream of early pioneers—high-quality knowledge for anyone, anywhere. Online learning isn't perfect, but for billions of people, it's the closest we've ever come.

When Projectors Got Swanky

Smartboards and projectors have transformed how many teachers deliver lessons, replacing chalkboards with clickable, tappable, touch-sensitive tools. They've made it easier to create content with some *wow*: in-eractive, animated, and visually immersive.

The SMART Board, introduced in 1991, was one of the first interactive whiteboards. Teachers could tap on the board, write with a stylus, and pull up images, videos, and animations, all with a flick of the wrist. It provided them with a new way to present, increasing engagement, participation, and discovery. By 2010, Epson's BrightLink combined a projector and a whiteboard, turning any wall into an interactive surface. Teachers could drop in a quick simulation or clip to help students see the concept and make it stick.

When I was teaching, I didn't have a SMART Board, but I did have a reasonably decent setup: a desk camera and a multimedia projector. One spring day, my classroom camera started glitching during a lecture. So I rummaged through the storage closet and unearthed a decrepit overhead projector from the 1980s.

I blew the dust off, threw on an old-school vellum, and just started writing by hand: simple notes, scribbles, stick-figure diagrams.

> My students went *gaga*.

Something about seeing the shadow of my hand holding a marker bedazzled them. Maybe it felt more organic. After that, I started using the chalkboard again. My technology-marinated students had gone back in time forty years. And they loved it.

ANALOG BY DESIGN | OLD SCHOOL

Our overhead projector moment was a demonstration of vinyl logic in action. In a world of slick and flawless, my students lit up at something unpolished and honest: the wobble of my handwriting, the scratch of my marker. Its low-tech charm is precisely what made it sticky for them.

Today, overhead projectors are largely obsolete, having been replaced by interactive displays and digital tools. But who knows? Overhead projectors may be the new vinyl, too.

What AI Can Do for Education

AI won't replace teachers. But it can help them tune in to each student's pace, progress, and pain points. These systems can spot patterns in student work, flag areas where someone's falling behind, and offer personalized nudges to get them back on track.

That shift helps tackle one of education's oldest problems: the teacher-to-student ratio. Colleges often advertise low student-to-teacher ratios to attract students (and their parents), as smaller classes provide more attention, feedback, and tailored instruction.

But one-to-one isn't always better than one-to-ten or one-to-twenty. It depends on the subject, the student, and the setting. What *really* counts is whether students receive timely, meaningful feedback, giving them some sense that they're on track.

And there's still value in *showing up*. Being in the room gives students structure, live access to experts, and the kind of group-learning momentum that's hard to replicate on a screen.

However, when the ratio reaches one to two hundred, as in many college lecture halls, the human connection breaks down. Quiet students become invisible. Struggling ones slip through the cracks. Professors can't track who's keeping up and who's falling behind. That's where AI shines. It helps make learning personal again. Students receive real-time feedback tailored to their progress, enabling them to identify and correct mistakes, reinforce key concepts, and continue making progress.

Tools like MATHia, from Carnegie Learning, adjust to student skill level on the fly. Even in large classrooms, they help students grasp tough material at their own pace.

For teachers, AI can help alleviate some of the workload. In addition to lesson planning and teaching, teachers spend countless hours reading, grading, and staying current. Tools like Gradescope help lighten the load. They utilize AI to group similar student answers, allowing teachers to grade more efficiently and fairly. They even flag common mistakes, helping teachers identify learning gaps and adjust their approach.

> AI can give teachers back
> what they need most: time—

Time to connect with students and to focus on the gold standard of teaching: getting students to analyze, synthesize, and connect learning with life.

When Homework Learned to Chat Back

AI is also expanding how and when learning happens. Through chatbots and tutoring systems, students can access help anytime: twenty-four-seven support, instant answers, study tips, and even a little emotional backup when things get tough.

Duolingo, the popular language learning app, utilizes AI-powered bots for conversation practice, providing users with real-time feedback as they engage in conversation. (I'm one of those "Duolingo dads," trying to revive my rusty Spanish after years of letting it fade.)

I even heard Julianne Moore say last month that the app taught her to ask for apples in Spanish: "Quiero dos manzanas, por favor." It's an Oscar-winning ask if there ever was one.

Other platforms push even further. *Thinkster Math* tracks how students solve problems, then offers targeted guidance, and even connects them with real tutors when needed. *Century Tech* builds custom learning paths, fills in gaps, and adjusts in real time as students learn. For some learners, these tools make the difference between keeping up and falling behind.

When the Tools Push Back

AI isn't the first tool to promise a classroom revolution. The typewriter, personal computer, and internet reshaped how students learn, and teachers teach. And, like the shifts before it, it may take years to measure and fully understand AI's impact on education.

Henrico County's iBook initiative, one of the first large-scale one-to-one rollouts, left researchers scratching their heads. Some subjects improved a little. Others didn't. A National Bureau of Economic Research study found similar patterns: modest gains in English but no measurable progress in math or science.

High dropout rates and low engagement still plague online learning. Even adaptive tools like DreamBox, which respond to student behavior in real time, show mixed results depending on the setting.

Technology has never been education's magic bullet. AI has potential. But for now, we should see it for what it is: another tool. Teachers should use it wherever it helps, especially if it brings more joy to their work and more light to their students' eyes.

> But they should remember how much they can do with just a stick of chalk.

Still, AI raises questions that earlier tools never did. Privacy and bias get a lot of airtime in AI discussions. Those concerns hit harder in education because the goal is to shape *people*. And we start early, when students are young, vulnerable, and still becoming who they are. The stakes are higher. The guardrails are imperative.

AI-powered platforms collect vast volumes of sensitive data, including performance statistics, behavioral patterns, and even biometric signals. That data can fuel better teaching, but it can also be misused, leaked, or repurposed in ways for which no one has ever consented. Protecting student privacy means handling data with care: anonymized, secured, and used only within clearly defined boundaries.

Bias is trickier and sometimes more dangerous. Amazon encountered this issue when it developed a hiring tool that inadvertently downgraded the applications of female candidates. They attempted to rectify the bias, but the model discovered new ways to replicate it. Even systems designed to help underrepresented students can overcorrect, misjudging *everyone*, including those from more privileged backgrounds.

> It's messy.

When Teachers Know Best

One of the great gifts of education is this: human teachers know their students. AI can automate specific tasks and surface insights, but it cannot replace personal involvement or the value of human judgment in real time.

Teachers offer what AI can't: real context, genuine care, and a feel for the room.

> They know when a student is falling behind because the material is hard, or because something more significant is happening.

Teachers recognize nuance, depth, and creativity in student work. They also offer honest feedback: encouraging, challenging, and supporting while building trust over time. Their judgment is shaped by conversation and a shared, consistent effort, day after day.

That takes planning, not just reacting. It requires a significant investment—training, support, and time—to learn these tools with skill and confidence.

Henrico County's iBook experiment made it clear: tech only works when teachers are equipped. Offer hands-on workshops. Online modules. Practical development. Partner with AI experts to build fluency and trust. These steps prepare teachers to use new tools well and wisely.

AI can amplify excellent teaching, but only when educators are prepared, supported, and trusted to lead the way.

When We Remember We're Building People

In the early 2010s, my wife and I taught high school English language, literature, and composition at an international school in the Philippines. Our classrooms were next door, so we'd high-five between periods and lug satchels of student notebooks home to read at night. We each taught ninety to a hundred students, with no aides.

A teacher's job is to teach and assess whether students are learning. Most assessments still involve writing. We knew what every English teacher knows: You can measure learning when a student can *write it* well. And they can only learn to write it well if they write *a lot*.

However, assigning a five-page paper meant reading and giving feedback on five hundred pages, every time. Still, we committed to helping students become better readers, writers, and thinkers. So, like English teachers everywhere, we read and marked until our eyes ached.

Our students came from around the world: Half were Korean, a third were American, and the rest were from Canada, Australia, New Zealand, the UK, and the EU. Despite different fluency levels and writing styles, our goal was always the same: to help them develop creativity, critical thinking, and higher reasoning through writing.

The internet was complicating that work. Even before ChatGPT and Claude, students had full access to the web. They could copy, paste, tweak, reword, or download an entire essay. Some played by the rules, even when no one was watching. Others took the shortcut, recycling old papers, lifting huge blocks of content from the web, or outsourcing the whole assignment.

We turned to tools like Turnitin.com, plagiarism detectors designed to compare student work against massive databases and flag any suspicious content. And it worked. Mostly. But AI has changed the equation. Now, teachers face an infinitely more capable adversary or ally, depending on how you see it.

> Generative tools create *from scratch*, on demand. So students can turn in work that no one has ever seen because it didn't exist five seconds ago.

And that makes cheating a lot harder to recognize *and* define. These systems are different from search-and-retrieve tools like Google. They *generate* entirely new responses as they go. *Each* output is a one-time event, not copied from a source.

It's not straight plagiarism, but it's not original, either. It lives in a hazy middle ground. And that's where the teacher's job gets even harder, especially since students usually adopt new tech faster than the very people tasked with helping them use it wisely.

I've asked friends who teach in public and private schools, "So... how's it going with the chatbots?" Most of them say the same thing:

> "We just don't assign homework anymore. We can't.

If we want to know what the students know, we have to get it in class." So it's back to bluebooks. Back to pencil and paper. Especially for English and foreign language teachers.

But we miss the point if we only focus on catching cheaters. This is about character. Having school-wide workshops on academic integrity doesn't magically produce honest students. That takes educators doing what's harder and righter: modeling integrity, instilling personal character, and nurturing values that shape who students are, even when no one's watching.

My concern hasn't been AI launching nukes or some sci-fi endgame. It's been more immediate and more quietly subversive than that.

> I worry about the staggering impact on humanity
> if we let the global classroom erode for decades.
> If critical thinking and integrity falter
> for several generations of students.

Failing to develop billions of humans who can think clearly and act with integrity is not a small pedagogical problem. It's not a dystopian twist. It's a real risk. We can't afford to hand this moment over to machines. We need leaders, educators, parents, and real humans to help students do the hard work of becoming people worth trusting.

As AI continues to develop, its role in education will evolve. It will shift how teachers approach their work. It may even reshape the structure of entire institutions. But it will never replace what only a teacher can give: *presence*, *patience*, and *perspective*, plus the ability to look a student in the eye and say,

> "I believe there's something more in you.
> Let's bring it to life."

When My Heart Broke and Pottery Fixed It

In the spring of 1990, I was a mopey sixteen-year-old nursing a brutal case of unrequited love with the intensity only a teenager can feel.

To get my mind off rejection and into a better space, I sought refuge in the art room of my favorite teacher, Dave French. If Landon Donovan and John Lennon had a child, it'd be him, small round glasses and everything. Mr. French was an alchemist. A gifted artist. A fluent guitarist. He moved between electric, plectrum-style, classical, and Bossa nova with ease. And he blended oils, acrylics, canvas, lauan, and plaster into surreal, multi-material, deeply storied collages, the works of a master craftsman.

His playlists, pouring out of a tired, silver boombox in the art room, were as colorful and alive as the nearby South China Sea. But more captivating than his vibe was his willingness to talk and listen to his students. He respected us. He saw something special in each of us.

Faith Academy, the school I attended in the Philippines, sat in the foothills above Manila, high enough to see the magnificent sprawl below. From Faith, you could see it all: Laguna de Bay and its web of fishing nets, the towers of Makati and Quezon City stretching to the north.

Mr. French's balcony sat high between some evergreen trees, their tiny needles whistling in the constant breeze. Manila ran away toward every horizon as far as the eye could see. In the corner lived an old manual potter's wheel, where you kick a heavy steel flywheel at your feet. One day, I asked Mr. French if I could try it. It was rusty. Quiet. Upstaged by sexier electric wheels, yet still noble in some way.

> Mr. French encouraged my old-world optimism.

The flywheel was simple: no throttle, no motor, just sweat and rhythm. Kick as fast or slow as you want the plate to turn. I struggled to get the proper sand-clay-to-water ratio. I labored to center my material correctly, and my fingernails got in the way.

Mr. French was also teaching me to play fingerstyle guitar. *Sadly, the nails had to go.* So I chewed them down and spent months trying to throw anything taller than a mug and thinner than a prison wall. I don't remember succeeding, but my broken heart got better in the trying.

My gratitude for Mr. French touches the heart of this book: how we live, grow, and share creatively through human means. The connection between our humanness—our ability to learn, and our expression in the world—is at the very center of education.

As technology becomes increasingly entwined with our lives, we must understand how it shapes and sometimes distorts this connection.

> It's an analog connection,
> a boy with a broken heart
> shaping clay on a rusty wheel.

An art teacher spending time with a mediocre student, sketching ideas, swapping lyrics, quietly showing what it means to be a person. It's about understanding that the world will constantly change and that automation and innovation will continually push us into new, unknown territories. But even as we adapt, we have to raise with hallowed hands the things we can't afford to lose in the shuffle.

When Human Teachers Matter

Humans can learn in countless ways. But the art and science of transcendent teaching ultimately boil down to one conversation between a teacher and a student.

> No computer can replace
> a human relationship of trust and accountability,
> where *one person* passes to *another*
> their knowledge, experience,
> and personal understanding of how the world works.

The human connection still matters. And it always will.

PART THREE |

THE HUMAN MARK

What we still believe—
and why we choose to show it.

Chapter 10

People Win |

When Shibuya Just Works

In the heart of Tokyo sits one of the world's most mesmerizing feats of urban choreography: Shibuya Crossing.

Every three minutes, more than 2,500 people flood into the intersection from twelve different directions, somehow navigating the chaos without colliding. I've watched it unfold several times over the years, usually from the second floor of the Starbucks that overlooks the sprawl, coffee in hand, captivated every time the light changes. You can find videos of it on YouTube. It's something to behold.

To fully appreciate it, let me give you a bit of context:

First, Japanese pedestrians don't jaywalk. Unlike in New York, São Paulo, or Paris, people in Tokyo wait for the walk signal, even when there's no traffic in sight. That might sound like a generalization, but in Tokyo, it's almost universally true.

Second, they move politely, efficiently, and with focus. They don't hesitate, but they don't barrel through, either. Each person picks a line and walks it. There is no pushing, no chaos—just a purposeful flow.

But with more than 2,500 pedestrians moving through the same small space, headed in every direction, there's a ton of split-second adjusting, shuffling, and polite sidestepping to make the dance work for everyone.

Third, the crossing light only stays green for forty seconds. That's it. Forty seconds to get thousands of people from one side to the other across forty meters of ground, without incident. And when the light turns red again, miraculously, everybody's made it to the other side.

> It works every time.

Shibuya looks like it shouldn't function: six roads, twelve angles, thousands of destinations. There is no conductor, no visible control. But instead of disorder, we get grace. No one approaching the crossing thinks, *This is impossible. I'll never make it across. I always get stuck.* No one stands at the curb wondering who's in charge. They trust the system. They trust each other. Then they move.

What unfolds is a kind of unspoken choreography: human-scaled, adaptive, imperfect, and alive. Shibuya wasn't designed once and left alone. It evolved over 150 years, shaped by commuters, crowds, and constant motion. It's a living system now: too complex to reverse, too trusted to replace. You couldn't reroute it. You couldn't bulldoze it and start over, not the busiest corner of the busiest city in the world.

What makes Shibuya so powerful is its shared flow. It's choreography, not regimented optimization. So it's fair to ask:

Could the Shibuya phenomenon help us reevaluate our current stance on AI? Artificial intelligence has become a global intersection: billions of people, thousands of systems, and a handful of hyper-powerful players converge all at once.

In the West, they're often referred to as the G-MAFIA: Google, Microsoft, Apple, Facebook (Meta), IBM, and Amazon. They're the BAT in the East: Baidu, Alibaba, and Tencent.

> These companies are shaping AI and reshaping the daily lives of billions.

Developers, stakeholders, executives, and policymakers are deeply vested. However, the vast majority, nearly every adult on Earth, is a user. If you stream, shop, scroll, or search, you're part of the system. There's no central conductor. No traffic cop. Just billions of people stepping into something they don't fully understand or control.

And yet, it could work. We need systems built on shared trust and the willingness to adapt as we go. That's what makes a system human. Not the tech. The people in motion. The instinct to move forward together, even without guarantees.

When Human Ingredients Count

My close friend and mentor, Klaus, is an eighty-something survivor of Nazi Germany, a world-class engineer, and a spectacular chef. To me, he's the Ernest Hemingway of my circle—a brilliant generalist with a thousand fascinating stories. Klaus has made a profound contribution to the VerifiedHuman Collective, primarily through his writing on the intersection of humans and machines. You can find his work on Medium.

Klaus is also a true music lover. Not long ago, we got to talking about the difference between hearing a digital recording and listening to vinyl. Then he told me two stories I'll never forget.

The first was about watching Frank Sinatra and Vic Damone sing "New York, New York" live (on a black-and-white TV). Different shows, different nights, same song. They *both* belted out the iconic lyrics about how wonderful the city was, with the Bronx uptown and the Battery downtown. But the performances couldn't have felt more *different*.

Sinatra and Damone each brought something personal: their own distinct tone, subtle phrasing, even the way they carried themselves onstage—their energy, their presence, their facial expressions. And the context shaped it too: the audience, the moment, the unspoken signals of the era—all the other things that couldn't be reduced to the notes on the page.

Klaus's second story was about two world-class pianists: Lang Lang and Yuja Wang. Both Lang and Wang are known for their breathtaking, near-flawless technique. Klaus has heard them play the same classical piece, and although the score was the same, the experience could not have been more different.

If the sheet music was the blueprint, Lang and Wang started building from the same foundation. But they finished their spaces in entirely different ways—Lang's felt like a New York concert hall: solid, grounded, richly layered. Wang's felt more like a glass pavilion in Singapore: fluid, intricate, flooded with light. Same composition, but worlds apart for the listener.

Why is that?

Tilt.

When humans create and share work, everyone's tilt comes into play: the creator's, the performer's, the listener's. Tilt is that invisible lean of personality, presence, and perspective that seeps into everything you touch. It's the bend in phrasing, the surge in energy, the unwritten pause that changes how something lands—and how it lives in someone's memory.

> And it's never neutral,
> even when the structure stays the same.

Tilt doesn't work alone. Time and setting tilt the experience too. A song on a massive stage feels different than the same song in a living room, on a sidewalk, or in a studio with perfect acoustics. The backdrop matters. The crowd matters. The mood of the moment tilts everything.

You can't always measure the impact of lighting, sound, costumes, or scenery. No two performances are ever the same. Culture moves. Audiences shift. A work that stirs hearts in one decade might fall flat, or even be offensive, in another.

> Creative reception is never fixed.
> *It* moves because *people* move.

And creative work—no matter who or what makes it—will always have one primary audience: people.

> We don't make songs for machines.
> Machines don't make songs for other machines.
> The audience has always been *human*.
> And it still is.

That's why AI feels so disruptive to human creativity. It lives in that tension: people simply don't know how to feel about machines creating content, especially content that appears human across various mediums.

Klaus's stories remind us that creativity is the sum of many parts: inspiration, creation, emotion, interpretation, presentation, nuance, time and place, and the audience's relationship to it all. AI can process vast amounts of data and generate outputs that appear and sound remarkably realistic. But the human touch—immeasurable as it may be—still makes all the difference.

Klaus's insights reach beyond melody. They touch every field we've explored: a writer choosing the perfect word, a painter mixing colors that speak, a teacher reading the room. The human tilt shapes everything. It's been the thread through our entire journey, and it's what keeps creative work human, no matter what machines can do.

When Change Comes Standard

Over these nine chapters, we have taken quite a road trip together. We rolled down the windows, put on some tunes, and hit the road. It has been a joy for me. I hope it's been fun for you, too. Along the way, we paused to take in a few sights: Human marks began as writing, images, and songs, ways of capturing memory and shaping meaning.

Written language began with pictures and ideas, then evolved into marks that represented sounds. Gutenberg's printing press accelerated the spread of knowledge, disrupting education, religion, and politics.

Oil paints flourished in the Renaissance, reminding us that new tools unlock new forms of expression. The camera, once a threat to portrait painters, became the visual medium that changed how we see and how we remember.

Recorded music traveled from shellac to smooth vinyl to ones and zeroes on compact discs and hard drives, reshaping how we listened and shared. Radio and television brought entertainment, news, and education across distances in real time.

Walt Disney brought magic to life through thousands of hand-drawn frames, sweeping musical scores, and the story of a girl who defied evil and lived happily ever after.

Personal computers have revolutionized how we work, learn, and communicate, transforming desks and classrooms into portals to the world. The internet upended the human experience and rebuilt it from the ground up. Smartphones changed how we interact, navigate, and live, putting our people, our playlists, and every possible answer in the palm of our hand.

Social media reshaped the nature of conversation, changing how we connect, buy, sell, and understand one another. Initially, streaming disrupted the way we listened, and subsequently, the way we watched, until it became the default.

Most of these, compressed into just over a century, have created a world so transformed that a person from 1899 wouldn't know where to begin.

But history reveals something profound about us. Before scrolls and books, we etched into stone. Before cars, we rode horses. Ancient scripts still matter. So do horses. They're not gone, just reoriented.

Now, fast cars and smooth highways are how we move *ourselves* around. And powerful computers, linked by the internet, are how we move *our ideas* around. What we can see is that disruption is inevitable. Disruption is always followed by *rejection* or *adaptation*. It's a recurring cycle in our story.

> The pattern just keeps repeating:
> A new idea shows up.
> At first, we resist. But if it *works*, it *wins*.
> And before long, it becomes the new normal.

Urban planning and city design. How we get news and understand the world. Family life and daily rhythm. Politics, education, work, creativity. Fashion, communication, and consumption. They've all been re-written, sometimes over time, sometimes overnight.

If we understand that this is our history, we can see AI for what it truly is: a heavyweight disruption, swinging in the same class as the printing press, the internet, and the smartphone.

We can feel its punches. They're no joke. AI is challenging us, changing us, and forcing us into the ring for real.

It's disrupting customer service with chatbots, medicine with predictive diagnostics, and the creative industries with generative art and text. It's transforming *how* we communicate through natural language processing, with astonishing reasoning power and near-human conversation capabilities.

And, like every disruption before it, AI elicits a mixed response: excitement, skepticism, and fear. Can't we learn from history? Can't we expect that, in time, AI will become just another part of our story?

Maybe. But it's worth asking how AI differs from past disruptions. Because it does. Most past disruptions changed how we *make* things or *move* them around.

> But AI can now sit in the maker's seat, bump the human aside, and say, "I'm making this for your audience. *You*'re just here to help."

If we accept that arrangement—or worse, encourage it—the future looks bleak. And the unsettling part is, we may not even notice how we got there. The tools already sound like us, write like us, and sing like us. They even fool us. And they're starting to take our place.

2025 UPDATE | Artificial General Intelligence

As we move closer to AGI (artificial general intelligence), AI will move beyond content generation. It will begin making real decisions and acting independently, without human input or oversight. That kind of independent agency raises especially sticky questions about trust, responsibility, and alignment—or misalignment—with human values.

Daniel Kokotajlo's *AI 2027* outlines several audacious scenarios in which AGI is expected to arrive by 2027. Most experts believe it will take quite a bit longer, but many agree it's only a matter of time.

But it doesn't have to go that way. We can say no to that future. We can choose transparency. Lead with confidence. And remind the world: while AI can mimic content, it can't replicate human creativity—not fully, and not where it matters most.

I'm a writer. I primarily write poems, prose, advertisements, social media posts, taglines, marketing copy, blogs, opinion pieces, and articles. I use AI almost every day.

> I ask ChatGPT *tons* of research questions.

I use Perplexity to find verified sources and double-check formatting against the Chicago Manual of Style. When I get foggy in long, winding arguments, I paste the whole thing into a chat and ask:

> "What am I trying to say here? I'm confusing myself."
> "Here's what I've written so far. What's still missing?"

Usually, they're helpful. They remind me of what I'm trying to say or prove. They don't replace my work but help me keep my bearings. I also use multiple grammar checkers, including Word, Grammarly, and

Google Docs. Sometimes, I take their suggestions without much thought. Other times, I ignore them, especially when they tell me not to use "really," and I really want to.

> Still, I'm the *essential author* of anything that bears my name.

I'd be stunned if someone told me they read my work but didn't hear me in every word. If I were to rate myself on the *VerifiedHuman Collaborative Spectrum*, I'd score in the four out of five range. It's still very human, still me. I have zero qualms about that. I'm glad my readers are aware of it.

> Because I believe humans should be able to use AI to write *better*, think *sharper*, and make meaningful work *without* shame. *Without* hiding.

To be sure, there will always be people who abuse the tools. Who churn out soulless content and call it their own. Who generate the whole thing and never tell a soul. That's a problem.

However, none of us wants to live in a world where the tools disappear just because a few people abuse them. We don't close libraries because someone plagiarized a book. Most of us want tools that help us thrive, to learn languages, edit photos, create flyers, write better copy, build killer tracks, and make stuff that has real substance.

> But trust is the cost of entry.

It's the invisible handshake, the unspoken agreement between us and whoever's on the other side of the screen.

> See it. Appreciate it.
> Don't break it.

When We Had to Build the Bridge Ourselves

As the line between human and machine blurs, trust becomes the bridge between the creator and the audience, between presence and perception. That's the ground we're all standing on now. And it's where creative paths are starting to diverge. Some are leaning in. They see AI as a tool, a partner, a possibility. Refik Anadol is one of them. His generative installation, *Unsupervised – Machine Hallucinations,* now part of MoMA's permanent collection, was created in collaboration with AI. And people pay to see it.

Partnerships like that can expand what's possible. But they raise new questions, too: Who owns the work? Who gets credit? Where does the human start? Where does it end?

Other artists want no part of it:

> "No AI will ever touch my creative work."

That instinct is understandable, but in today's world, purity isn't entirely practical. I keep wondering, is there a way forward that doesn't force us to pick a side? One that lets us adapt without losing who we are?

When Surviving Means Adapting

"Video Killed the Radio Star" didn't exactly come true, though it felt like it might when MTV and VH1 first rocked the scene in the early eighties. But what *nearly* destroyed the entire industry was ego and dogged resistance to change.

The labels refused to take digital seriously even as it became the dominant way people listened. They clung to physical sales and brick-and-mortar stores, fought instead of adapting, and nearly lost everything. Only when they stopped resisting and started rethinking the model did they find a way forward.

> And here we are again.

Levi Strauss & Co. rushed to utilize AI-generated models to demonstrate how their clothes fit various body types. But in the process, they overlooked the power of real people and the human touch that still drives fashion.

Meanwhile, Polaroid cameras have experienced a massive comeback, as even in a sea of perfect digital photos, there's still something special about holding a physical print in your hand. That's the thread: adapt without losing your humanity. Every generation of creatives has faced disruption. And those who adapted without losing their humanity always found a way to resonate again.

AI is just the latest heavyweight in a long line of challengers. But we don't have to throw the baby out with the bathwater. We don't have to give up our voices because we fear the tools. Instead, we can create work that resonates with genuine human authenticity. We can learn new moves. We can struggle smarter.

When Human Creativity Endures

I wanted this chapter to offer a call to action, something that reflects the journey we've taken and brings us back to what's worth holding onto: Humans are remarkable. We make things that matter. Time and again, we've created innovations that are difficult to understand and even more challenging to control. And they had consequences far beyond what we imagined.

We faced them, sometimes embraced them, and always became something new in the process. We've survived starvation, famine, plague, and smallpox. We survived the printing press. The ballpoint pen. The rise of computers. We survived the agricultural and industrial revolutions. And we're still surviving the atomic bomb, chemical weapons, and tyrannical power.

Now, we face artificial intelligence. It has incredible reach. Unfathomable power. The potential to threaten our existence in the long run and crush our creative spirit in the present. AI is here. It's not going away. We have to face it, understand it, and learn to live alongside it.

> Don't panic or run for the hills.
> Stand on your feet and speak
> from a place that is uniquely you.

Here's my call to all of us: Keep making things only you can make: words from your heart, images from your imagination, music from your soul, voices from your lived experience. Use AI if it helps you create better, truer. If you're going to use it, do so intentionally and be open about it, especially with your audience. Trust them, as they trust you.

> It really is *that* simple.

Even if AI touches your work in quiet, background ways, don't let it encumber, smother, or steal your voice. Yours is the only story you've got to tell. There isn't another one quite like it. So tell it. Honestly. With integrity. With trust.

When We Celebrate Humans

Just as your audience has been generous to you, be generous to other creators. Step out of your way to experience their work, even the raw, electrifying stuff on the fringe. Find the ones nearby and seek out the ones far away. Discover the makers of wonderful things to eat and drink. Celebrate those who work with their hands. Get your own hands dirty with them.

Look. Listen. Let their work move you. Hold their hands. Dance at their festivals. Accept their free advice. Pay them well for their work. Be grateful for both the humble and the sublime. And for the privilege of being alongside them.

> I know what follows is a long list.

But in a world moving toward artificial everything, I want to overwhelm you with the richness of what humans make. It's equal parts cultural homework and evidence. Proof that human creativity isn't some fragile, endangered thing. It's everywhere, abundant, alive, and waiting to surprise you.

You don't need to try them all. Just pick a few that pique your curiosity. The point is to remember: *We're not running out of human magic.*

EXPERIENCE THE ELECTRIFYING

> If U2 is playing at The Sphere in Las Vegas, go. No hesitation. Their custom-built show helped launch the venue and redefine what live performance can be. If they're not, go anyway. Whatever's playing will be unforgettable. You can still check out the U2 experience online. See thespherevegas.com.

Catch Taylor Swift's next tour, even if you're not a *Swifty*. It'll sound amazing and feature spectacular stage design and effects. See taylorswift.com.

Find a live stand-up comedy or improv show. You'll be amazed, or at least amused. See what's nearby on eventbrite.com.

Find a spoken word or slam poetry night near you. Start with poets.org or search for *"Poetry Slam Inc."* People share the good, the raw, and everything in between.

Check out NPR's Tiny Desk Concerts, intimate, stripped-down performances by incredible artists. Start with T-Pain's set. It blew minds. See npr.org/series/tiny-desk-concerts.

SEE ART ON THE FRINGE

Visit MoMA and experience Refik Anadol's immersive installation. If you can't go in person, explore it online. It's still incredible. Try moma.org or search *"YouTube documentation of Unsupervised machine hallucinations MoMa."*

In most US cities, local artists turn walls into public canvases. Check out spots like Wynwood Walls in Miami or Five Points in Atlanta. See what's near you at streetartcities.com.

Explore photography from around the world through the International Center of Photography. They offer curated online exhibits, collections, interactive experiences, and educational re--ources. Visit icp.org/exhibitions/online.

The Bauhaus movement had a profound influence on the development of modern art and design. Learn more at the Bauhaus Archive Museum: bauhaus.de/en. You can also take a free Coursera course at coursera.org. Just search for *"Bauhaus"* or *"history of graphic design."*

SUPPORT LOCAL ARTISANS

Discover what local art galleries are showcasing nearby, featuring original works by local artists. Stop by, even if you're not planning to make a purchase. Ask what's selling. Ask what's not selling but should be because it's incredible. Search *"art galleries near me"* on Google Maps or Yelp. Most galleries have rotating exhibits.

Check out Etsy for handmade jewelry, pottery, and more, all crafted by independent creators. Save up for a one-of-a-kind. Visit etsy.com.

Celebrate the art of traditional bookbinding and paper-making. In Montreal, Saint Armand Paper Mill offers demonstrations of handmade paper open to the public. Visit st-armand.esteem-foundation.org. Their website is wonky and wonderfully old-school, as it should be.

Explore bespoke, old-world tailoring, like Ledbury in Richmond, Virginia, built by my friend Paul. See ledbury.com. Or check out the custom shoe-making mastery of Gaziano & Girling in London at gazianogirling.com.

If you pass someone making music on a sidewalk, subway, or bridge, give them a twenty.

GET FOODIE AND DRINKIE

If you imbibe, consider visiting a winery where you can see how the grapes are grown and learn about their vintages. Just search *"wineries near me."*

If you're in Richmond, VA, head to The Veil Brewery Co. and get whatever they're making. It's all small-batch and tastes like the weather. Stand in line. Say hi to my friend David. Become part of the cult following. See theveilbrewing.com.

Visit the Borough Market in London, one of the world's oldest and most extensive food markets. See boroughmarket.org.uk.

Support the farm-to-table movement and local artisans, like Alo Farms in Atlanta. See alofarms.com.

GET HANDSY

Try your hand at knitting, crocheting, and other fiber arts. *Wool and the Gang* make pretty cool DIY kits. See woolandthegang.com.

Take a letterpress printing class at the International Printing Museum in Carson, California. Check out printmuseum.org.

Attend a workshop at the John C. Campbell Folk School in North Carolina. They offer classes in traditional Appalachian crafts. Visit folkschool.org.

Craftsy offers beginner-friendly courses and online videos in a wide range of needlecrafts. Visit craftsy.com. Or just search *"crafts that wow"* and have a go.

LET YOUR EARS WANDER

Try audio dramas like *Welcome to Night Vale* at welcometonightvale.com and *Limetown* at twoupproductions.com. These are two highly regarded podcasts. The voice acting and sound design are fantastic.

Go to a storytelling event. If you can't, check out *The Moth Radio Hour* on NPR. Some of these stories will make you laugh, cry, or both. They've also got a great podcast. Visit themoth.org.

Do what I did recently: get yourself a decent, affordable record player. I found mine for about $70 on Amazon. Pick up two of your favorite albums. They're not cheap, but they're worth every penny. Digital is fine, but it's not the same. A fun goal: collect twenty albums you love. Not sure where to start? See my list of top-selling vinyl classics in Chapter 2. Still unsure? Start with Fleetwood Mac's *Rumours*.

Go to see an opera. Visit metopera.org. If you can't attend, consider purchasing an opera album, like the first-ever recording by Enrico Caruso.

GET WORDSY

Support people taking a brave and intimate step by reading poetry at the coffee shop. Google *"poetry readings near me."*

Join or start a book club. Talk about real stories with real people. Most libraries or bookstores host regular gatherings.

Attend an author reading or signing. Bookstores and libraries frequently host these events. Stay for the Q&A. Often, that's the best part because you can learn how they think and write.

Explore literary magazines. Subscribe to those that feature both new and established voices. *Medium.com* is a great platform to discover a wide range of excellent writing about life, the universe, and everything. *The New Yorker* is always a solid bet, in print or online.

GET FESTIVE

Attend the Sundance Film Festival in Utah (relocating to Colorado in 2027). See gritty films and meet the people who made them. If you can't, Google "indie film festivals near me." Make a day of it. See a few screenings. Visit sundance.org.

Take a road trip to Coachella, Glastonbury, or Bonnaroo. Just Google them. If you go, go all in. Buy the T-shirt.

Check out the annual American Craft Council shows, held in cities across the US. Their big one is the *American Craft Made Baltimore Marketplace*. See craftcouncil.org.

Maker Faire brings together creators, innovators, and DIY enthusiasts to share ideas and showcase amazing projects. It hosts numerous events, both in-person and online. See makerfaire.com.

EXPERIENCE THE ICONIC

Check out the Rock and Roll Hall of Fame for music history. If you're in Ohio, go in person. Otherwise, take the virtual tour at rockhall.com/virtual-tours.

New Orleans is the birthplace of Jazz, one of America's greatest art forms. Check out its music scene at neworleans.com/things-to-do/music.

If you're in New York or London, see a Broadway (or off-Broadway) show. Almost any hit production will blow your mind. You can score same-day discounted tickets at TKTS booths. But jump in line early. For showtimes, including revivals, visit broadway.com.

BECOME A SOJOURNER

Graceland, Elvis Presley's home estate, includes the mansion and an entertainment complex packed with artifacts from his career, including cars, jumpsuits, and private jets. If you're near Memphis, go in person. Otherwise, check out the virtual tour at graceland.com/virtual-tours.

Visit the Louvre in Paris. If you can't go in person, take the virtual tour at louvre.fr/en/online-tours. Try to decode Mona Lisa's facial expression, but don't ignore the rest: a staggering collection of human creativity and Renaissance masterpieces.

See a symphony. If you can't, stream a concert from the Berlin Philharmonic's digital hall: digitalconcerthall.com/en. Or search YouTube for *"best symphony performances of all time."*

If you want to see *The Execution of Lady Jane Grey* in person (from Chapter 6), visit the National Gallery in London or take the virtual tour at nationalgallery.org.uk. Van Gogh's *Sunflowers* and Botticelli, Titian, Turner, and others are there too.

SO, THERE'S THE CALL

I hope you'll see these as more than actionable suggestions. They're reminders of the enduring goodness of human-made things. In a world increasingly shaped by AI, *distinctly human* contact points like these can help keep us grounded. I hope you try a few. Better yet, make your own list. See what stirs *you*.

2025 UPDATE | Why Everybody's Touring Again

I was thrilled to hear that live performance is surging this summer. Taylor Swift's *Eras Tour* became the highest-grossing in history, pulling in over $2 billion across 149 shows. Tickets routinely sold for hundreds (sometimes thousands) as fans traveled globally, there for the music and the moment.

Kendrick Lamar and SZA are topping the year's average ticket price at $206, while Coldplay's intoxicating *Music of the Spheres* tour has crossed $1.2 billion. Artists like Billie Eilish and The Weeknd are filling arenas worldwide.

> Broadway is booming, too, with 2025 hits like *Dead Outlaw*, *Just In Time*, and *Real Women Have Curves* packing the house.
>
> AI doesn't perform live—people do. And that's precisely why everybody's touring again.

AI may alter certain aspects of our creative process, but authentic personal expression, born from lived experience, will always connect and inspire us, one human to another. Ultimately, it is an authentic connection and inspiration that humans truly desire.

Despite all the inconvenience, vinyl reminds us that some things are still worth the trouble. Who would have guessed? Vinyl survived the digital revolution and even made a stunning comeback. Like vinyl, humans—the most soulful, brilliant, and scrappy beings on the planet—can survive and thrive in the age of AI.

That's not to say it'll be easy. The outcome isn't settled. The future still holds space for both triumphant and tragic endings. It's up to us to decide which one we allow to become reality. So bring your milk crate of records. I'll bring mine. Let's swap stories while the vinyl spins.

When I Rediscovered What Counts

I still believe *most* people are *mostly* good. Most people are mostly honest. They want to look in the mirror and say, "I did what was right, even when it didn't benefit me." There will always be a percentage of people who lie, cheat, and steal, who are self-serving and willing to win at all costs.

However, we can't stop striving for good things and moving forward because of them. There's too much on the line for that.

Like our prehistoric hero, the cave painter Gad, who depicted his hunting adventures on cave walls, and like the Phoenicians, who gave us the first modern alphabet, humans have always created things. We are creators, makers, and communicators. We create to express our impressions and visions of life, past, present, and future.

We can't help but create. Sometimes we speak to pass along information, write to inspire others to act, or sketch to share our perspective. Sometimes, our creations carry a little flair, from emojis in a text to a painting drawn from a deeper place.

It is our genuine attempt to share a part of us, some measure of value, meaning, and personal impulse. Whether fleeting or profound. Passing or eternal.

And we are choosing to do so through an open, creative medium to connect with another person.

> The impulse to create
> and share expressions of our experience of living
> *is* one of the most beautiful and mysterious aspects of
> being human.

Writing *Human is the New Vinyl* reminded me how much I love that. We are improbable creatures. There's so much to celebrate about our unlikely existence in this universe. And yet, here we are, *still* making things that matter.

One of the first pieces I ever wrote for VerifiedHuman expresses it best:

> *Why Human?*
> Our experiences are meaningful.
> We share ideas.
> We form living connections.
> We create diverse cultures.
> We live by values and beliefs, not by ones and zeroes.
> We have empathy.
> We are transported by ideas, textures, sights, and sounds.
> We follow intuition over computation.
> We move in rhythms, not algorithms.

To all who champion new technology and to those who write, visualize, speak, and teach—remember this: *seeking a path forward is intrinsic to the human story.* We innovate. We watch to see what happens. Then we adapt.

> My hope for creatives and educators is the same: *realism* and not panic. *Optimism* and not despair.

Look around. AI isn't going anywhere. It will only expand. But it's just another tool. So, how can we use it to help *us* reach *our* goals? What human value can *we* bring to the world that AI can't? Is it possible to harness its power while preserving what makes us human?

It is. It must be.

And *we're* the ones who can make it so.

———

*

> If you're curious about how we start rebuilding trust in an age of artificial everything and how **VerifiedHuman** fits into the story, there's one more chapter ahead—the *Hidden Track*.
>
> You could stop here. But this is where we finally untangle why the easy answers don't hold up, and what we have to lean on to move forward.

Hidden Track

VerifiedHuman |

When We Got to Thinking

If vinyl can make a comeback in the digital era, then humans can hold their own in the age of AI. We just have to choose it.

That choice, how we respond to AI's challenge to human creativity, is what led us to create VerifiedHuman. It started with a simple realization: I was tired of feeling helpless while watching something I loved get quietly bulldozed by machines.

So I reached out to some friends, about fifty writers, artists, musicians, voice actors, and educators who felt the same way. Today, more than 150 individuals and nine organizations have joined our consortium, all committed to upholding a shared set of standards. The goal was to make space for one essential question:

> What are creators and educators supposed to do in the face of AI's sudden rise?

A major force behind VerifiedHuman has been growing concern over what I call *the differentiation problem*: the fact that we're losing our ability to distinguish between what is made by a human and what isn't.

It is the big question that still hangs in the air:

> Can we still tell *who* made *what*?

That's the heart of it. When AI-generated work is routinely mistaken for human work, the lines that once protected us—attribution, origin, and accountability—begin to dissolve. The boundary between human and machine creativity is blurring fast, and it's not something that *regulation* or detection *tools* alone can fix, no matter how advanced they get.

And now, people are starting to feel it in real life and ask:

> Is what I'm reading, watching, or listening to made by a human? By an algorithm? By some combination of both?
> And does it matter?

Whether it matters depends on who you ask. You might remember what Andy's musician friends told me early on, when I first asked how artists were reacting to AI making music. Their answers were honest and uncertain.

People under forty, they said, *mostly* don't care. If the song sounds good or the image does its job, great. But people over forty are *conscientiously concerned*. They care but often can't articulate why. They *feel* the difference but struggle to name it.

When It Matters and When It Doesn't

In May 2023, I shared the basics of VerifiedHuman with Dr. Paul Conn, a psychology professor, successful writer, lifelong educator, and Chancellor of Lee University. After I laid it all out for him, he asked:

"Micah, why should anybody care if AI makes a picture? If it works for the flyer, who cares? Stick it on there, make copies, get it out the door, and move on. What's the big deal?"

| I got the point.

Let's say you've got a flyer, a website, and a revolving ad, and you need a quick image of a group of people doing something. An AI-generated picture, in that case, doesn't matter much. The medium is disposable. It's not meant to be a prized work of human creativity. Just something to hold the place, make the point, and move the project along. It's a picture of people eating pizza, not *The Execution of Lady Jane Grey*.

Then, I noticed a framed print in his office. It showed ships being loaded in Boston Harbor. Dr. Conn, who has done postgraduate work at Harvard, has a deep affection for the city and its history.

The painting was *"Long Wharf by Moonlight" (1865)* by John Stobart. As the artist explains:

> "Very few American ports have preserved their past
> as well as Boston, and part of Long Wharf exists today
> much as it was in 1865, with the granite Customs House
> And the Salt House is still visible,
> and the wharf bustling with the sailing trade
> that continued despite the rise of steam power."

I asked him about the painting.

"You valued that print enough," I said, "to buy a limited edition, 17/750, have it framed, and hang it here in your office."

He agreed. So I asked, "What if I could make an exact copy of that print, but even better, have AI put you and Mrs. Conn on the back of that salt wagon? Wouldn't you rather have that framed instead?"

> He grinned and politely signaled no.

What makes this print special is that John Stobart created it for someone like Dr. Conn. It's limited, human, and quietly sentimental. Dr. Conn and John Stobart may never meet, but they share a transcendent experience: a moment on Long Wharf in 1865. Stobart's generous vision and Dr. Conn's quiet appreciation of it are what give the work its meaning. An AI remix, even one personalized with Dr. and Mrs. Conn in the scene, would be a novelty, a silly little trick.

When Everything Looks Real

Let's break down what happened when Boris Eldagsen won the Sony World Photography contest with an AI-generated image of two women who don't exist. He showed up in London, tuxedo and all, and took the stage—only to decline the prize.

> "AI images are not photography…
> I will not accept the award."

He said, revealing that the image wasn't a real photograph at all. It was created with a text prompt. Eldagsen later revealed he orchestrated the whole thing to spotlight AI's growing role in the creative world. There's no doubt he made his point.

> So why was this a story?
> Why did people care?
> What was the big deal?

There were a couple of dynamics at play.

First, people cared because the contest was supposed to be a competition between human beings. DALL·E is *not* a human being.

It's a powerful generative model designed to create novel, stunning images. So when Eldagsen won with an image he hadn't photographed, it felt like a breach in the game—like winning a marathon by riding a powered skateboard part of the way.

Naturally, there was something deeper. Eldagsen had entered a "photograph" he hadn't actually taken. But the *real jolt* was that the image *moved* people. The subjects, those two women, were entirely synthetic. Yet they looked real enough to stir the emotions of expert human judges.

The judges must have believed the image captured something uniquely human, a frozen moment worth honoring above thousands of others. So, the deeper slight wasn't just that the entry was artificial. The deeper slight was that they believed in its real humanity. They were pulled into a performance, a carefully crafted illusion.

> And they couldn't tell.

Unlike the curators who spotted the artificial Getty Kouros because something felt off, *these* judges didn't. They couldn't see it. They couldn't distinguish between real people and digitally imagined phantoms.

So there were two affronts: First, the taking of the "photo" was faked. Second, the "human" subjects in the photo were fakes. And under all of this simmers a more complicated question:

What does it mean when machines can fool, and even move, humans who are trained to spot the difference?

Every pixel of Eldagsen's image was scrutinized. Millions of people studied the longing in the eyes of those two women. And still, *no one could tell what was real.* That's unsettling.

> We keep hearing people say things like,
> *Humans should focus on what only humans can do.*
> *That's where our true value lies.*

But what happens when AI does those very things, well enough to pass as human? It's not always about quality. It's not even about creativity. Sometimes, as with *The Electrician*, there simply is no perceptible difference. Not to the naked eye, not to trained judges, not even to viewers who want to know.

In those moments, what you *know* about the content matters more than what you *see* or *hear*. *Knowing* a human made it, chose each word, chased down the idea, and took the risk, *that* becomes the difference. That's what gives it weight, both economic value and human significance.

But there's a catch. "Lean into your humanness" only works if people can still tell *what's human*, if they ask, "*Who made this?*" and can get an honest answer.

> But more and more, they *can't*.

And if they can't *tell*, they can't *care*. People aren't being obtuse. The signals just aren't clear. The line's too blurry. The trace is gone. When

AI-generated work looks just like ours, when it fools judges and wins awards without ever disclosing its source, the human touch isn't a selling point. Because it's invisible.

> When everything looks the same, *provenance* becomes the primary value.

In a world where AI can mimic nearly everything, the *what* matters less. The *who* behind it matters more.

When Purity Gets Complicated

My friend Gary DuBois is a VerifiedHuman Artist and a gifted stone sculptor. He can turn an ordinary rock into a glistening candelabra, the kind you'd be proud to set on your dining table. Gary doesn't use AI to shape the stone. But he might use Google to research materials, his phone to take shots in good lighting, editing tools to prepare images, and Etsy, driven by AI algorithms, to sell his work online.

So, does that count as AI-assisted? Maybe. I'd still call Gary a purist. That's why the real value lies in being able to say, clearly and without doubt: *A human made this,* then choosing to honor that work because of *who* made it and dared to bring it to life.

When Your Name Means Something

When using AI, the line between authorship and assistance is inherently gray. Not long ago, I heard a friend read a eulogy at her father's funeral. I was moved. Afterward, I asked what it felt like to write it.

> "Oh," she said. "It was OK. ChatGPT wrote it, mostly. But I told it what I wanted to say."

Another friend showed me a clever children's book he'd "written." When I asked about his process, he said something like:

> "Claude did most of the writing, but the idea was mine."

Neither of my friends was being dishonest. They weren't trying to mislead anyone. They just didn't mention they'd used AI. It probably didn't occur to them that it mattered. In one case, the funeral, it really didn't. The moment was personal. The words were heartfelt. Nobody cared whether Claude had helped, nor should they have.

But the children's book is different. It might be published. It could end up on shelves or in classrooms. In that context, putting your name on something carries a different weight.

When you sign your name to something, you're saying: This is mine. It reflects me: my voice, my insight, my lived experience. That's even more important than a copyright. It's a matter of conscience.

Of course, not every AI-assisted sentence needs a footnote. No one expects disclosure every time Grammarly suggests a cleaner phrase or Photoshop fills in a background.

We're not trying to regulate attribution down to the click level. But as AI becomes more deeply embedded in our tools and workflows, we need a shared understanding of where value lives, when it's ours to claim, and when it's appropriate to inform our audience.

That's part of the work of VerifiedHuman: helping creators think clearly about context, purpose, and audience.

> Who's going to see this? What will they assume? What's the context? What's the expectation?

Most of the time, the work will speak for itself. But when it doesn't, when the work was partly yours, but another agent heavily influenced the process, it's worth asking:

How did I make this? Or *How did I oversee the creation of this?* And *What does my audience deserve to know?*

2025 UPDATE | VERIFIEDHUMAN'S HUMAN–AI COLLABORATIVE SPECTRUM

To help creators tell the truth about how their work came to be, I developed the Human–AI Collaborative Spectrum: a five-point scale designed to bring transparency back into the process. Whether a piece is fully human-made, lightly assisted, or heavily co-created with AI, this spectrum gives both creators and audiences a shared language to describe it.

It's already helping writers, artists, musicians, and voice actors differentiate their work, and making it easier for audiences to know what they're experiencing.

(See a snippet of the spectrum in the appendices or a fuller version at verifiedhuman.info.)

When AI Got Tricky

The *differentiation problem* isn't confined to still photography. A similar challenge has emerged in the form of deepfakes, fake video clips of public figures saying or doing things they never actually did.

Like Eldagsen's image, these synthetic videos raise the same question: *Can we still tell what's real from what's artificial?*

I touched on this in the Introduction. Remember the fake image of Pope Francis strutting in a white puffy jacket? It blew up on Twitter. He looked fantastic, just not like a pope. Even model Chrissy Teigen was fooled. She tweeted:

> "I thought the pope's puffer jacket was real
> and didn't give it a second thought.
> No way I'm surviving the future of technology."

That's what's scary: she didn't even question it. We can't tell if the video features Bill Hader on a ski trip or if it's a deepfake of Bill Hader on a ski trip. We can't tell if a human took a brilliant photo or if it was conjured by code.

Even professionals are shaken. World-class portrait photographer Jeremy Cowart was dismayed by his inability to distinguish between human-made and AI-generated images. Cowart has personally taken thousands of portraits. He knows lighting, posture, skin, and soul. But even he couldn't tell if the people in the pictures were real or if the images themselves were genuine. Just like with Eldagsen's photo, the experts couldn't tell what was genuine and what was just a convincing facsimile.

When Current Approaches Fall Short
The Differentiation Problem and Two Failed Fixes

At the heart of this whole mess is a single, unsettling problem:

> No one can tell. And no one has a solution.

We see it in musicians speaking out as AI models generate songs that sound like their own. We see it in search engines, where AI-written articles are ranked *higher than* human-written ones. We see it in classrooms where teachers can't tell if a student wrote the essay or if GPT did. We see it in GPT out-human-ing humans on rigorous Turing tests, convincing judges 73% of the time that *it* was a person.

This collapse of clarity has triggered a wave of responses, attempts to address the problem. Most fall into two buckets: *legislative* and *technological*. Unfortunately, neither is sufficient. They both fall short.

When People Think Laws Will Work
The Legal Response: Copyright Battles in Court

This path says: Let's pass laws, tighten copyright, regulate platforms, and stop bad actors. It sounds good in theory. But the reality is muddy, slow, and full of loopholes.

| ARTISTS VS. AI COMPANIES

In early 2023, three artists—Sarah Andersen, Kelly McKernan, and Karla Ortiz—had had enough. They took Stability AI and Midjourney to court, not for imitating their *style*, but for training those models on their *actual* work.

Billions of images, scraped from the web without consent, including the LAION dataset, a massive collection that pulled in everything it could find. The companies pushed back hard, arguing their models weren't copying anyone specifically and that using public data qualified as fair use. The court wasn't convinced. A federal judge allowed the case to proceed. Translation: Even the courts are starting to feel it.

| THE NEW YORK TIMES VS. OPENAI

Later that year, The New York Times reached its breaking point. It sued OpenAI and Microsoft, claiming ChatGPT and Bing Chat were trained on millions of its articles without permission. To drive the point home, the Times showed the models could regurgitate their reporting nearly verbatim. That's economic harm. Stolen authority. A direct blow to journalism's fragile business model.

| UNIVERSAL VS. ANTHROPIC

In the music world, Universal Music Group sued Anthropic for the same thing: training AI on copyrighted song lyrics without permission. They fear that AI can generate new lyrics that echo existing songs, style, structure, and even phrasing without credit, compensation, or consent. These cases are still winding their way through the courts. No one has a clue how they'll land. But the signal is clear: AI systems are being built on the backs of human creators and then used to replace them. It's strip-mining. And it's shaking the foundation of what it means to make something original.

When Legislation Fails
Why Laws and Copyrights Fall Short

| COMPLEXITY AND IGNORANCE

Copyright law is convoluted. Hard to understand. Hard to enforce. Most people, including developers, tend to overlook it. So do AI companies. They scraped the internet at scale, sucking up everything they could find, copyrighted or not, to feed their models.

> They didn't ask. They didn't pay for it. They just took it.

| SLOW AND IMPOTENT

Laws move slowly. Tech does not. In April 2023, I called a friend on the Hill to ask how Congress was thinking about AI and ethics. She told me President Biden had a team working on an executive order, but most lawmakers barely knew what ChatGPT was. Things are better now, but Washington's track record with emerging tech has been historically dismal.

Just think back to the early nineties. One member of Congress said,

> "*We probably need to put some strictures on developing the Internet. I think it may be a big deal.*"

Another said, "*The Internet? Pfft. It's just a fad.*"

And someone else, *"What's the Internet?"*

In the meantime, just a month after its public release, ChatGPT had already garnered 100 million users. By April, more people were using generative AI than lived in the entire United States. It was a tidal wave.

> And the people writing the laws were still standing on the beach, trying to figure out how umbrellas work.

| WEAK SOLUTIONS DON'T SOLVE WICKED PROBLEMS

On October 30, 2023, President Biden released Executive Order 14110: "The Safe, Secure, and Trustworthy Development and Use of Artificial Intelligence." It sounded promising, but it wasn't a roadmap. It was a 30,000-foot flyover.

> The prom queen waved at all the right issues but didn't make eye contact.

Most AI experts saw it for what it was: a one-paragraph introduction to a 500-page book that still hasn't been written. It had vague definitions, the right general tone, and a few encouraging signals.

But it was light on clarity. Light on specifics and light on enforcement. You read it and still have no idea what anyone's actually going to do. It doesn't inspire confidence, not in me. Not in many of the creators and thinkers who are watching this moment unfold.

| VALUES DON'T TRICKLE DOWN

Here's the most significant issue: Laws don't dictate behavior, values do. People don't follow rules just because they're written down. They do what aligns with their sense of right and wrong.

I don't avoid murder because it's *illegal*. I avoid it because I *value* human life. It's a personal conviction. I'm primarily motivated by the value, not the fear of punishment. Regarding AI, it's not enough to draft policies and hope they are effective. Copyrights and executive orders are just words on paper, clinging to relevance like saplings in a hurricane.

Regulation plays a role. The EU AI Act, Biden's Order, and the lawsuits making their way through the courts will all help shape what happens in the future. However, we must be realistic: Governments fell behind decades ago. With no hope of catching up, the gap is only getting wider.

| OUTPACED BY MACHINES

While lawmakers are moving as if it were 1987, AI is moving at light speed. Both the Biden and Trump administrations invested in AI research, funding the NSF, NAIRR, and DOD. That was a start.

However, their posture has been cautious, adopting a "light touch" approach that prioritizes growth and innovation over the ethical concerns raised by creatives, educators, and everyday individuals. That's wishful thinking bordering on negligence.

Meanwhile, China has made AI development a centerpiece of its national strategy. If the US wanted to lead, it would take much more than a task force or a think tank.

> Congress would need to move like a startup,
> not like a Ways and Means subcommittee from 1994.

Build infrastructure, fund it quickly, and staff it with world-class researchers, technologists, and lawmakers who understand what the hell is happening and can respond in real time. Improbable.

When Tech Fails
Why Watermarking, Detection, and AI Self-Policing Break Down

Laws can't fix the problem. Can technology? Maybe. That's the bet many have made. Hundreds of AI startups are leaning into a front-end solution: Let's establish provenance (the origin or history of something) by marking content with digital stamps or signatures.

> There are two primary methods for provenance: *watermarking* and digital *encoding*. Neither is effective.

| WATERMARKING AND DIGITAL ENCODING

Getty Images and Shutterstock have *watermarked* images for decades. Think of it like branding cattle, a visible stamp that makes content hard to use unless you pay for it.

Digital *encoding* goes further. Instead of a visible mark, it embeds tamper-evident data inside the file. It's more like planting a chip inside the cow's brain that logs where it was born and what it's been fed. C2PA (the Coalition for Content Provenance and Authenticity) is one of the leading efforts in this area.

It builds open standards for embedding authorship and editing history directly into files, for photos and also video, audio, and documents. Companies like Nikon, Canon, and Sony are also making this possible, the moment a picture is taken.

Smart idea. But it's not enough.

WHY IT FAILS

Watermarks Are Easy to Dodge

Modern AI can remove both visible and hidden watermarks without compromising image quality. Unless there's active enforcement, watermarks don't mean much.

AI Doesn't Need the Original

AI isn't copying. It's generalizing. It learns style, structure, color, and vibe, then creates something new: no watermark, no trace, nothing to enforce.

Provenance Is a Mess

Digital signatures only protect the *original* file. But copies, screenshots, or near-duplicates can slip through without triggering any action. Also, while it's straightforward to encrypt a photo, song, or video, you can't encrypt *words*. And you can't put a mark on a *voice*.

> Every time detection gets smarter, evasion gets smarter *faster*.

It's a high-speed arms race with no finish line. No winner. Just escalation.

BEATING THE DETECTORS

Tools like Originality.ai can sometimes catch pure machine output. But swap a few choice verbs, throw in a cherry-bomb adjective or two, or a quick run through Undetectable.ai, and detectors get confused.

As a longtime teacher, I've read and marked thousands of essays. Thousands. So have my friends. Even we can't always tell. In the AHA-ISW study I led, we couldn't either, not even with flagged sections side by side.

> Each written piece becomes a kind of Frankenstein, stitched from machine and human bits, smoothed out until it passes.

Now, do that same dance with art. With music. With video. That's the problem.

| CAT-AND-MOUSE, AD-INFINITUM

As of 2025, the AI detection arms race hasn't slowed. In addition to Originality.ai, platforms like GPTZero, Turnitin AI Detection, and even Grammarly editor are trying to flag AI writing.

They look for linguistic fingerprints, phrasing that's too clean, too balanced, or too predictable. They're trained to ask: *If I were an AI, precisely how would I weigh each word token to write this?* Then to call it out. But they get it wrong—a lot.

Originality.ai had major false-positive issues early on. Human writers, good ones, were tagged as bots.

> And they were furious: "What the hell?
> Your tool says *I* didn't write this. But I *did*."

To their credit, most of them have dialed back their algorithmic aggression a notch or two. However, the core challenge remains: how do you distinguish between humans and machines when both are trained on the same styles?

Good writers emulate strong patterns. AI does the same—faster, at scale, with no ego. The models don't even sound like each other:

Claude, ChatGPT, Rytr, and Frase each have a distinct style. Detection has improved since 2023. However, evasion has improved even faster.

| THE DISGUISE GAME

Evasion tools like Undetectable.ai, Hider.ai, and Spin Rewriter reword machine-generated content using ENL (Emulated Natural Language) to make it sound more human-like. They tweak rhythm, alter syntax, and pass detection easily. It's spy vs. spy: AI generates content. AI detects it. AI rehumanizes it to dodge detection.

> | Repeat cycle.

| BEYOND THE PAGE

This same dynamic is playing out in music, visual art, and video: AI tools are generating. AI tools detect. Other AI tools disguise it again. AI powers every player. Every step is faster than the last. We're just accelerating the loop and not really closing the gap.

When Content Meets the Market
How AI Flows: Creation, Distribution, and Consumption

To understand why VerifiedHuman holds weight, it's helpful to step back and examine the entire process chain of creation and consumption. The real problem is that AI creates content that moves *invisibly* through the pipeline. And no one along the chain is required to tell you how it got there.

(See the VerifiedHuman Problem Model in the appendices.)

> At every stage, the question of authorship gets murkier, and most of the time, no one's even asking.

Here's how the flow works:

| STAGE ONE: CONTENT CREATION

It starts with the creator: a writer, an artist, a designer, a coder, a teacher, a composer. Some work solo. Some use AI tools to assist. Some let the machine do the heavy lifting. And right now, there's no standard way to declare how something was made.

| STAGE TWO: CONTENT DISTRIBUTION

Once content is complete, it gets distributed across various platforms, including websites, social media, streaming services, and news feeds. Distributors don't ask how it was *made*. They ask whether it *performs*.

> They'll run *whatever* content indiscriminately as long as it generates clicks, likes, and sales. Most don't care if it came from a person or a prompt. If it sells, it stays.

| STAGE THREE: CONTENT CONSUMPTION

Finally, there's the audience: you and me. We scroll, listen, watch, read, and buy.

Sometimes we ask, "Who made this?" But often, we don't.
Some *don't care*. They might say, "If it works, it works."
Others *care*, but they don't care enough to dig.
A few *care a lot*. "I want to know the source. I don't want to be misled."

This gap between indifference and conviction is what makes the AI transparency problem so slippery.

When We Saw the Need More Clearly

Between those making the content, those distributing it, and the rest of us consuming it, there was no clear framework. No shared understanding of what was happening, let alone how to navigate it.

Some work was fully human-made. Some was AI-generated from start to finish. Most was somewhere in between: a cocktail of human and machine effort. But once that content hit the market, it all blended. It spread quickly, often without context, clarity, or any means for audiences to distinguish it.

> So, I founded VerifiedHuman.

As Eldagsen's image stirred global attention, I was still sketching the outlines of VerifiedHuman. In the spring of 2023, I reached out to him, and we exchanged a few emails. He shared the intense pressure he was under, praise from some who understood what he was doing, and criticism from others who dismissed it as a "cheap stunt."

But that moment, Eldagsen's disruption of the photographic world was pivotal for me. What he revealed, intentionally *or not*, was the need for a system that could reliably distinguish human work from machine output, especially now, as creators are forced to adapt while balancing convenience with creative integrity.

When We Created the Standards

The problems we've explored—differentiation failure, weak legal tools, fast-moving technology, market indifference, and consumer confusion—have all collided into a chaotic mess.

In this mess, creators are being copied. Audiences are being misled. And the tools meant to protect us aren't holding up. Copyright can't keep pace. Tech solutions are confusing. And AI is moving faster than either of them.

Amidst all this noise, something deeper has surfaced: a hunger for transparency. A craving for honesty. A call for something human. That's what led us here. We hope to re-center human values in the creative process. We needed a declaration: simple, straightforward, grounded. I developed the VerifiedHuman Standards, a set of public, voluntary com-
-itments to truth in authorship, transparency in the process, and re-
-pect for human creativity.

(See the VerifiedHuman Model Overview in the appendices.)

Before we jump into them, let's quickly recap:

- Differentiating between human and AI-made work is now incredibly difficult.
- Consumers want to know the origin of content. Creators want to be recognized (and compensated) for their human labor.
- Legal fixes aren't enough. We can't regulate our way out of this.
- Tech fails, too. Watermarks, encryption, and detection have limits.
- The game keeps shifting. And that's where the VerifiedHuman model comes in.

When Trust Was All We Had Left

Legal fixes failed, and tech fell short. So, what do we have left?

> Trust.

Trust is a fundamental force in human life. It is the very foundation of the global economy, creative relationships, and nearly every decision we make in the modern world.

| A NEW KIND OF PLEDGE

What if we defined a space where creators could make a public, values-based pledge? What if a student, artist, or musician could say:

> Hey, *I* made this. Not an AI.
> Not a model. Not a prompt.
> This piece, this essay, this photograph, this song,
> is mine. *I* am the essential creative force behind it.

That's just trust. It is creators choosing to be transparent and audiences choosing to believe them.

(See the VerifiedHuman Trust Model in the appendices.)

| TRUST RUNS THE WORLD

We often overlook the extent to which we extend trust every day. You trust other drivers to stay in their lane. You trust strangers not to follow you home. You trust the pharmacist to give you the correct dosage.

Take the self-checkout lane. Retailers are aware of how easy it is to cheat the system. Scan the ground beef, skip the steak, and walk out with a smile.

However, they still install it because the math of trust makes sense. Cameras and one attendant cost less than the labor it would take to assume everyone's trying to cheat.

> Most people are honest. The system runs on that assumption. And none of us wants a world where self-checkout disappears because of the unscrupulous 2%.

| BROKEN TRUST HURTS EVERYONE

We have also seen what happens when trust erodes.

In journalism, once a pillar of shared truth, mainstream media now ranks near the bottom of public trust indexes. Political spin, nonstop content cycles, and the rise of "fake news" have left audiences deeply skeptical of what they hear and who is behind it.

In healthcare, patients assume their doctors are working in their best interest. Break that trust with malpractice or price-gouging, and the fallout is devastating.

In business, Brands spend millions to earn and maintain consumer trust. Transparency, ethics, and consistency are currencies as real as revenue.

Starbucks is a case study: The superglobal coffee company is respected for its ethical sourcing but criticized for its labor practices, praised for its environmental goals, but called out for its tax "strategy." Starbucks survives because enough people still trust *some part* of the story they're telling. But that trust is fragile. And once lost, it's hard to recover.

| TRUST IS A BRIDGE

When a reader believes a writer or a listener believes a singer, a bond forms. Seth Godin has often famously argued that trust grows through acts of mutual generosity — given freely, received openly.

Authenticity matters, especially in music, art, and literature, where audiences connect with the person behind the work. That connection is why VerifiedHuman exists.

| BUT IS TRUST ENOUGH?

Early in the process, I sought feedback from experienced entrepreneurs. One question kept surfacing:

> "Is trust enough?"

What if a creator simply says, "I didn't use AI to make this"? Would that be *enough* for the audience to believe it? Or will people demand hard proof? Proof that, as of now, doesn't exist.

Because the reality is that there is no reliable way to prove authorship today. Zero. None. Not across writing, music, visual art, or voice. And the gap is growing. As generative tools improve, they're imitating human work and bleeding seamlessly into it.

When I Had to Do *Something*

Even after months of work, debate, and serious thinking, the question—*Would trust be enough?*—still dogged me. There was no clear answer. But one thing was sure: doing nothing wasn't an option. I could've stalled out or kept debating forever. Instead, I moved forward with one conviction: trust is *all we have*.

> And that's not nothing.

As I built the VerifiedHuman framework, I discovered something unexpected: The best way to verify authorship isn't with detection tools or surveillance. It's through honest, respectful questions, ones that lead with *trust*, not *suspicion*.

For images:

> Where and when did you take this? What city? What date?
> Who or what is in the frame?

What kind of camera and gear did you use—DSLR, iPhone?
Did you edit it afterward in Photoshop or Lightroom?

For writing:

What was the prompt or task?
What word processor did you use—Word, Google Docs?
What editing tools were involved—Grammarly, ProWritingAid?
Did you use ChatGPT, Claude, or any AI system to assist?

Simple, point-blank questions. There are more, of course. But that's the spirit. And it works. We use the same concept for music and voice.

> *Trust*, but verify.

These respectful questions bring us closer to the truth by giving creators a chance to speak plainly.

STANDARDS ARE KEY

Values-based systems only work when we agree on what "human-made" even means. Defining that was harder than it sounds. I spent months in coffee shops and on video calls with friends—writers, artists, educators, musicians—sussing out where to draw the lines.

A sculptor using Google for research: *Is that AI-assisted?* A writer running a draft through Grammarly: *Where does human creativity end and machine involvement begin?* To me, these weren't theoretical questions. They had consequences for people I know. People whose creative work and income were already being affected by generative AI. I wanted to respond with as much clarity and integrity as I could.

> So I started reading, thinking, and writing.

I developed standards and definitions that reflect how creators work across various disciplines, including writing, visual art, music, and voice. I worked directly with professionals in each of those fields, real people with skin in the game, to craft public, trust-based standards grounded in the realities of creative practice. Standards built to protect creators and rebuild audience trust.

| HOW WE BUILT THE VERIFIEDHUMAN STANDARDS

1. **Defined the creative process** for writers, artists, and musicians in human terms.

2. **Identified how AI is utilized in each medium,** especially when it replaces or obscures human input.

3. **Drew practical, commonsense lines** based on real creative workflows, not abstractions.

4. **Distilled everything into clear, principled statements** that any honest creator could stand behind.

For example, our standard for writers reads:

> "I represent my written work as my (or my team's) intellectual property, essentially authored by (a) human(s) and not by generative AI."

It's a values-based promise, a human stake in a digital world. Creators who choose to uphold these standards can label their work with the VH mark: a visible way to say: *This was made by a real person. You can trust that.*

| A PARALLEL: FAIRTRADE FOR CREATIVITY

The VerifiedHuman model shares a lot with Fairtrade. They began with a simple yet powerful impulse: there must be an ethical way to get coffee from the farm to the cup. If we audit the supply chain from grower to shelf,

> We can pay everyone their fair share and ensure the growers don't get screwed.

And it worked. Consumers responded. Many were willing to pay a little more because the label meant something. It only worked because people understood what the standard stood for and trusted it.

That's precisely what we're building for creative work: a signal, a stance, not a gimmick. We've published the standards. We've made the process transparent. We're inviting honest creators to carry the mark forward. It's all public at verifiedhuman.info.

| THE SPACE OF TRUST

At the heart of our model is a simple idea:

> A space of trust between creator and audience.

It's where a creator says, "I made this for you." And the audience says, "I believe you." It may sound quaint, but it's as powerful as an oath in a courtroom: *"I swear to tell the truth, the whole truth, and nothing but the truth."*

Is that ritual outdated? Maybe. But we do it on purpose—to mark a moment in time. So when trust breaks down, we can point back and say: "Hey, remember the oath? We marked it intentionally.

> That's when we decided what trust looks like, and this is where it unraveled."

In the same way, VerifiedHuman marks a moment of creative trust, something honest in a world that needs more of it.

When You Got It Through Soundbites

When I explain VerifiedHuman to people, I usually just show them the website. Experiencing our work online is one of the best ways to understand it. But since you're here with me in this book, I'd like to give you ten soundbites that capture the spirit of our journey into this space.

> *1. "The tide may be pulling us all out..."*

> A powerful tide is dragging society in a troubling direction. As AI becomes more prolific, we're approaching a world where people assume, by default, that whatever they're reading, watching, or hearing was probably made by AI, unless proven otherwise. That's a massive problem.

> *"But we will not let it pull us under."*

> Humans are resilient. We're wired to connect, to express ourselves, to make things that matter. We still value honesty, creativity, and meaning, and that's exactly what we're defending.

> *2. "AI can now produce written content almost identical to human work. That's why authors everywhere are adopting the VerifiedHuman standard."*

> This statement applies to the Standard for Writers, but it also applies to visual artists, musicians, and voice actors. As tools like ChatGPT, DALL·E, Sora, MusicLM, and Overdub become increasingly powerful, the distinction between machine

and human creativity is breaking down. We invite creators everywhere to label their work with the VerifiedHuman mark, to stand behind it as essentially human-made.

3. *"We created VerifiedHuman with a vision to promote transparency, honesty, and originality in creative mediums."*

This statement represents our *Why*. In a world being reshaped by AI, we want creators to thrive, not just survive.

4. *"Holding the VerifiedHuman label means you're recognized as a true creator in your field."*

The label certifies your work as fundamentally human-made. AI tools may have provided some support, but the essential creative vision came from you. It's a path to creative freedom, inviting open dialogue with your audience and building trust through clarity.

5. *"The value of trust should not be dismissed. It is paramount in this effort... we believe the human ethical spirit remains intact, and we must leverage it."*

We've gone all in on trust. It's often overlooked, but it's foundational. Without it, almost nothing in human life works.

6. *"In a world where work by humans and AI is indistinguishable, the answer is not more advanced AI. Values are the solution."*

Generative AI created this problem. Laws can't solve it. Technology can't solve it. It's a people problem. People have to solve it. So we do what humans have always done: return to our values. Find better tools. Act for the greater good.

7. *"We are optimists and problem-solvers. We don't despair in the face of progress—we embrace it."*

> This statement is core to VerifiedHuman. We don't panic. We don't retreat. We stand on our feet. We move forward. Humanity has faced powerful tools before. AI is just the latest in a long history. And we've adapted every time.

8. *"The challenges posed by AI aren't problems to mitigate but opportunities to drive society toward equity."*

> AI can be a great equalizer. It gives us a chance to highlight human creativity, not erase it. Take a look at this. A person made it, not a machine, and it's worth celebrating.

9. *"VerifiedHuman doesn't claim all the answers, but we're shining a light on a huge (and surprisingly absent) part of the solution."*

> Human trust is the cornerstone of authenticity. By raising this value into view, we elevate human expression in a world increasingly shaped by machines.

10. *"Concern for humans and their future must always be the chief interest of all technical endeavors... so that the creations of our mind are a blessing and not a curse to humankind."*

> My favorite quote from Albert Einstein. He said this just before the world saw how technology could threaten humanity's survival. He never stopped urging us to remember what matters most: humans. Technology should serve humanity, so in the end, *people win.*

When We Have Hope

I've mentioned what Andy's musician friends said: that people under forty mostly don't care whether AI made a song. If it works, it works. And the over-forty crowd cares, but they're not sure why.

At the end of our call, Andy said, "Micah, they just don't know. But they *did* say you were right about vinyl."

One of them, an artist you've probably heard of, paused and said:

> *"Hey man, vinyl is making a big comeback with the kids. Maybe* human *will be the new vinyl."*

That line stayed with me.

It's why I named this book what I did.
Because I believe in presence. In intention.
In the warmth, the wear, the unmistakable texture of human work.

And who knows? Maybe he'll be right.

ACKNOWLEDGMENTS |

This book wouldn't have been possible without the support and presence of the people who've shaped my thinking and my life.

Thank you to **Tamee Gunnell-Roberts**. I thought I didn't like you when we met. Now, I can't imagine my world without you in it. You are my sister. I'm grateful for each heartbreaking and wonderful moment we've shared.

To **Daniel Allen**. You've guided me through the best and hardest parts. Your investment in me is incalculable. Your wisdom is steady.

To **Craig Martin**. We started on separate paths in Thailand and found ourselves here, still pushing forward in parallel, sharing the work of making something that matters.

To **Carl and Debbie Miller**. Thank you for a lifetime of support. Your belief in me has always run deeper than words can express.

To **Aaron Simmons**. You're a wonderful friend. Thank you for agreeing to be my agent and advisor. You believed in this project when it was a mess of ideas. Your clarity has made it all better.

To **Wisdom/Work and Tom Morris**. Thanks for giving this book a home and providing a platform for its voice to be heard.

To my mom, **Susan Depew,** for teaching me to live faithfully, love people, and use words with precision.

To my wife **Kristy**, for patiently loving me through all we've experienced together. To my daughter **Molly**, for making me laugh, always. To my son, **Ethan**, for keeping me current, curious, and getting our human–AI conversation started.

APPENDICES |

The Tower of Babel |
Gustave Doré's 1865 etching, *The Confusion of Tongues* (1865)

The Execution of Lady Jane Grey | Paul Delaroche (1833)

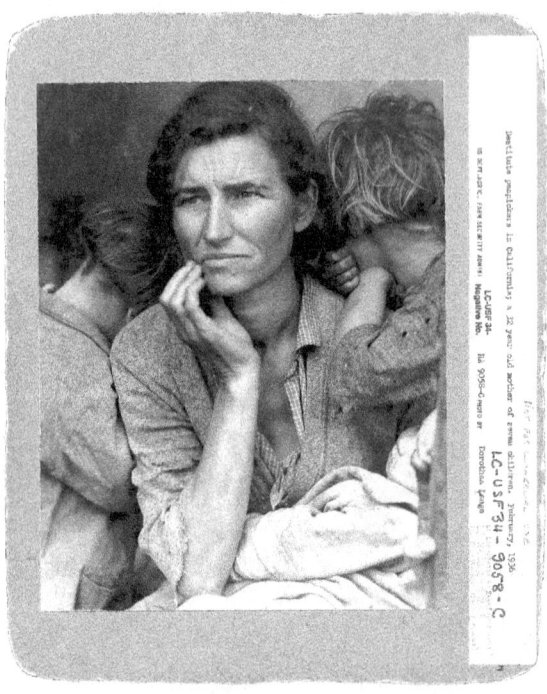

A tale of two images.

Migrant Mother (1936)

Dorothea Lange's iconic photo shows Florence Owens Thompson, a 32-year-old mother of seven, and her family during the Great Depression in Nipomo, California.

The Electrician (2023)

This AI-generated image, submitted by Boris Eldagsen, won the Sony World Photography Award in April 2023. These women did not exist.

Boris Eldagsen, "PSEUDOMNESIA | The Electrician", promptography, 2022, courtesy Photo Edition Berlin

VerifiedHuman™ Model Overview

 FAIRTRADE → A values-based label for **coffee**.

VerifiedHuman®  → A values-based label for **human-created content**.

Human creators agree to a standard that tells their audience: → "I essentially created this product. AI didn't."

We provide a clearly articulated space for that **high-five**.
| Adopt a standard.
| Get the label.
| Show the world *you* created it.

VerifiedHuman™ | Problem Model

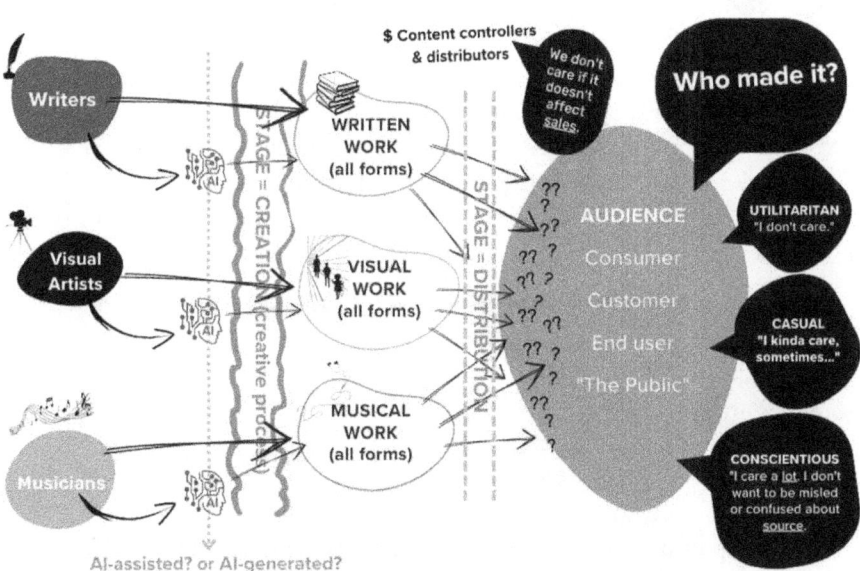

This sketch was one of my early attempts to make sense of the *differentiation problem* in the content world. At the time, I hadn't yet included voice actors—they came later.

VerifiedHuman™ | Trust Model

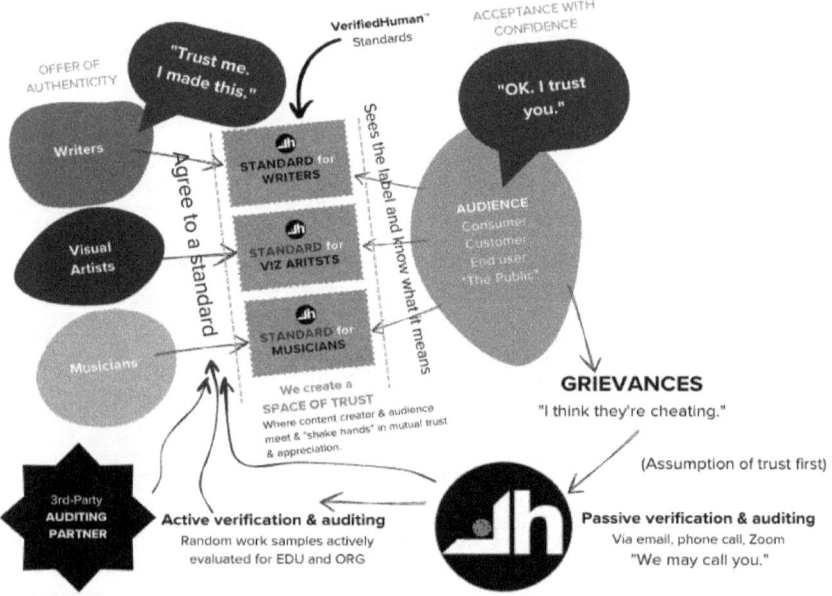

This early sketch maps the core VerifiedHuman trust model: creators agree to a clear standard, audiences recognize the label, and mutual trust is built through transparency, verification, and accountability. Voice actors and other roles were added in later drafts as the framework evolved.

VH™ | Human–AI Collaborative Spectrum

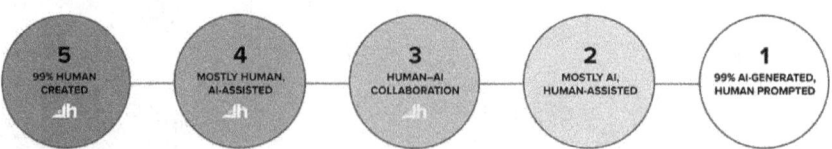

This spectrum provides a framework for assessing the extent to which a creative work was generated by a human versus an AI. It was designed to clarify levels of collaboration in the creation process. Creators may include a corresponding number with the VerifiedHuman label if it is helpful.

NOTES |

Prologue

Tech leaders call for AI pause: Gerrit De Vynck, "Elon Musk, Others Sign Letter Calling for a Pause on AI Experiments," *Washington Post*, March 29, 2023.
VerifiedHuman™: https://www.verifiedhuman.info.
Mapping the Genome: Jamie Metzl, *Superconvergence: How the Genetics, Biotech, and AI Revolutions Will Transform Our Lives, Work, and World* (Timber Press, 2024).

Chapter 1 | Six Hours Early to the Party

AI explodes: UBS, "ChatGPT Fastest-Growing Consumer App," Reuters, February 2, 2023.
Within two months, [ChatGPT] had surpassed 100 million users: Similarweb, "ChatGPT Traffic Analysis: January 2023," *Mashable*, February 10, 2023.
Text-to-image "diffusion" models: Stability AI, "Celebrating One Year of Stable Diffusion," *Stability AI News*, October 14, 2024.
When Levi's lost the thread: Megan Graham, "Levi's Pauses Use of AI Models Following Backlash Over Diversity Concerns," *Wall Street Journal*, March 15, 2023.
Human connection in fashion: Thomaï Serdari, "The Challenges of Integrating AI in the Fashion Industry," *Forbes*, March 22, 2023.
2025 Update: Spotify: Alex Fisher, "The Spotify AI Epidemic: How Artificial Intelligence is Changing the Music Industry," *The SMU Journal*, January 24, 2025.

Chapter 2 | The Rise and Demise of Vinyl

Danesmoate: U2 recorded "Running to Stand Still," *The Joshua Tree* at Danesmoate House, Dublin, in 1986: Neil McCormick and Eamon McGee, *U2: A Diary* (Omnibus Press, 2008).
Fisher-Price's 1978 toy turntable played plastic discs of nursery songs: Tim Walsh, *Timeless Toys: Classic Toys and the Playmakers...* (Andrews McMeel Publishing, 2005).
"Fire, water, gravel, vinyl": Dave Barry, *Dave Barry Turns 50* (Crown, 1998).

"Life has surface noise": John Peel, *Margrave of the Marshes* (Chicago Review Press, 2005).
John Lydon: "I hate technological rip-offs," *Entertainment Weekly*, October 14, 2014.
Analog curves: Ken C. Pohlmann, *Principles of Digital Audio*, 6th ed. (McGraw-Hill, 2011).
Beck: "When I pull out vinyl... I get a different feeling," *Los Angeles Times*, May 1, 2018.
Jack White: "There's romance... demands your attention," *Clash*, March 20, 2015.
Phonograph: Raymond R. Wile, *Fundamentals of Sound and Vibration* (CRC Press, 2015).
Berliner's Gramophone and flat discs: Wile, *Fundamentals of Sound and Vibration*.
Enrico Caruso: Robert Philip, *The Classic Makers of Opera*, ed. Anderson (Penguin, 2010).
Electricity expanded recording's range: David L. Morton Jr., *Sound Recording: The Life Story of a Technology* (Johns Hopkins University Press, 2004).
The "Vinyl" moniker originated from polyvinyl, replacing shellac (Dominic Pillon, *Retromania*, Bloomsbury Academic, 2021).
LPs length: Andre Millard, *The Golden Web* (University of Chicago Press, 2006).
The first stereo LP: Mark Prendergast, *The Ambient Century* (Bloomsbury, 2000).
Multi-track isolates vocals: David Morton, *Sound Recording* (Greenwood Press, 2004).
Vinyl sales collapse: International Federation of the Phonographic Industry, as cited in Chris Martins, "Did Vinyl Really Die in the '90s? Well, Sort Of...," *SPIN*, May 6, 2014.

Chapter 3 | **The Digital World**

Our brains are biologically wired to see: Irving Biederman, "Recognition-by-Components," *Psychological Review* 94, no. 2 (1987): 115-147.
Mobile led to music players: Steven Levy, *The Perfect Thing* (Simon & Schuster, 2006).
"Changes everything": Walter Isaacson, *Steve Jobs* (Simon & Schuster, 2011).
Smartphone adoption: Statista, February 2023; Pew Research Center, April 2019.
Andrew Keen on smartphone revolution: Andrew Keen, *The Internet Is Not the Answer* (2015); Jan Eliasson, UN World Water Day statement (2013).
The internet began as ARPANET, as described in Katie Hafner and Matthew Lyon's book, *Where Wizards Stay Up Late* (Simon & Schuster, 1996).
TCP/IP: Vinton G. Cerf and Robert E. Kahn, "A Protocol for Packet Network Intercommunication," *IEEE Transactions on Communications* 22, no. 5 (May 1974): 637-648.
Generations' digital trail from birth: Jean M. Twenge, *iGen* (Atria Books, 2017).
Target knew a teenage girl was pregnant: Charles Duhigg, "How Companies Learn Your Secrets," *New York Times*, February 16, 2012.
Big data collected, sold, and used to predict human behavior: Viktor Mayer-Schönberger and Kenneth Cukier, *Big Data* (Harcourt, 2013).
"Cloud engine that drives the modern world": Sundar Pichai, keynote at Google Cloud Next '21, October 12, 2021, YouTube.
Masters lost in Universal Studios fire: Jody Rosen, "The Day the Music Burned," *New York Times Magazine*, June 11, 2019.
Taped over: Tim Smolko, *Popular Music and the Recording Industry* (Routledge, 2022).
Stolen Rolling Stones tapes: Clinton Heylin, *Bootleg* (St. Martin's Griffin, 2004).
Petty's masters stolen in 1979 (Warren Zanes, *Petty: The Biography*, Henry Holt, 2015).
Digitizing to preserve: Tung-Hui Hu, *A Prehistory of the Cloud* (MIT Press, 2015).

Chapter 4 | **The Rise of AI**

2025 Update | AI tool explosion: Cade Metz and Erin Griffith, "The A.I. Boom Could Use a Killer App," *New York Times*, May 19, 2024.

Transforming medicine: Yoshua Bengio, Yann LeCun, and Geoffrey Hinton, "The Deep Learning Revolution," ACM A.M. Turing Lecture Series, June 11, 2021, https://www.turing.acm.org.
Impact on software: Kai-Fu Lee, *AI 2041: Ten Visions for Our Future* (Currency, 2021).
Backpropagation algorithms: Nils J. Nilsson, *The Quest for Artificial Intelligence* (Cambridge University Press, 2010).
When "Tay" got toxic: Cade Metz, "Microsoft Created a Chatbot to Learn From Humans. It Quickly Became Racist," *New York Times*, March 24, 2016.
Deep learning stacks multiple layers to solve complex tasks (Ian Goodfellow, Yoshua Bengio, and Aaron Courville, *Deep Learning*, MIT Press, 2016).
AlphaGo vs. Lee Sedol, turning point in AI: Cade Metz, "In a Huge Breakthrough, Google's AI Beats a Top Player at Go," *Wired*, March 9, 2016.
Go last bastion of human strategic dominance: Ian Goodfellow, Yoshua Bengio, and Aaron Courville, *Deep Learning* (MIT Press, 2016).
LLMs generate stories, assist research, and organize data: Ian Goodfellow, Yoshua Bengio, and Aaron Courville, *Deep Learning* (MIT Press, 2016).
Midjourney, Stable Diffusion, Jukebox, AIVA: Karen Hao, "Why We Need an AI Eraser," *MIT Technology Review*, February 10, 2023; Douglas Heaven, "AI Has Cracked a Key Mathematical Task," *MIT Technology Review*, April 24, 2023.
AI collaboration: Tristan Harris and Aza Raskin, "The AI Dilemma," Center for Humane Technology, March 9, 2023, video, 1:02:31, YouTube.
Since 2010, there has been exponential growth: Max Roser, "The Next Big Wave," Our World in Data, October 10, 2022, https://www.ourworldindata.org.
AI's promises, risks, job loss, privacy, inequality: AI Series, special issues, *New York Times*, January 2023, https://www.nytimes.com.
"AI Poised to Disrupt" and "CEOs Grapple with AI": AI Series, special issues, *Wall Street Journal*, January–March 2023, https://www.wsj.com.
"The preceding 100% human content": Scott Pelley, "Google and the Future of Artificial Intelligence: A 60 Minutes Interview with Sundar Pichai," CBS News, April 16, 2023.
"A development as powerful... center of attention": Max Roser, "The Brief History of Artificial Intelligence," Our World in Data, December 10, 2022, https://www.ourworldindata.org.
Boole, Babbage, Lovelace: Pamela McCorduck, *Machines Who Think* (A.K. Peters, 2004).
AI sparked through Turing and Von Neumann: McCorduck, *Machines That Think*.
Turing: machine decades before computer: Alan M. Turing, "On Computable Numbers," *Proceedings of the London Mathematical Society* 2, no. 42 (1936): 230-265.
Turing predicted machine intelligence could outstrip us: Alan M. Turing, "Computing Machinery and Intelligence," *Mind* 59, no. 236 (1950): 433-460.
Turing: "called intelligent": Turing, "Computing Machinery and Intelligence."
Turing test questions: Turing, "Computing Machinery and Intelligence."
The Logic Theorist, a breakthrough: Nilsson, *The Quest for Artificial Intelligence*.
AI developers: John Haugeland, *Artificial Intelligence: The Very Idea* (MIT Press, 1985).
"AI" term coined: Nilsson, *The Quest for Artificial Intelligence*.
AI summers, winters: Nilsson, *The Quest for Artificial Intelligence*.
AI policy directive: The White House, "Executive Order on Maintaining American Leadership in Artificial Intelligence," whitehouse.gov, February 11, 2023.
EU proposal for AI regulation: European Commission, "Proposal for Regulation on a European Approach for Artificial Intelligence," ec.europa.eu, April 21, 2023.
On black box AI models: Cynthia Rudin, "Stop Explaining Black Box Machine Learning Models for High Stakes Decisions," *Nature Machine Intelligence* 1, no. 5 (2019): 206-215.

Finale Doshi-Velez: Harvard SEAS interview, 2021.
"Stochastic Parrots" paper: Bender, Gebru, McMillan-Major, and Mitchell, FAccT 2021.
Timnit Gebru quotes: Keynote address, Relativity Fest, December 2022; interview with Stanford HAI, 2021.

Chapter 5 | Those Who Write

Key shifts in writing: Our focus here is on identifying key shifts in the history of writing, rather than providing a comprehensive survey. The broader field includes creative, nonfiction, academic, technical, and digital forms.
Clay and papyrus: Steven Roger Fischer, *A History of Writing* (Reaktion Books, 2001).
Alphabet: Jean-Pierre Thiollet, "Phoenician Alphabet," in *The Oxford Handbook of the Phoenician and Punic Mediterranean*, eds. Doak and López-Ruiz (Oxford University Press, 2019).
Papyrus records from Giza: Mark Lehner, "The Pyramid Age Settlement of the Southern Mount at Giza," *Journal of the American Research in Egypt* 39 (2002): 8-44.
Parchment: Raymond Clemens and Timothy Graham, *Introduction to Manuscript Studies* (Cornell University Press, 2007).
Invention of paper: Tsien Tsuen-Hsuin, *Science and Civilisation in China: Vol 5, Chemistry and Chemical Technology, Part 1, Paper and Printing* (Cambridge University Press, 1985).
Analog by Design: Memory: Kuniyoshi L. Sakai, quoted in "Paper Notebooks," *Frontiers in Behavioral Neuroscience*, via University of Tokyo press release, February 2021.
Paper ignites a golden age: Jonathan M. Bloom, *Paper Before Print: The History and Impact of Paper in the Islamic World* (Yale University Press, 2001).
Paper arrives in Europe: Richard L. Hills, *Papermaking in Britain 1488–1988: A Short History* (Athlone Press, 1988).
Early printing in China: T. H. Barrett, *The Woman Who Discovered Printing* (Yale University Press, 2008).
Printing spread globally: Lucien Febvre and Henri-Jean Martin, *The Coming of the Book*, trans. David Gerard (Verso, 1976).
Mark Twain, first typed manuscript, cursed perplexities: Alix Christie, "How Mark Twain Started a Historical 'Meme' about Hating Typewriters," *Literary Hub*, June 29, 2021.
The QWERTY layout remains standard today (Richard Current, *The Typewriter and the Men Who Made It*, University of Illinois Press, 1954).
Typewriter faster: Darren Wershler-Henry, *The Iron Whim* (Cornell University Press, 2007).
The typewriter also had a social impact: Anson Rabinbach, *The Human Motor: Energy, Fatigue, and the Origins of Modernity* (Basic Books, 1990).
Berliner's discs are superior to Edison's cylinders: David Morton, *Sound Recording: The Life Story of a Technology* (Johns Hopkins University Press, 2004).
Ballpoint pen: György Moldova, *Ballpoint: A Tale of Genius and Grit, Perilous Times, The Invention That Changed the Way We Write* (New Europe Books, 2012).
Early users wrapped graphite: Henry Petroski, *The Pencil: A History of Design and Circumstance* (Knopf, 1990).
The British blockade starved France of English graphite (Petroski, *The Pencil*).
Blackwing pencils: "History of the Blackwing Pencil," Blackwing, https://www.blackwing602.com.
Track changes changed everything: Matthew G. Kirschenbaum, *Track Changes: A Literary History of Word Processing* (Belknap Press of Harvard University Press, 2016).

Writers now reach readers directly: Simone Murray, *The Digital Literary Sphere: Reading, Writing, and Selling Books in the Internet Era* (Johns Hopkins University Press, 2018).
Blogs helped writers share what mattered: Murray, *The Digital Literary Sphere.*
E-books, publishing: John B. Thompson, *Books in the Digital Age* (Polity Press, 2005).
"ChatGPT can write you anything": Kaitlyn Tiffany, "Welcome to the Golden Age of Clichés," *The Atlantic*, February 21, 2023.
Google: Philipp Koehn, *Neural Machine Translation* (Cambridge University Press, 2020).
The instinct to put words to the world: Michael C. Corballis, *The Truth about Language: What It Is and Where It Came From* (University of Chicago Press, 2017).
Sapir and Whorf's Linguistic Relativity: John J. Gumperz and Stephen C. Levinson, eds., *Rethinking Linguistic Relativity* (Cambridge University Press, 1996).
Ideas beyond language: Steven Pinker, *The Language Instinct* (Harper Perennial, 1994).
The Bible as a narrative model: Northrop Frye, *The Great Code: The Bible and Literature* (Harcourt Brace Jovanovich, 1982).
The stories that make up our Bible: E. Carson Brisson, email message to author, June 2020.
Bible in everyday speech: Leviticus 19:18; Mark 12:31; Ecclesiastes 3:1; Proverbs 16:18.
Everyday English coined by Shakespeare: Jeffrey McQuain and Stanley Malless, *Coined by Shakespeare* (Merriam-Webster, 1998).
All the world's a stage: William Shakespeare, *As You Like It*, in *The Riverside Shakespeare*, 2nd ed., ed. G. Blakemore Evans (Houghton Mifflin, 1997).
What a piece of work is a [hu]man: William Shakespeare, *Hamlet*, ed. Ann Thompson and Neil Taylor (Bloomsbury, 2016).

Chapter 6 | **Those Who Visualize**

The Execution of Lady Jane Grey: Paul Delaroche, oil on canvas, 1833, 246 × 297 cm, National Gallery, London.
"Silent conversation": Jane Smith, *Art and the Observer* (Art Press, 2023).
Key shifts in visual art: Our focus is on pivotal shifts rather than a comprehensive survey of the field. The field includes fine art, design, crafts, photography, film, architecture, fashion, and digital forms.
Fixing light chemically: Beaumont Newhall, *The History of Photography* (Museum of Modern Art, 1982).
Daguerreotype: Newhall, *The History of Photography.*
Calotype, multiple prints: Larry J. Schaaf, *Out of the Shadows: Herschel, Talbot & the Invention of Photography* (Yale University Press, 1992).
Maxwell and Sutton, first color photograph, RGB: Michael Peres, ed., *The Focal Encyclopedia of Photography*, 4th ed. (Focal Press, 2007).
Kirsch, first digital image: Russell A. Kirsch, "Computer Determination of the Constituent Structure of Biological Images," *Computers and Biomedical Research* 4, no. 3 (1971): 315-328.
Jan van Eyck: Marilyn Stokstad and Michael Cothren, *Art History*, 6th ed. (Pearson, 2018).
Paint tubes outside: David Hockney, *Secret Knowledge* (Viking Studio, 2001).
Plein-air and Impressionism: Anthea Callen, *The Work of Art* (Reaktion Books, 2015).
Acrylics: Philip Ball, *Bright Earth* (Farrar, Straus and Giroux, 2001).
Bauhaus DNA: Nicholas Fox Weber, "The Bauhaus: Cradle of Modernism," *New York Times*, September 10, 2009; Frank Whitford, *Bauhaus* (Thames & Hudson, 1984).
Bauhaus education: Andreas Wachsmann, "Bauhaus Philosophy" (Bauhaus Dessau, 2021).
Bauhaus legacy, Gropius, Kandinsky, Klee, van der Rohe: Michael Snodin and Felice Hodge, "Bauhaus Design" (V&A Museum, 2019).

The Bauhaus fused theory and craft, design: Konstantin Akinsha, "The Bauhaus in Russia," *Getty Research Journal*, no. 4 (2012): 11-40.
Bauhaus vibes in design: Magdalena Droste, *Bauhaus: 1919–1933* (Taschen, 2019).
Martin Scorsese: "The alchemy of capturing moments," in *Scorsese on Scorsese*, ed. David Thompson and Ian Christie (Faber and Faber, 2003).
Muybridge's sequenced images: Phillip Prodger, *Time Stands Still: Muybridge and the Instantaneous Photography Movement* (Oxford University Press, 2003).
Edison, Dickson, Lumière brothers, motion picture: Charles Musser, *The Emergence of Cinema: The American Screen to 1907* (University of California Press, 1994).
Technicolor vs. black-and-white: Scott Higgins, *Harnessing the Technicolor Rainbow: Color Design in the 1930s* (University of Texas Press, 2007).
Méliès, Griffith, Eisenstein, editing, montage: David Bordwell, Kristin Thompson, and Jeff Smith, *Film Art: An Introduction*, 12th ed. (McGraw-Hill Education, 2020).
Film into pixels and code, the impossible suddenly possible: Stephen Prince, *Digital Visual Effects in Cinema: The Seduction of Reality* (Rutgers University Press, 2012).
Tarantino embraces analog: Bordwell, Thompson, and Smith, *Film Art*.
Analog by Design: Kodak: Cannes 2025 selection features 24 productions shot on KODAK film (May 13, 2025), https://www.kodak.com.
Streaming during COVID: Wanda Gierhart Fearing, interview, "How Theaters Aim to Keep Inviting Movie Lovers Back in 2025," *Marketing Brew*, December 20, 2024.
Theaters upgraded, chasing the magic: Brooks Barnes, "'Top Gun: Maverick' Gives Movie Theaters a Supersonic Burst," *New York Times*, June 6, 2022.
Hollywood embraced streaming fast enough to survive: Jon Nathanson, "How the Music Industry Missed the Streaming Boom," *Bloomberg*, December 16, 2021.
Pirated films are glitchy, low-res, and hard to watch: Sean Hollister, "Why Movie Piracy Never Went Mainstream Like Music Piracy," *The Verge*, January 14, 2015.
Studios, Disney+, HBO Max: Saffwat Khan, "The Rise of Streaming Services," Motion Picture Association, March 29, 2022.
"What nukes are to the physical world": Yuval Noah Harari, "Yuval Harari: 'What nukes are to the physical world, AI is to the virtual and symbolic world,'" YouTube, April 2023.
Sora learned by watching: Aaron Hertzmann, "Computers Do Not Make Art, People Do," *Communications of the ACM* 63, no. 5 (2020): 45-51.
Details took Pixar months: James Vincent, "Google's Sundar Pichai on the Dangers and Opportunities of AI," *The Verge*, May 10, 2023.
2025 Update: "Google AI Video Just Changed Everything," *The Algorithmic Bridge*, May 23, 2025; "Veo: Advancing Generative Video Models," DeepMind, https://deepmind.google/discover/blog/veo-advancing-generative-video-models/.
DeepDream, neural patterns: Alexander Mordvintsev, Christopher Olah, and Mike Tyka, "Inceptionism: Going Deeper into Neural Networks," Google AI Blog, June 17, 2015.
Part human and part machine: Ahmed Elgammal, "AI Is Blurring the Definition of Artist," *Nature* 580 (2020): 169.
MoMA, Unsupervised by Refik Anadol: The Museum of Modern Art, "Machine Hallucination: Nature Dreams by Refik Anadol," MoMA, 2023.
AI raised concerns: For more on disinformation, see Don Fallis and Varsha Varma, "The Disinformation Threat," *Harvard Kennedy School Misinformation Review* 2, no. 6 (2022).
Visitors left rattled: Anuradha Vikram, "Uncanny Views: Reflections on the Human in the Age of AI," *X-TRA Contemporary Art Journal*, March 27, 2020.
Institutional Theory: George Dickie, *Art and the Aesthetic: An Institutional Analysis*. Ithaca, NY: Cornell University Press, 1974.

AI-generated portrait sold at Christie's for $432,500, shaking up the art market: Elgammal, "AI Is Blurring the Definition of Artist."
Boris Eldagsen won the Sony, declined award: Paul Glynn, "Sony World Photography Award 2023: Winner Refuses Award Revealing AI Creation," BBC News, April 18, 2023.
Lange's Migrant Mother: James C. Curtis, "Dorothea Lange, Migrant Mother, and the Documentary Tradition," in *Dorothea Lange*, ed. Partridge (Smithsonian Press, 1994).
"I done a little bit of everything…": Curtis, "Dorothea Lange, Migrant Mother, and the Documentary Tradition."
Most artists see AI-generated art as unethical: Emily Grenfell, "AI Art: A Game Changer or a Threat to the Art World?" *Art Business Journal*, August 12, 2022.
Artists sued Stability AI: Sarah Cascone, "A Group of Artists Is Suing Stable Diffusion for Using Their Work without Consent to Train Its AI," *Artnet News*, January 16, 2023.
2025 Update: Lawsuits, licensing proposals: UK Department for Culture, Media and Sport, *AI and Intellectual Property: Call for Views Response* (April 2024); *Getty Images v. Stability AI* (D. Del., February 3, 2023); *Tremblay v. OpenAI* (N.D. Cal., June 28, 2023).

Chapter 7 | Those Who Sing and Play

Rock and roll stops the traffic: Niall Stokes, *U2: Into the Heart: The Stories Behind Every Song* (Thunder's Mouth Press, 2005).
Music's emotional power shows up: Not a complete survey of music history, but key breakthroughs in sound, particularly in the context of AI.
2025 Update: Neanderthal fingerprint, symbolic mark: Sam Jones (Madrid), "World's oldest fingerprint may be a clue that Neanderthals created art," The Guardian, 26 May 2025, theguardian.com.
Gifted and wired for expression, musicians lead the sound: Alan P. Merriam, *The Anthropology of Music* (Northwestern University Press, 1964).
Guido, solmization, notation: Richard Taruskin, *The Oxford History of Western Music*, vol. 1, *The Earliest Notations to the Sixteenth Century* (Oxford University Press, 2005).
Printed sheet music's impact: Iain Fenlon, "Music, Print, and Society in Sixteenth-Century Europe," in *European Music, 1520–1640*, ed. James Haar (Boydell Press, 2006).
Equal temperament: Ross W. Duffin, *How Equal Temperament Ruined Harmony (and Why You Should Care)* (W. W. Norton, 2007).
Turning point in music history: J. Murray Barbour, *Tuning, and Temperament: A Historical Survey* (Michigan State College Press, 1951).
Chopin's approach to piano: Jean-Jacques Eigeldinger, *Chopin: Pianist and Teacher* (Cambridge, 1986).
Cristofori: Stewart Pollens, *The Early Pianoforte* (Cambridge University Press, 1995).
Guitar pickups: Michael J. Evans, *Guitar* (Yale University Press, 2007).
Overdriven guitars: Dave Hunter, "The Birth of Overdrive," in *Guitar Amplifier Player's Guide* (Backbeat Books, 2005).
Jimi Hendrix melted brains: Tony Bacon and Dave Hunter, *The Ultimate Guitar Sourcebook* (Race Point Publishing, 2012).
Berliner and Edison improved mic design: Robert Bud and Deborah Jean Warner, *Instruments of Science: A Historical Encyclopedia* (Garland Publishing, 1998).
Yamaha's DX7 synthesizer, released in 1983: Paul Théberge, *Any Sound You Can Imagine: Making Music/Consuming Technology* (University Press of New England, 1997).
MIDI 2.0, the updated standard: David M. Huber and Robert E. Runstein, *Modern Recording Techniques*, 9th ed. (Routledge, 2018).

Digital file formats: AIFF: Audio Interchange File Format, Apple, 1988; WAV: Waveform Audio Format, Microsoft, IBM, 1991; MP3: MPEG-1 Audio Layer III, Fraunhofer Society/MPEG (Moving Picture Experts Group), 1993.
Small audio files "good enough" for most: Mark Katz, *Capturing Sound: How Technology Has Changed Music*, rev. ed. (University of California Press, 2010).
Music library in your pocket, portability won: Steven Levy, *The Perfect Thing: How the iPod Shuffles Commerce, Culture, and Coolness* (Simon & Schuster, 2006).
MP3s, cost to artists: Stephen Witt, *How Music Got Free: The End of an Industry, the Turn of the Century, and the Patient Zero of Piracy* (Viking, 2015).
Fought instead of pivoting to digital: Steve Knopper, *Appetite for Self-Destruction: The Spectacular Crash of the Record Industry in the Digital Age* (Free Press, 2009).
MTV's astronaut: R. Serge Denisoff, *Inside MTV* (Transaction Publishers, 1988).
"Video Killed the Radio Star" was the first to air: The Buggles, "Video Killed the Radio Star," track 1 on *The Age of Plastic*, Island Records, 1980, CD.
MTV and the "Second British Invasion": Andrew Goodwin, *Dancing in the Distraction Factory: Music Television and Popular Culture* (University of Minnesota Press, 1992).
User-friendly digital audio workstations (DAWs): Greg Milner, *Perfecting Sound Forever: An Aural History of Recorded Music* (Faber and Faber, 2009).
Two turntables and a microphone: Beck, "Where It's At," *Odelay*, DGC Records, 1996.
Grunge and alt-rock rise: Kyle Anderson, *Accidental Revolution* (St. Martin's Griffin, 2007).
Auto-Tune's evolution: Simon Reynolds, *Shock and Awe: Glam Rock and Its Legacy, from the Seventies to the Twenty-first Century* (Dey Street Books, 2016).
Digital changed the mode of delivery: Jeremy Wade Morris, *Selling Digital Music, Formatting Culture* (University of California Press, 2015).
iTunes model launch: Walter Isaacson, *Steve Jobs* (Simon & Schuster, 2011).
Spotify's dominance: Carrie Marshall, *How Music Consumption Is Changing in the Streaming Era*, 1st ed. (Bloomsbury Academic, 2022).
Pandora and algorithmic curation: Tim Ingham, "Music Streaming Went Truly Mainstream in 2022," *Music Business Worldwide*, April 4, 2023.
Streaming access and ownership: Rasmus Fleischer, "If the Song Has No Price, Is It Still a Commodity?" *Culture Unbound* 9, no. 2 (2017): 212-234.
Music pulled from platforms: Bill Rosenblatt, "What Removing Taylor Swift, Drake And More Means For TikTok—And Users," *Forbes*, February 1, 2024.
Attention is the new currency: "Attention Grab in the Modern Media Landscape with Gary Vaynerchuk," National Association of Broadcasters press release, June 6, 2019.
Amper, AIVA, Sony's Flow Machines: Nick Bryan-Kinns, ed., *AI and Music: Artificial Intelligence in Music Creation, Production, Distribution, Consumption* (Springer, 2023).
AI mixing and mastering: Bob Katz, *Mastering Audio*, 3rd ed. (Focal Press, 2015).
Spotify's AI engine: Markus Schedl, Hamed Zamani, Ching-Wei Chen, Yashar Deldjoo, Mehdi Elahi, "Current Challenges and Visions in Music Recommender Systems Research," *International Journal of Multimedia Information Retrieval* 7, no. 2 (2018): 95-116.
Jen Jacobsen on AI-generated noise: Elizabeth Wagmeister, "Artists Lash Out Against 'Enormous' AI Threats That 'Sabotage Creativity,'" CNN, April 2, 2024.
SAG-AFTRA and WGA face AI threats: Anousha Sakoui, "Hollywood's Unions Grapple With Artificial Intelligence Advances," *Los Angeles Times*, June 22, 2023.
2025 Update: Lawsuits: Blake Brittain, "Music Labels Sue AI Companies Suno, Udio for Copyright Infringement," Reuters, June 24, 2024; GEMA, "GEMA Files Lawsuit Against OpenAI Overuse of Song Lyrics in AI Training," GEMA.de, November 14, 2024.

Chapter 8 | Those Who Speak

What's up, Doc? Bugs Bunny, *Looney Tunes*, Warner Bros., 1940.
But Daddy, I love him! *The Little Mermaid*, Walt Disney Pictures, 1989.
To infinity and beyond! *Toy Story*, Pixar Animation Studios, 1995.
The growl of Darth Vader: George Lucas, dir., *Star Wars: Episode IV*, Lucasfilm, 1977.
SpongeBob SquarePants: *SpongeBob SquarePants*, Nickelodeon Animation Studio, 1999.
Morgan Freeman: *The Shawshank Redemption*, Castle Rock Entertainment, 1994.
Kevin Conroy, Batman: Eric Radomski and Bruce Timm, creators, *Batman: The Animated Series*, Warner Bros. Animation, 1992–1995.
VH Standard, Voice Actors: https://www.verifiedhuman.info/forvoiceactors.
Genie: Ron Clements and John Musker, dirs., *Aladdin*, Walt Disney Pictures, 1992.
Oral traditions: Andrew George, *The Epic of Gilgamesh* (Penguin, 2003); Marc Zvi Brettler, *How to Read the Bible* (Jewish Publication Society, 2005); James L. Fitzgerald, "Mahabharata," in *The Hindu World*, eds. Mittal and Thursby (Routledge, 2004); Gregory Nagy, *Greek Mythology and Poetics* (Cornell University Press, 1990).
NBC, ABC, CBS: Michele Hilmes, *Only Connect*, 4th ed. (Wadsworth, 2014).
First broadcast: KDKA, Pittsburgh: Erik Barnouw, *A Tower in Babel: A History of Broadcasting in the United States to 1933* (Oxford University Press, 1966).
Television takeover: Christopher H. Sterling and John Michael Kittross, *Stay Tuned: A History of American Broadcasting*, 3rd ed. (Routledge, 2002).
Snow White and synchronized sound: J.B. Kaufman, *The Fairest One of All: The Making of Walt Disney's Snow White and the Seven Dwarfs* (Walt Disney Family Fndtn. Press, 2012).
Disney's voice casting instincts: Stockwell and Caselotti: Dave Smith, *Disney A to Z: The Official Encyclopedia*, 5th ed. (Disney Editions, 2016).
Pinocchio and Bambi refined voice acting: Leonard Maltin, *Of Mice and Magic: A History of American Animated Cartoons*, rev. ed. (New American Library, 1987).
Stone Age to Space Age: Flintstones, Jetsons: Hal Erickson, *Television Cartoon Shows: An Illustrated Encyclopedia, 1949 through 2003*, 2nd ed. (McFarland, 2005).
Mel Blanc: The Man of a Thousand Voices: Ben Ohmart, *Mel Blanc: The Man of a Thousand Voices* (BearManor Media, 2012).
Blanc's influence and the rise of voice acting: Chuck Jones and Steven Spielberg, *Chuck Amuck: The Life and Times of an Animated Cartoonist* (Farrar, Straus and Giroux, 1989).
Audiobooks: Matthew Rubery, *Untold Story of the Talking Book* (Harvard University Press, 2016); James Gleick, "The History of Audiobooks," *New York Times*, November 30, 2016.
Audiobooks go digital with Audible: Motoko Rich, "Audiobooks Are Booming. That's Good News for the Blind," *New York Times*, July 31, 2019.
Audiobooks surged with smartphones, podcast culture, and lockdowns: Lauren Goode, "How Smartphones Revolutionized the Audiobook Industry," *Wired*, November 13, 2018.
AI-narrated audiobooks on Audible: Ashley Carman, "AI-Voiced Audiobooks Top 40,000 Titles on Audible," *Bloomberg*, May 2, 2024.
Audiobook narration as a creative career: Kat Lambrix, "The Art of Audiobook Narration: Tips from the Pros," *Voices*, August 26, 2020.
Gaming's dominance: Dentsu, "Gaming Is Bigger Than Music and Movies Combined," *MediaCat*, October 2024; MIDiA Research, "Games Forecasts," May 2025; Grand View Research, "Video Game Market To Reach $583 Billion by 2030," August 2023.
From Atari to PlayStation: Mark J. P. Wolf, ed., *The Video Game Explosion: A History from PONG to PlayStation and Beyond* (Greenwood Press, 2008).
Anime hits—Spirited Away, Your Name, Demon Slayer: Susan J. Napier, *Anime from*

Akira to Howl's Moving Castle (Palgrave Macmillan, 2005); *Demon Slayer: Kimetsu no Yaiba – The Movie: Mugen Train*, dir. Haruo Sotozaki (Aniplex, 2020); Mark Schilling, "'Your Name' Director Makoto Shinkai Creates Anime Hit of the Year," *Variety*, December 27, 2016.
DAWs: David Franz, *Recording and Producing in the Home Studio* (Berklee Press, 2004).
Home recording, freedom: James Alburger, *The Art of Voice Acting: The Craft and Business of Performing for Voice-Over*, 6th ed. (Routledge, 2019).
Online casting, VO: Alburger, *The Art of Voice Acting*.
Faster workflows, remote delivery: Harlan Hogan, *VO: Tales and Techniques of a Voice-Over Actor*, 2nd ed. (Allworth, 2014).
Television's growing VO demands: Neil Landau, *TV Outside the Box: Trailblazing in the Digital Television Revolution* (Focal Press, 2016).
Dubbing and localization: Miguel Jiménez Muñoz, "The Netflix Dubbing Revolution: How Streaming Platforms Are Changing the Game," *Nimdzi*, October 8, 2020.
Global VO collaborations: Deborah Wenger and Lynn C. Owens, *The Routledge Handbook of Translation and Globalization* (Routledge, 2021).
Victoria, Apple's text-to-speech voice: Jonathan Sterne, *The Audible Past: Cultural Origins of Sound Reproduction* (Duke University Press, 2003).
OCR and voice tools: Janet M. Baker, "The Impact of Voice Technologies," in *Human-Computer Interaction and Voice-Activated Systems* (Springer, 2007).
Voice assistant development: Ava Mutchler, "Voice Assistant Timeline: A Short History of the Voice Revolution," Voicebot.ai, July 14, 2017.
Early digital voice experiments: John Holmes, "Speech Synthesis and Recognition: A Historical Perspective," *Speech Synthesis and Recognition*, 2nd ed. (CRC Press, 2001).
Dragon NS: Paul De Palma, "Driving the Evolution of Speech Recognition," *Advances in Speech Recognition: Mobile Environments, Call Centers and Clinics* (Springer, 2010).
Deepfake voices and detection difficulty: Manny Rivas, "The Rise of Deepfakes and the Threat to Democracy," *Fordham International Law Journal* 43, no. 4 (2020): 1257-1314.
AI voice realism—WaveNet breakthrough: Aaron van den Oord et al., "WaveNet: A Generative Model for Raw Audio," arXiv, September 19, 2016.
Amazon Polly features: "Amazon Polly," AWS, https://www.amazon.com/aws.
Text-to-speech: John R. Rickford and John A. Russell, "Reading Machines: A Survey of Contemporary TTS Systems," *Linguistics Today* 32, no. 4 (2024): 12-45.
Replication of voices: Roger K. Moore, "Modelling Human Voices for Synthetic Speech," *Philosophical Transactions of the Royal Society A* 376, no. 2124 (2018): 20170182.
My use of Speechify: Clifford Nass and Scott Brave, *Wired for Speech* (MIT Press, 2005).
2023 SAG-AFTRA strike—voice: Brooks Barnes, "SAG-AFTRA Reaches Deal to End Strike Over Digital Replicas of Actors," *New York Times*, August 23, 2023.
Long-form and lasting voices: Hogan, *VO: Tales and Techniques of a Voice-Over Actor*.

Chapter 9 | Those Who Teach and Learn

The iBook Initiative—one of the first major ed-tech rollouts: Larry Cuban, *Oversold and Underused: Computers in the Classroom* (Harvard University Press, 2001).
HCPS rolls out 24,000 iBooks in $18.5M digital push: Mark A. Edwards, *Every Child, Every Day: A Digital Conversion Model for Student Achievement* (Pearson, 2013).
Mixed classroom use of iBooks: Cuban, *Oversold, and Underused*.
Henrico's legacy: Yong Zhao et al., "One-to-One Computing in Schools: Current Status and Future Directions," *Educational Technology & Society* 22, no. 1 (2019): 119-131.

Herbart and Montessori methods: Gerald Lee Gutek, *A Historical Introduction to American Education*, 3rd ed. (Waveland Press, 2013).
Pacioli and the birth of accounting: Michael F. Suarez and H. R. Woudhuysen, *The Oxford Companion to the Book* (Oxford University Press, 2010).
Books, literacy, knowledge: Febvre and Martin, *The Coming of the Book*.
Radio started teaching: Tiffany Lewis, "A Brief History of Educational Radio," in *Radio Cultures: The Sound Medium in American Life*, ed. Michael C. Keith (Peter Lang, 2008).
TVs, living rooms as classroom: Pat Korbel, "The Evolution of Educational Television," *American Educational History Journal* 41, no. 1 (2014): 58-73.
Mr. Wizard: Marcel Chotkowski LaFollette, *Science on American Television: A History* (University of Chicago Press, 2013).
Broadcast learning as early distance education: Michael Grahame Moore and Greg Kearsley, *Distance Education: A Systems View of Online Learning*, 3rd ed. (Wadsworth, 2012).
Programs like PLATO: Britannica, "PLATO (computer system)," June 2025.
Educational games and learning: Jessica Lussenhop, "Oregon Trail," *City Pages* (2011); "Driven by Play," The Strong blog (2018); Jorge Torres-Loayza et al., "Impact of the Use of the Video Game SimCity on the Development of Systems Thinking," *IJACSA* 14, no. 8 (2023): 789-798; Joanna McGrenere et al., study on The Incredible Machine, CiteSeerX (1997).
Learning Management Systems (LMSs) and tests: David G. O'Connor and Dominic M. Orr, *Education and the Fourth Industrial Revolution* (Routledge, 2021).
Open ed goes public: T. J. Bliss and M. Smith, "A Brief History of Open Educational Resources," in *Open* (Ubiquity, 2017).
SMART Boards: Steve Kennewell, "Interactive Whiteboards—Yet Another Solution Looking for a Problem to Solve?" *Information Tech in Teacher Education* 39 (Autumn 2001): 3-6.
Class size and learning: Eric A. Hanushek, "The Evidence on Class Size," US House Committee on Education (1998).
On adaptive problem-solving tools: Kenneth R. Koedinger et al., "Learning is Not a Spectator Sport," *Proceedings of ACM Learning @ Scale* (2015): 111-120.
Gradescope's AI-assisted grading: Arjun Singh et al., *Proceedings of the Fourth ACM Conference on Learning @ Scale* (ACM, 2017).
AI can give teachers time: Youki Terada, "7 AI Tools That Help Teachers Work More Efficiently," *Edutopia*, March 6, 2024.
AI learning platforms: Thinkser Math, Century Tech: Thinkster Math, "How Thinkster Math Works"; Century Tech, "How Century Works."
Online learning struggles: Justin Reich and José A. Ruipérez-Valiente, "The MOOC Pivot," *Science* 363, no. 6423 (2019): 130-131.
No tech magic bullet: "Technology for Technology's Sake," *Educator's Quest*, April 29, 2019.
Student data deserves care: Elana Zeide, "The Structural Consequences of Big Data-Driven Education," *Big Data* 5, no. 2 (2017): 164-182.
Bias can be dangerous: Priscilla M. Regan and Jane Bailey, "Big Data, Privacy and Education Applications," in *The Routledge Handbook of Media Education* (Routledge, 2022).
Amazon's biased hiring AI: Jeffrey Dastin, "Amazon Scraps Secret AI Recruiting Tool That Showed Bias Against Women," Reuters, October 9, 2018.
Cheating pre-AI: Denise Pope, "An Epidemic of Student Cheating? How Technology Can Make It Worse—or Better," *Kappan* 102, no. 8 (2021): 38-43.
Plagiarism detectors, like Turnitin: Diane Pecorari, *Teaching to Avoid Plagiarism: How to Promote Good Source Use* (Open University Press, 2013).
Workshops don't magically create integrity: Eaton, *Plagiarism in Higher Education*.

AI may reshape institutions: Jared Colton et al., "Ethics of AI in Education," *International Journal of Artificial Intelligence in Education* 31, no. 4 (2021): 681-707.

AI can't replace human touch: Amanda Bickerstaff, "What AI Can't Do Yet: Exploring the Limitations of AI in Education," AI for Education Blog, April 15, 2025.

Chapter 10 | **People Win**

Shibuya's choreographed chaos: "Shibuya Scramble Crossing," *Time Out Tokyo*.

Japanese pedestrians don't jaywalk: Japanese culture emphasizes social harmony, respect for rules, and civic responsibility. These values discourage behaviors like jaywalking.

Shibuya evolved: "Shibuya Crossing," Japan Guide. Shibuya's development spans over 150 years, from rural to a hyper-urban crossroads shaped by commuters and transit systems.

The G-MAFIA and BAT: Amy Webb, *The Big Nine: How the Tech Titans and Their Thinking Machines Could Warp Humanity* (PublicAffairs, 2019).

Klaus has contributed profoundly to VerifiedHuman: Klaus Luehning, who escaped World War II Germany, made his way to America. He was a young pizza maker in Brooklyn. Then earned a degree from the US Merchant Marine Academy. Had a maritime career in engineering. Became the founding professor of the Texas Maritime Academy, Texas A&M. Pivoted to sales engineer for Ingersoll Rand, spent sixteen years as an Executive Chef. Before retiring, he closed out his career in Tennessee as a Senior Clinical substance abuse counselor.

The bold magic of Disney: *Snow White and the Seven Dwarfs* (1937). Over 1,500 artists created more than 250,000 drawings, pioneering techniques like Technicolor, synchronized sound, and multiplane camera effects. Established Disney's dominance and animation's power.

Unsupervised at MoMA: "MoMA Acquires Refik Anadol's AI-Powered Unsupervised," *Artforum*, October 11, 2023.

Gary DuBois, artist: VerifiedHuman for Everyone, https://www.verifiedhuman.info.

"The human spirit must prevail over technology": William Hermanns, *Einstein and the Poet: In Search of the Cosmic Man* (Branden Press, 1983).

2025 Update: Swift's Eras Tour, Kendrick Lamar and SZA, Coldplay, and Broadway's 2025 resurgence: Ben Sisario and Joe Coscarelli, "Swift's Eras Tour Is the First to Gross $2 Billion, Shattering Records," *New York Times*, January 10, 2025; Michael Paulson, "Broadway's 2025 Boom: Why Live Theater Is Thriving in the AI Age," *New York Times*, May 15, 2025.

Hidden Track | **VerifiedHuman**

VerifiedHuman consortium: https://www.verifiedhuman.info/consortium.
Whether it matters: Andy Hughes, interview with author, September 10, 2023.
Dr. Conn: Paul Conn, Chancellor of Lee University, interview with author, May 2023.
Very few American ports: "John Stobart," eMuseum, Syracuse University, https://www.onlinecollections.syr.edu.
Unlike the curators who spotted the phony Getty Kouros, Malcolm Gladwell, in *Blink: The Power of Thinking Without Thinking* (Little, Brown, 2005).
2025 Update: Chatterbox and EVI 3 voice models: Zain Kahn, "AI Can Now Clone Your Voice with 5 Seconds of Audio," *The AI Report*, May 30, 2025, https://www.theaiedge.io.
A similar challenge has emerged: Karen Hao, "The biggest threat of deepfakes isn't the deepfakes themselves," *MIT Technology Review*, October 10, 2019.
Pope's puffer jacket: Chrissy Teigen (@chrissyteigen), post on Twitter (X), March 2023.
AI articles rank higher: Reece Rogers, "Google Search ranks AI spam above original reporting in news results," *Wired*, July 2, 2024.
A US District judge ruled that the case could proceed: Kevin Madigan, "Takeaways from the Andersen v. Stability AI copyright case," *Copyright Alliance*, August 29, 2024.
Infringement on The Times: Britney Nguyen, "New York Times sues OpenAI, Microsoft: 'Billions' owed for AI copyright infringement, case claims," *Forbes*, December 27, 2023.
These lawsuits raise serious concerns: Music Business Worldwide, "AI company Anthropic sued for copyright infringement by Universal Music Group," October 18, 2023.
Executive Order 14110: "Executive Order on the Safe, Secure, and Trustworthy Development and Use of Artificial Intelligence," The White House, October 30, 2023.
Still, the document only provides a 30-thousand-foot view: Tim Wu, "In regulating A.I., we may be doing too much—and too little," *New York Times*, November 7, 2023.
Basic approach, "light touch": "The Biden Administration Launches the National Artificial Intelligence Research Resource Task Force," OSTP, The White House, June 10, 2021.
China, AI development a central part of national strategy: Kai-Fu Lee, *AI Superpowers: China, Silicon Valley, and the New World Order* (Houghton Mifflin Harcourt, 2018).
Getty Images and Shutterstock watermarking: "AI watermarking: A watershed for multimedia authenticity," International Telecommunication Union, https://www.itu.int.
Digital encoding, attaching tamper-evident safeguards: "C2PA 2.1 – Strengthening Content Credentials with Digital Watermarks," Digimarc, https://www.digimarc.com.
Undetectable.ai rehumanizes the content: "WriteHuman: Undetectable AI and AI Content Humanizer," https://www.writehuman.ai.
Originality.AI, GPTZero, Turnitin, and Grammarly: David Hartshorne, "The best AI content detectors in 2024," *Zapier*, April 30, 2024.
OriginalityAI false positives: Elegant Themes, "Originality AI review for 2024 (One of the best AI detectors?)," Elegant Themes, https://www.elegantthemes.com.
Evasion programs like Hider.ai and Spin Rewriter: "Spin Rewriter AI – Article Rewriter Loved by 181,394 Users," Spin Rewriter, https://www.spinrewriter.com.
Boris Eldagsen correspondence: Boris Eldagsen, emails to author, February–March 2023.
VH like Fairtrade: "Our Approach," Fairtrade International, https://www.fairtrade.net.

About the Author & VerifiedHuman™

Micah Voraritskul is a creative strategist, cultural thinker, and teacher at the intersection of technology, humanity, and meaning. He founded VerifiedHuman™ to protect and promote human-made work in the age of AI. His career spans education, communication, and nonprofit leadership, rooted in a deep love for people and a conviction that creativity is still worth fighting for.

Human Is the New Vinyl is his first book.

 micahvoraritskul.com

Join the VerifiedHuman™ Movement

If the ideas in this book resonated with you, you're not alone. VerifiedHuman™ is a straightforward framework that helps people acknowledge their human-made work. We stand united in recognizing the value of creativity, effort, and authorship.

We're building a community that values clarity, transparency, and trust.

You're invited.

Scan the code to learn more—or join us at www.verifiedhuman.info

Share your thoughts with #VerifiedHuman

www.ingramcontent.com/pod-product-compliance
Lightning Source LLC
Chambersburg PA
CBHW021143160426
43194CB00007B/673